MW00809738

The Crisis in America's Criminal Courts

The Crisis in America's Criminal Courts

Improving Criminal Justice Outcomes by Transforming Decision-Making

William R. Kelly

ROWMAN & LITTLEFIELD
Lanham • Boulder • New York • London

Published by Rowman & Littlefield
An imprint of The Rowman & Littlefield Publishing Group, Inc.
4501 Forbes Boulevard, Suite 200, Lanham, Maryland 20706
www.rowman.com

6 Tinworth Street, London SE11 5AL, United Kingdom

British Library Cataloguing in Publication Information Available

Library of Congress Cataloging-in-Publication Data

Names: Kelly, W. R. (William Robert), 1950- author.
Title: The crisis in America's criminal courts : improving criminal justice
   outcomes by transforming decision-making / William R. Kelly.
Description: Lanham : Rowman & Littlefield, [2021] | Series: Applied
   criminology across the globe | Includes bibliographical references and
   index. | Summary: "This book highlights the variety of problems that
   judges, prosecutors, and public defenders face within a criminal justice
   system that is ineffective, unfair, and extraordinarily expensive. Much
   of the dysfunction originates from crushing dockets and caseloads
   combined with the lack of time, expertise, and resources for effective
   decision-making"— Provided by publisher.
Identifiers: LCCN 2020057523 (print) | LCCN 2020057524 (ebook) | ISBN
   9781538142165 (cloth) | ISBN 9781538142172 (epub)
Subjects: LCSH: Criminal justice, Administration of—United States. |
   Criminal courts—United States.
Classification: LCC KF9223 .K428 2021 (print) | LCC KF9223 (ebook) | DDC
   345.73/01—dc23
LC record available at https://lccn.loc.gov/2020057523
LC ebook record available at https://lccn.loc.gov/2020057524

♾️™ The paper used in this publication meets the minimum requirements of
American National Standard for Information Sciences—Permanence of Paper
for Printed Library Materials, ANSI/NISO Z39.48-1992.

Contents

Acknowledgments

First and foremost, I must once again express my profound gratitude to my wonderful wife, Emily, who has been so encouraging and supportive in this effort and those that preceded this one. She has also been an excellent sounding board for many of the ideas contained herein. More importantly, she is the best life partner one could imagine.

I also want to thank several undergraduate students who provided very able research assistance over the course of this project. Michaela Capplleo was indispensable in assisting with the interviews I conducted with progressive prosecutors. Echo Nattinger, Taryn Shanes, Clemens Finger, Saskia Reford, Emily Schuerman, Jordan Ludzenski, Peeyal Kumar, and Maura Evans were extremely valuable in reducing the literal mountains of research I had collected into meaningful summaries. Molly Karten, Jake Wigel, and Brianna Goodfriend conducted extensive background research on the prosecutors I interviewed as well as compiled summary data on their elections. I also want to thank Saskia Reford and Emily Schuerman for reading earlier drafts of the manuscript and offering terrific criticisms and edits. It is so encouraging to know that there are such smart students who are really interested in criminal justice reform.

I'd like to express my gratitude to Dan Mears for his usual extraordinarily insightful comments. I also thank the Charles Koch Foundation for financial support for conducting the prosecutor interviews.

As usual, Rowman & Littlefield has been wonderful, especially Kathryn Knigge and Becca Beurer. Thank you for all you have done to help make this book a reality.

Introduction

The reach of the American criminal justice system is staggering. Today, one-half of the adult population in the United States has an immediate family member who currently is or has been incarcerated in the criminal justice system.[1] Two-thirds have had an immediate family member or an extended family member incarcerated.[2] Nearly one-half of Black males and 40 percent of White males have been arrested by the time they reach age twenty-three. All told, one in three working-age Americans has a criminal record, as many as have college degrees. Moreover, a young adult today is 36 percent more likely to be arrested than a young adult born in the 1960s.[3]

We have racked up these statistics by creating the largest and arguably most punitive criminal justice system in the world. Over the past forty years, the US prison population has increased 500 percent. Today, the United States has the largest prison and jail population and the highest incarceration rates in the world. The incarceration rate for the United States as a whole (including the federal system and all fifty state prison systems and jails) is currently about 860 per 100,000 adults.[4] Our incarceration rate substantially exceeds that of Cuba, China, Rwanda, Russia, Turkey, and all of the states of the former Soviet Union. It is three and one-half times that of our European allies, and it is far greater than that of Japan, Canada, Australia, and New Zealand.

Our penchant for punishment is not just reflected by the sheer number of offenders incarcerated. The United States is a world leader in the severity of punishment. For example, approximately one-third of all offenders serving life sentences in the world are in the United States.[5] Another way of looking at it is that the number of people serving life sentences in prison today in the United States exceeds the total prison population in the United States in 1970.[6] Moreover, the average sentence length is greater in the United States compared to other Western nations.[7]

The footprint of American criminal justice is not limited to incarceration. Over the past forty years, the number of people on probation and parole (referred to as community supervision or conditional release to the community under supervision) has more than tripled. Today, the United States has the highest number and rates of community supervision known in the world. There are currently 4.5 million people under community supervision, a number well over the entire population of Los Angeles. The community supervision rate in the United States is close to 2,000, compared to 375 in Canada, 480 in England and Wales, 26 in Finland, 78 in Switzerland, and 25 in Japan.[8]

We have not always been the world leader in criminal punishment. In the 1950s, 1960s, and early 1970s, for example, the prison population hovered around 200,000 inmates and the incarceration rate was between 100 and 160, remarkably below the rate today. Moreover, US incarceration rates during this era were in the neighborhood of the rates of other Western democracies.[9]

How did we get here? And why? A variety of unprecedented policy, statutory, procedural, and funding changes at all levels of government coincided to create a criminal justice system with one overriding priority—to punish bad behavior out of those who break the law.

The "how" involves the dramatic expansion of prisons and jails to accommodate the increases in the prison population. Federal, state, and local governments joined in an astonishingly aggressive campaign of capital investment in prison and jails. For example, in 1990, the Texas prison system had a capacity for 50,000 inmates. By 1997, it had exploded to 150,000. Tough-on-crime policies also required the commensurate enhancement of probation and parole resources, as well as significant increases in officer caseloads.[10]

The creation of this new, punishment-focused criminal justice system was also facilitated by a radical restructuring of sentencing laws, which took discretion away from judges and made many crimes subject to mandatory sentences. Examples include mandatory life sentences, repeat offender laws such as three strikes, and mandatory minimum drug sentences. Even in states where judges still have significant discretion in sentencing, the statutes are heavily populated with mandatory sentences where judicial discretion is radically limited. The end result of the changes to sentencing laws during this era of tough on crime is that average sentence length increased. For example, between 1979 and 1986, the length of federal prison sentences increased by 32 percent.[11] Between

2000 and 2014, the average sentence length in state prisons increased by five years.[12] In 1984, there were 34,000 prison inmates in the United States serving a life sentence. In 2016, that number had risen to 162,000.[13]

Not only did the changes to sentencing laws and the more punitive decisions of tough-on-crime prosecutors and judges increase up-front sentences for those convicted of crimes, but revisions to release laws required that offenders serve greater percentages of the sentences imposed. Sixteen states accomplished this by simply eliminating parole release, which is early release from prison under the supervision of a parole officer. Other states implemented so-called "truth in sentencing" laws, which require that inmates serve a greater percentage of the sentence imposed before they are eligible for parole consideration. A common provision of truth-in-sentencing laws is the stipulation that certain violent offenders serve 85 percent of their sentence before they are eligible for parole consideration. In the end, these changes increased the amount of time an offender actually spent in prison—between 1990 and 2009, the average time served in state prisons increased by 36 percent.[14]

The war on drugs has played a key role in creating demand for correctional control. In 1980, there were 41,000 individuals in state and federal prisons and local jails for drug offenses. In 2017, there were 453,000, representing a 1,000 percent increase.[15]

Revocation policies for offenders on probation and parole have also contributed to the incarceration explosion. Probation is a post-conviction sentence in lieu of incarceration. It is conditional release under the supervision of a probation officer. The conditions are imposed by statute and by the court during sentencing. Violation of the conditions may subject a probationer to revocation, which means incarceration.

Parole is supervised, conditional release after incarceration in prison. If an offender on parole violates the parole conditions, he is subject to reincarceration, typically to serve out the remainder of the sentence. The federal system eliminated parole in the 1980s, meaning federal offenders serve the entirety of their sentence behind bars. However, a period of post-incarceration supervised release is often imposed on federal offenders, and violation of the supervised release conditions can result in additional prison time.

In 1980, 17 percent of prison admissions were parole violators—individuals on parole who were revoked to prison for violation of conditions or a new offense. By 1990, that had risen to 29 percent. Over one-third of prison admissions in 1999 were parole violators.

As the probation population expanded to unprecedented levels in the 1980s, 1990s, and 2000s, failure rates increased in a similar manner. In 1985, for example, roughly 80 percent of probationers in the United States successfully completed their period of supervision. By 2005, that had dropped to 59 percent, and most of those who failed were revoked to incarceration.[16]

The irony is that both parole and probation were designed in part to reduce the demand for incarceration by diverting individuals from prison or jail (probation) and by releasing offenders early from prison (parole). Unfortunately, for a variety of reasons, both versions of community supervision contributed substantially to prison admissions, or in the case of parole violators, prison readmissions.

The reach of the US criminal justice system has been increasingly extended by the expansion of the criminal code, the set of laws that define what behaviors are criminal. At both the federal level (controlled by Congress) and the state level (controlled by state legislatures), the trend has been more and more to identify problems for which the criminal justice system is the solution. For example, the Pennsylvania Crimes Code, which was codified in 1972, identified 282 criminal offenses. By 2010, the Pennsylvania State Legislature had added 354 criminal offenses for a total of 636 crimes. In 2019, it had increased to more than 1,500 offenses.[17]

Research by the Manhattan Institute confirms the trend of the ever-expanding criminal code. A six-year analysis in 2014 of the state legislatures of North Carolina, Michigan, Oklahoma, South Carolina, and Minnesota revealed that they added an average of forty-two new crimes annually, the majority of which were felonies.[18] A 2015–2016 update of the analysis demonstrated that the code expansion continues, with Michigan, North Carolina, and South Carolina adding an average of thirty-seven new crimes per year.

The expansion of state and federal criminal codes has resulted in the widening of the net of criminal liability. As more behaviors are criminalized, the number of people subject to arrest, prosecution, conviction, and punishment increases.

The purpose of the justice system—criminal and civil—is to right wrongs, to provide remedies for parties harmed by the actions of others. While civil and criminal law are considered distinct, there are many ways in which the criminal law has expanded into what we may think of as traditionally civil matters, blurring the line between civil and criminal liability.

A surgeon makes a mistake during surgery and as a result the patient dies. This sounds like a medical malpractice civil case, an error by the surgeon. However, it is possible under criminal statutes to charge the surgeon criminally if the prosecutor is inclined to charge criminal negligence. An electrician is hired to fix the wiring in a house. He forgets to cap off a live wire and as a result, the house catches fire several hours later. The resident is badly burned. This sounds like a matter for civil court, but a prosecutor could once again charge the electrician with criminal negligence.

My point is simply to question the wisdom of criminal prosecution in such matters. What do we gain by turning an accident into a crime? Do we need to deter surgeons or electricians from making mistakes? Isn't that the job of licensing or certification or professional associations? Criminal liability has a variety of negative consequences, and I am suggesting that we understand and appreciate those consequences before we invoke criminal liability in a matter that can be resolved in civil court.

The extension of criminal liability through expanding the criminal code reflects an increasing reliance on criminal law to manage the consequences of a variety of circumstances that have resulted from policy decisions that have profound impacts on the administration of criminal justice. These include decisions to seriously underfund public health, resulting in increasing numbers of untreated and undertreated individuals with mental illness and substance-use disorders. For a variety of reasons, many of these individuals end up in the criminal justice system, often because there is nowhere else for them to go. I will discuss this in more detail below.

The failure of local and state governments to adequately fund the criminal court system has given us the shortcut mechanism of criminal prosecution known as plea bargaining. Plea negotiation, or the exchange of benefits for both the government (avoiding a trial) and the defendant (lesser punishment) is what allows the criminal court system to operate. It expedites prosecution and conviction and, I suggest, perpetuates tough-on-crime policies, in part because punishment is the currency of the exchange.

Another consideration that has facilitated the unprecedented expansion of American criminal justice is the considerable political leverage associated with being tough on crime. Most state judges and District Attorneys are elected locally, in county elections. For decades, the safe position for a judge, sheriff, or DA has been to run on a tough-on-crime platform.

The circumstances of the 1960s, 1970s, and 1980s—historically high crime rates, race riots across the nation, campus protests over the Vietnam War and the draft, the expanding use of illicit drugs in urban areas and college campuses, the crack epidemic of the early 1980s, as well as the political salience of being tough and punitive regarding perceived problems all spelled a fundamental shift in criminal justice policy toward the expansion of punishment. It was an easy sell—punishment makes sense. Either lock up offenders so they cannot commit crimes (incapacitation) or punish them severely enough so they will not want to reoffend (deterrence).

But let's be clear. The massive increase in correctional control in the United States, seen most notably in terms of incarceration, was not largely due to increasing crime. Yes, crime rates in the 1960s, 1970s, and early 1980s were historically high, but they then dropped precipitously through the 1990s and forward. Crime victimization data show that criminal victimization was higher in England and the Netherlands than in the United States, and essentially the same as the United States in Canada, Sweden, and Australia.[19] None of these nations pursued punitive policies on the scale of the United States. Rather, tough on crime was a result of a variety of policy decisions to admit more people to prison for longer periods of time. It is estimated that this explains about 80 percent of the increase in incarceration.[20]

It was also a policy that was best delivered in a top-down strategy from federal to state, and from state to local. States would see changes to federal policies, such as the expansion of the criminal code and implementation of the harsh guidelines and the elimination of parole release, and the message was clear. States modified sentencing laws, implemented mandatory sentences, restricted parole, and expanded prison and jail capacity, among other changes. Local counties adopted this new way of doing business in the day-to-day administration of justice. Importantly, all of this changed how we think about crime and punishment—criminal offenders make bad decisions. What better way to motivate better decision-making than punishment?

Today, we find ourselves in a new era of criminal justice reform, and things are quite different this time around. First, while there is much discussion about changing the policy path, there is a lack of clear consensus about what that means. Most reform advocates argue for ending mass incarceration through such things as eliminating mandatory minimum and mandatory sentences, expansion of parole release, facilitating successful reentry from incarceration, and reducing technical parole violations that return offenders to prison. However, it is very important that we understand that "ending mass incarceration" is not just a matter of numbers. Cutting the prison population by 50 percent may seem like a reasonable goal, but it is not just a simple matter of placing fewer people behind bars.

I admit that I have strong beliefs when it comes to criminal justice reform. My take is that meaningful reform needs to be big, bold, and aggressive. I believe that we need to reinvent how we go about the business of criminal justice, which includes substantial changes to law, policy, procedure, funding, and importantly culture—how we think about crime and punishment. Fine-tuning may make some elected officials and policy makers feel like they are solving the problem, but, at the end of the day, timid policy fails to produce the changes necessary to effectively reduce crime and recidivism. Let's take the very recent federal First Step Act as an example.

On November 14, 2018, the editorial board of the *New York Times* declared the First Step Act: "A real chance at criminal justice reform." About a month later, the editorial board of the *Chicago Sun Times* stated "With First Step Act, Jared Kushner taps into our common humanity." The November 16, 2018, headline on the Senate's Committee on the Judiciary's website proclaims *"Wall Street Journal, New York Times* Praise Trump-Backed First Step Act."

The White House proclaimed

President Donald J. Trump Secures Landmark Legislation to Make Our Federal Justice System Fairer and Our Communities Safer. The First Step Act will make communities SAFER and SAVE tremendous taxpayers dollars. It brings much needed hope to many families during the holiday season. President Donald J. Trump's signing of the First Step Act marks a monumental bipartisan win for the American people.[21]

Van Jones, a television commentator and criminal justice reform advocate, called the First Step Act "a Christmas miracle"[22] and coauthored an op-ed on the CNN website entitled "10 Reasons to Celebrate the First Step Act."[23] The United States Conference of Catholic Bishops also joined in on the praise, as have a variety of other religious and nonprofit criminal justice reform organizations such as the American Civil Liberties Union (ACLU), Families Against Mandatory Minimums, The Prison Fellowship, Right On Crime, #cut50, and the Fraternal Order of Police.

The United States Conference of Catholic Bishops declared, "This bill contains many more fine provisions which will help foster a more just and merciful justice system."[24]

All of this praise and affirmation may be well-intentioned, but I fear it's a bit like President Bush's vastly premature declaration of job done regarding the war in Iraq. On May 1, 2003, from aboard the aircraft carrier USS *Abraham Lincoln*, President George Bush declared, "In the battle of Iraq, the United States and our allies have prevailed." He made this statement directly under a very large banner that shouted Mission Accomplished.

History tells a very different story regarding the war in Iraq, and I suspect that careful observers of US criminal justice policy will see the First Step Act in a similar perspective.

The First Step Act is restricted to addressing criminal law and policy at the federal level. The federal system accounts for only about 10 to 12 percent of the total US criminal justice system. There are also fifty state criminal justice systems that deal with the vast majority of all crimes, criminal offenders, prosecutions, convictions, sentences, and punishments, as well as more than 3,100 counties that are essentially self-contained criminal justice systems. They are unaffected by the First Step Act.

Perhaps more important than the quite limited footprint of the First Step Act is its utterly modest reform effort. At first glance, the First Step Act's reductions of the rather draconian federal mandatory minimum sentences sounds like a very positive step toward a more sensible punishment scheme. However, the changes are minimal and do not affect the sentences of many federal offenders. Examples of the changes include:

- expansion of the safety valve provision that gives judges discretion to bypass certain mandatory sentences for nonviolent drug offenders with limited criminal histories
- the mandatory minimum for violent or more serious drug convictions is reduced from twenty to fifteen years
- the federal mandatory habitual offender or three strikes sentence is reduced from life to twenty-five years
- a serious drug conviction that used to result in a twenty-year sentence is now reduced to fifteen years
- the sentences of individuals convicted of crack cocaine charges have been reduced by making retroactive the 2010 Fair Sentencing Act, which lowered the (100 to 1) disparity between crack and powder cocaine; this has resulted in the early release of about 3,000 federal crack cocaine offenders and shortened the sentences of 1,700 more
- the development of risk and needs assessments that can determine what rehabilitative programming will help reduce recidivism

The federal prison system consists of approximately 180,000 offenders. To date, the First Step Act has measurably affected less than 3 percent of the federal prison population.

I have three additional concerns regarding the First Step Act. First, I would not be a bit surprised if the First Step Act is also the Last Step Act in terms of federal criminal justice reform legislation passed by Congress for the foreseeable future. Mission accomplished for criminal justice reform.

My second concern is that the First Step Act involved a top-down strategy. Congress has ordered those in the trenches to use (yet to be developed) risk and needs assessments to determine what rehabilitative programming (also largely yet developed) selected federal offenders should receive. Assuming the assessments and programs are eventually developed, actually implementing these provisions does not guarantee they will be properly executed and effective. As I will argue later, there are a variety of reasons why bottom-up (i.e., local) reforms have a higher likelihood of proper implementation and effectiveness compared to top-down mandates.

My third concern is that the First Step Act can set the standard of what criminal justice reform should look like at the state level. While the federal government cannot mandate what states do in reforming criminal justice, federal law and policy serve as examples that states may emulate. Sentencing expert Doug Berman, a professor at the Ohio State University Moritz College of Law, puts it: "Even though the federal system only represents 10% of our criminal justice systems, anything the feds do garners attention in the states. It allows advocates to say, 'Look, the folks at the national level thought this was a good idea. Let's do our own version.'"[25]

This clearly has been the case historically with states following the federal lead on national tough-on-crime policies, and there is some evidence that versions of the First Step Act are surfacing in some states. For example, legislators in North Carolina and Florida have drafted legislation labeled the Florida First Step Act and the North Carolina First Step Act. These efforts have faced opposition from state prosecutor associations and law enforcement organizations. A version of the Florida First Step Act passed, but it does not provide judges with discretion to override or modify mandatory sentences, a keystone of the federal act. The North Carolina version, which has passed the state senate as of this writing, provides judges limited discretion to reduce mandatory sentences for low-level, nonviolent drug offenders.

Let's take a look at another example of criminal justice reform, the so-called Texas Miracle. Former Texas governor Rick Perry has promoted policy changes in Texas and calls on other states to follow the Texas example and "eliminate our incarceration epidemic."[26]

So, in 2007, with broad support from Republicans and Democrats alike, Texas fundamentally changed its course on criminal justice. We focused on diverting people with drug addiction issues from entering prison in the first place, and programs to keep them from returning . . . The results have been remarkable . . . I am proud that in Texas, criminal justice policy is no longer driven solely by fear, but by a commitment to true justice, and compassion for those shackled by the chains of addiction. My hope is that all states will do likewise. States across the country can follow the successful example of Texas.

The Texas Public Policy Foundation, a conservative policy think tank in Texas, claims Texas has become a model for criminal justice reform around the nation.[27]

The push for criminal justice reform based on conservative principles—improved public safety, consideration for victims, redemption, fiscal restraint and liberty—continues to grow. Texas spearheaded many of these reforms and has continued to strive each [legislative] session to remain a guiding light for the rest of the nation.

Despite the acclaim, I just don't get it. Yes, Texas has made some changes, in particular investing more resources in probation, prison reentry, and diversion programs for some offenders with substance-use problems. What did all of this accomplish in terms of incarceration? The prison population is down 4 percent from its peak in 2010. However, Texas still has the largest prison population and the fifth highest incarceration rate in the nation. Moreover, there has been a 66 percent increase in the use of force by prison staff between 2006 and 2019, from 6,624 to 10,990. The number of mentally ill inmates also increased dramatically over this period, up by one-third, or 7,000 inmates.[28]

The state jail system, which was designed to avoid hard time in prison by diverting low-level felons to special facilities called state jails, where a variety of rehabilitation options were to be available, has been an utter failure.[29] There are very few rehabilitation resources available in the state jails, and the recidivism rates of those released from state jails are nearly 40 percent higher than for offenders released from prison.[30] Importantly, more than 25 percent of all admissions to the Texas prison system in 2018 were admissions to state jails, so we are talking about a significant chunk of the prison population.[31] To make matters worse, a December 30, 2019, headline in the *Houston Chronicle* proclaims, "'The Place Is a Jungle': Texas Youth Prisons Still Beset by Gangs, Violence, Abuse."

A recent (end of year 2019) assessment of criminal justice reform initiated by state legislatures concludes that efforts have been universally modest.

> But criminal justice reform remains an uneven patchwork. States that make bold moves on one issue can be harshly punitive on others. And while some set new milestones, elsewhere debates were meager—and in a few states driven by proposals to make laws tougher.[32]

Legalization and decriminalization of marijuana continued to occupy legislative agendas, and a couple of states took decriminalization beyond just marijuana possession. For example, Colorado made possession of most drugs a misdemeanor. Oklahoma made retroactive their "defelonization" drug bill of 2016. There was not much else accomplished regarding sentencing except for some very limited repeal of mandatory minimums (North Dakota) and modification of other mandatory sentences (Washington and Delaware). Several states tried to abolish life-without-parole sentences but those efforts were defeated.[33] That is essentially it for the 2019 state criminal justice reform report card. Underwhelming indeed.

The point is that any change or reform to date, whether the First Step Act, the Texas Miracle, or the very modest reductions in state prison populations in the aftermath of the recession of the late 2000s, simply amounts to tinkering around the edges. To put it in perspective, if we continue at the recent rate of decline in the prison population, it will take seventy years to cut the prison population in half, which would reduce it to 750,000, the level it was in 1990.[34]

Modest change is where I part company with most current criminal justice reform efforts. As will become clear in the following pages, my version of justice reform is a good bit more comprehensive, ambitious, and aggressive than what we have seen or heard to date.

There are many ways to think about criminal justice reform. Some raise questions about the ethics of criminal procedure, the morality of harsh punishment, and the increasing reliance on the criminal justice system to solve social problems. Many express concerns about fairness regarding the poor and racial and ethnic minorities in the criminal justice system. Still others are concerned with effectiveness and the extent to which criminal justice policy is producing sufficient dividends in terms of crime and recidivism reduction. Then there is the cost issue and the extent to which the criminal justice system is a good return on investment.

When we fundamentally changed the criminal justice system fifty years ago by embracing tough-on-crime, punitive policies, the goal was clear and simple—more punishment for more people. Today, there seems to be less consensus about what reform means. Many advocates argue for ending mass incarceration. Bail reform and reducing pretrial detention are front and center today. Others focus on enhancing and facilitating reentry from prison, changing sentencing laws such as eliminating mandatory minimums, ending the war on drugs, improving probation and other diversion programs, and addressing such policing issues as use of force, racial profiling, and arrest versus citation practices, among others. Many cite the racial inequalities that define American criminal justice and the need to address these inequalities in everything from policing to punishment.

In 2019, the Brennan Center for Justice invited national leaders to provide their solutions for ending mass incarceration in the criminal justice system.[35] This effort was a follow-up to a similar Brennan Center initiative in 2015. The leaders selected include many of the original contenders in the 2020 Democratic primaries (Harris, Booker, Castro, Gillibrand, Klobuchar, O'Rourke, Warren, and Sanders), as well as other high-profile individuals such as Jared Kushner, Van Jones, and Sherrod Brown. As one might expect, the ideas are all over the map, ranging from cutting the prison population by 50 percent, reducing the policing of minority neighborhoods, providing treatment for addiction, fair wages and housing, implementing the First Step Act, eliminating private prisons, ending the war on drugs, eliminating racial disparities, and reducing the incarceration of women.

The good news is that in this election cycle, criminal justice reform has gained a seat at the table. For the first time in decades, questioning how we go about the business of crime and punishment and offering solutions seems to be a mainstream element of national politics. All of the Democratic candidates have identified justice reforms in their campaign materials, although some have more extensive proposals than others. Acknowledgment on a national stage that the criminal justice system is broken and in need of substantial change goes a long way in advancing the conversation.

On the other hand, what the Democratic candidates and other national leaders (the Brennan Center document) recommend constitute a fairly standard set of reforms. There is nothing wrong with that per se. Advocating for these reforms will move the needle in terms of traditional criminal justice goals—reducing inequity, enhancing fairness, and reducing recidivism. However, I fear I must disagree with the president of the Brennan Center, who characterized the results of the input from national leaders in the following way: "After decades in which fear of crime and 'tough on crime' were the ultimate wedge issue, now there's a competition to see who can have the most transformative reform."[36] My disagreement is in part a matter of degree—I just don't view what was proposed as necessarily transformative. Moreover, words are one thing, implemented policy reform is another. We now turn to an introduction of meaningful, comprehensive criminal justice reform, a topic that will consume subsequent chapters of this book.

There is a relatively short list of circumstances that go a long way in accounting for criminality in the United States—poverty and income inequality, inadequate education, underemployment and unemployment, substance abuse and addiction, homelessness, mental illness, neurodevelopmental and neurocognitive impairment, and intellectual deficits, among others. The unfortunate truth is that we have failed at the federal, state, and local levels to effectively address these circumstances and have increasingly relied on the criminal justice system to manage the impacts of poverty, mental illness, addiction, poor educational outcomes, and so on.

The vast majority of criminal offenders come from origins of poverty and disadvantage. Eighty percent of individuals in prison and jail today in the United States have a substance-use disorder (abuse, dependence, or addiction). That percentage is six to eight times the prevalence of substance abuse disorders in the general population. More than 50 percent of those in jail and prison have a diagnosable mental illness and nearly 20 percent have a serious mental illness (schizophrenia, bipolar disorder, and major depression).[37] These percentages are two to three times the prevalence compared to the general population. A stark reality is that the Los Angeles County Jail is not only the world's largest jail, it is also the world's largest mental health facility. The Cook County (Chicago) Illinois Jail is the largest mental health facility in Illinois. That is the case for essentially any jail in any metropolitan area in the country. Today, jails and prisons are the mental health asylums in the United States.

So, why is there such as over-representation of the disordered (mental illness, substance abuse, cognitive impairment) in the criminal justice system? The primary reason is the failure to develop adequate public health capacity.

DJ Jaffe, a mental health policy expert and author of *Insane Consequences: How the Mental Health Industry Fails the Mentally Ill*, puts it bluntly:[38]

> America's mental health system is insane, expensive, and ineffective. Under the guise of increasing freedom, it is increasing incarceration. Under the guise of facilitating recovery, it ensures that fewer recover. America treats the least seriously ill ("the worried well") and forces the most seriously ill to fend for themselves. The ability to get help is inversely related to need. We move sick people from hospitals to jails and label it progress . . . Our mental health system is not based on science and has nothing to do with compassion. As a result, there are ten times more people with mental illness incarcerated as hospitalized. Being mentally ill has essentially become a crime.

We as a nation have made very conscious decisions at the federal, state, and local levels to inadequately fund public health resources for treatment of such things as mental illness and substance abuse among the poor.[39] A recent health-care ranking (2019) puts the United States at thirty-seventh, behind all of Western Europe, as well as such nations as Costa Rica, Chile, Oman, Morocco, Saudi Arabia, Columbia, and Cyprus.[40] Another assessment of US health care relative to eleven comparable nations, such as the United Kingdom, New Zealand, Canada, France, and Australia, found that the United States performed poorly in terms of affordability, access to care, health outcomes, and equality between rich and poor.[41] The picture gets worse if we consider children. As Paul Krugman recently wrote in an op-ed entitled "Why Does American Hate Its Children?":[42]

> Most advanced countries devote substantial sums to benefits for families with children; in Europe these benefits average 3% to 4% of gross domestic product. The corresponding number for the United States is 0.6% of GDP. Even where the United States does help children, the quality of that help tends to be poor.

As I write this in mid-April of 2020, the COVID-19 virus has not peaked yet in the United States. The strain on public health resources is quite evident. News reports indicate that the federal Strategic National Stockpile is essentially depleted and the US Department of Health and Human Resources is asking for public donations.

There is other evidence from the COVID-19 pandemic that underscores the lack of an adequate public system in the United States. The limited COVID-19 mortality data that are currently available indicate a dramatic racial/ethnic disparity (as of April 10, 2020, only eight states were reporting COVID-19 mortality data by race/ethnicity). Nearly one-third of all COVID-19 deaths were of African Americans. The Black mortality rate is 2.6 times what would be expected based on their relative prevalence in the population.[43]

Again, the data are preliminary, but what is suggested is the relatively higher incidence of high-risk health conditions among African Americans, such as diabetes, heart disease, and lung disease, among others. Race and ethnic differences in morbidity and multimorbidity have been well established, highlighting inadequate access to health care.[44]

> Middle-aged non-Hispanic black adults start at a higher level of chronic disease burden and develop multimorbidity at an earlier age, on average, than their non-Hispanic white counterparts. Hispanics, on the other hand, accumulate chronic disease at a faster rate relative to non-Hispanic white adults. Our findings have important implications for improving primary and secondary chronic disease prevention efforts among non-Hispanic black and Hispanic Americans to stave off greater multimorbidity-related health impacts.

For the past fifty years, we have been using the criminal justice system to try to manage the drug problem, a matter that the American Medical Association and the American Psychiatric Association defined as a medical disorder decades ago. I challenge you to try to find anyone with any knowledge of the war on drugs who can conclude with a straight face that it has been successful. This includes most judges, prosecutors, and several previous Drug Czars, the individuals in charge of the Office of National Drug Control Policy. Yet, day after day, we continue our efforts to arrest, convict, and punish our way out of a public health crisis.

We also have been using the criminal justice system as a way to handle some of the consequences of an underfunded and poorly performing system of public education. The phrase "school to prison pipeline" is an unfortunate reality. It refers to educational underachievement as a correlate of criminal justice involvement. The vast majority of prison inmates failed to graduate from high school. Those who drop out of school are four to six times more likely than high school graduates to be arrested.

Human capital, the education, training, and health of the workforce, is an important determinant of economic productivity and growth. In 1990, the United States was ranked sixth in the world in terms of education and health. In 2016, the US ranking dropped to twenty-seventh. This reflects the relative lack of effectiveness of public education and public health and helps us understand why the US criminal justice system is the repository for the consequences of poor educational outcomes and lack of adequate mental health care and substance abuse treatment.

We continue to use the criminal justice system to try to manage homelessness. Homelessness is increasingly being criminalized in many jurisdictions through laws that regulate where the homeless can sleep or congregate. A new report by the National Law Center for Homelessness and Poverty concludes that about three-quarters of cities in the United States have outlawed camping or sleeping in public.[45] They also note that there has been a 15 percent increase in such laws since 2016.

There are several factors that have contributed significantly to the homeless crisis today. Affordable housing capacity in the United States has dwindled. There has been a 60 percent reduction in affordable housing stock in the United States between 2010 and 2016.[46] A more recent assessment by the National Low Income Housing Coalition reports a shortage of seven million affordable rentals for extremely low-income renters.[47] Moreover, the recession of the later 2000s pushed tens of thousands of previously housed individuals and families onto the streets, many of whom remain homeless today.

The criminal justice system has been used to mitigate a crisis that began in the 1980s and shows few signs of abating. In fact, there has been a 50 percent increase in homeless individuals between 2016 and 2018.[48]

We have, in effect, criminalized the consequences of these public policy decisions, and it is no coincidence that the US criminal justice system has an extraordinarily high prevalence of disordered and disadvantaged individuals. Instead of adequately funding public health, substance abuse treatment, public education, and affordable housing, among other things, we have tried to punish our way out of the consequences. There is nothing about punishment that makes the mentally ill mentally healthy, the addicted or substance abusers drug free, the homeless housed, or those with educational deficits educated, and it does nothing to address poverty and disadvantage. In fact, the evidence is clear that punishment itself is criminogenic. Rather than reducing recidivism, punishment actually increases the risk of reoffending.

There is no indication that there will be any comprehensive, fundamental positive change to public health, public education, affordable housing, or other social and economic programming for the disadvantaged. The political reality is that these are just not a priority. It is equally unfortunate that the criminal justice system is ill-prepared to deal with the fallout.

The bigger picture I mentioned earlier involves the realization that many criminal offenders enter the justice system with complex, comorbid conditions. Poverty, addiction, and mental illness tend to co-occur. Periodic homelessness is not unusual, nor are educational deficits and employment problems. Unfortunately, criminal offenders leave the justice system in no better shape than when they went in, and often in worse shape. That perpetuates the cycle of reoffending.

It is time to appreciate the scope and scale of the challenges that have been dumped on the criminal justice system. We have spent the past fifty years trying to punish bad behavior out of criminal offenders. It has not worked.[49] Recidivism rates provide a reasonable indication of that failure. Today, 85 percent of offenders are rearrested.[50] Unfortunately, in all likelihood, this is an underestimate of recidivism since it is based on those who are caught. Only about 50 percent of crimes are ever reported to the police. Of those crimes that are reported, the arrest rate is highly variable. On average, about 40 percent of violent crimes known to the police lead to an arrest or clearance; about 20 percent of reported property crimes lead to an arrest.

Despite what some policy makers may wish, the criminal justice system as currently designed and operated does a horrible job of reducing crime and reoffending. It does an even worse job of returning individuals back to the community in any condition to be productive members of society. It does that at an annual direct cost of one trillion dollars.[51] Other cost estimates have expanded the crimes included as well as the indirect costs to victims and their families such as pain and suffering and quality of life. These recent analyses show that the 121 million crimes committed in 2017 are estimated to have a $2.1 trillion annual price tag, $625 billion in direct costs and $1.5 trillion in indirect victim costs. The vast majority of the cost (80 percent) is attributed to violent crime.[52]

The cost of criminal justice is not just financial. An extensive evidence base indicates that criminal justice involvement has a variety of negative collateral consequences. Recent studies indicate a number of effects of incarceration on the individuals incarcerated, their families, and their communities.[53] They include:

- poor physical and mental health outcomes for those incarcerated and their families
- employment problems and compromised future earnings
- family disruption
- reduced civic engagement
- financial and material insecurity and reliance on public assistance
- housing problems and residential instability
- compromised education and health outcomes for children of the incarcerated
- loss of neighborhood/community informal social control

Very recent research documents the relationship between parental incarceration and the psychiatric and functional outcomes of young adults.

The evidence shows higher rates of psychiatric diagnoses including attention-deficit/hyperactivity disorder, conduct disorder, anxiety disorders, illicit drug-use disorder, having a felony charge, incarceration, failure to complete high school, and being socially isolated. It is clear that parental incarceration has significant intergenerational consequences regarding mental health, functional outcomes, criminality, and criminal justice involvement.[54] The authors conclude "parental incarceration is associated with a broad range of psychiatric, legal, financial and social outcomes during young adulthood. Parental incarceration is a common experience that may perpetuate disadvantage from generation to generation."[55]

Another study looks more broadly at incarceration and public health across counties and concludes, "Consistent with findings from prior research on individuals, families and at the state level, results of our analyses indicate that higher levels of incarceration are associated with higher levels of both morbidity and mortality."[56]

While much of the research focuses on the effects of incarceration on a variety of negative outcomes, a comprehensive review of the evidence implicates other forms of contact with the criminal justice system, including arrest, conviction for misdemeanors, and placement on probation.[57] For example, the New York City health commissioner recently declared that criminal justice involvement, "even brief contact with the police or indirect exposure, is associated with lasting harm to people's physical and mental health."[58]

But it just gets worse. Negative collateral consequences are also a result of deliberate, statutory, and regulatory restrictions placed on criminal offenders because of their criminal status. These "hidden sentences" are independent of and in addition to the official sentences imposed by the courts, sentences such as incarceration or probation.[59]

The American Bar Association's Criminal Justice Section in collaboration with the US Department of Justice's National Institute of Justice created the National Inventory of the Collateral Consequences of Conviction (NICCC). The NICCC is a compilation of codified regulations and restrictions imposed on offenders subsequent to their discharge from the criminal justice system. These regulations and restrictions are for all fifty states, the District of Columbia, and the federal government.

Joshua Kaiser has provided the first comprehensive analysis of the NICCC. He defines these hidden sentences as adverse restrictions or requirements, imposed by law as a consequence of a criminal status. What distinguishes these from criminal sentences is that hidden sentences are external to the criminal law and/or imposed by someone other than a sentencing judge.[60]

All told, there are more than 42,600 post-release restrictions or regulations across fifty-two jurisdictions included in the NICCC. For example, there are 23,715 restricting employment, 15,623 restricting occupational licensing and certification, 15,180 restricting business licensing and other property rights, 4,579 affecting political and civic participation, and 3,499 restricting residency. These restrict, limit, or regulate things ranging from employment and occupation licensing (more than 60 percent), ability to own businesses, participate in government programs, engage in contractual services or sell and distribute goods (40 percent), limit access to government loans and grants, including job training and business loans, and limit access to public assistance, unemployment, and workers' compensation benefits. Drug convictions can drastically limit access to public housing and other federal benefits, including Social Security and food stamps.[61]

The point is straightforward and compelling. Not only does incarceration produce a variety of negative collateral effects at the individual, community, county, and state level, so does criminal justice involvement more broadly. On top of that are tens of thousands of deliberately imposed limitations, restrictions, and regulations on individuals who we have finished officially punishing. These hidden sentences dramatically expand the number and variety of collateral consequences imposed on criminal offenders.

The obvious irony is that the system presumably intended to reduce crime and recidivism produces, through a stunning variety of collateral consequences, precisely the opposite effect. In retrospect, an 85 percent re-offense rate should not be the least bit surprising.

The task is enormous—essentially reinventing criminal justice as we know it. In effect, this effort perhaps should be guided by the axiom from the American medical community—"first do no harm." This probably sounds like an absolutely contrary concept for the criminal justice system, which has been designed to inflict more harm on more people.

To be clear, "do no harm" should not apply to everyone who enters the criminal justice system. Some people deserve harsh punishment in the form of lengthy prison sentences, even life without parole. For the rest, it is important to appreciate that punishment has consequences. Not the consequences that were envisioned, such as deterring future crime. The research is clear that rather than reducing recidivism, incarceration actually increases the probability of reoffending once released. We must also appreciate that the vast majority of people we incarcerate or otherwise punish will leave prison or leave correctional control, so an obvious question is what risks to public safety do they pose when they exit the justice system.

What I am suggesting is careful thought about downstream consequences associated with decisions made in the moment, decisions such as what cases to prosecute, what to charge, what to plea negotiate, and what to impose at sentencing.

I find the medical metaphor also relevant for how offenders are treated while in custody and under correctional control. There is overwhelming evidence that identifying and mitigating the criminogenic circumstances associated with an individual's criminality is key to reducing the risk of reoffending. The goal should be to return those who have been through the justice system back to the community in a position to remain crime free, as well as to be a contributing, productive member of society, earning a living and supporting a family.

While I have spent a fair amount of time here discussing correctional outcomes, this is not a book about how prisons should be run. The first two books I wrote about criminal justice reform (*Criminal Justice at the Crossroads* in 2015 and *The Future of Crime and Punishment* in 2016 and updated in 2019) took on the big picture of reform, including a good bit on reforming corrections, especially prisons, parole and reentry, as well as probation.

By way of reference, there are excellent models for prison reform that have come to US policy makers' attention in the past ten years. For example, Norway shifted its incarceration policies about twenty years ago, to get away from a retribution-focused, punitive system to what they have today, which emphasizes rehabilitation.

> The idea is to give them a sense of normality and to help them focus on preparing for a new life when they get out . . . We start planning their release on the first day they arrive. In Norway, all will be released. So we are releasing your neighbor. If we treat inmates like animals in prison, then we will release animals onto your street.[62]

Norway has transformed incarceration policy as well as how they think about crime and punishment. They use incarceration sparingly (the incarceration rate is around 65 per 100,000 Norwegians). Most remarkably, for those who have been incarcerated, the recidivism rate is an extraordinarily low 20 percent.

I am not suggesting that we should immediately transform all US prisons to the Norwegian model, but their experience does provide a compelling approach that states and the federal government should investigate and seriously consider.

Let me be very clear about my take on criminal justice reform. While I will be proposing aggressive change, especially to the court system, that does not mean I recommend that we shut down prisons and eliminate punishment. On the contrary, punishment plays a very important role and prisons are absolutely necessary. Punishment is one way of holding offenders accountable and extracting revenge. There is a place for retribution—an eye for an eye. Some people just commit horrible crimes, and exacting vengeance may be entirely justified and proper. However, I will suggest that we need to be more selective and more reserved in our use of retribution. It has its place, but it also has limited utility in terms of positive criminal justice outcomes. It is not designed to reduce recidivism or desistance from crime.

Incarceration is necessary. There are people that commit very bad crimes and they need to be separated from society. Others are at a very high risk of reoffending and for them, prison is the only reasonable way to manage that high risk. Then there is retribution, where certain offenders simply deserve to be incarcerated.

On the other hand, incarceration should not be automatic. It should not be the default decision. Not everyone needs to be incarcerated in order to preserve public safety. Moreover, the evidence is overwhelming that 1) punishment does not effectively deter, as evidenced by our extraordinarily high recidivism rates; and 2) incarceration (prison and jail) is criminogenic, actually increasing the probability of reoffending rather than reducing it. What I am suggesting in the following pages is careful thought about the downstream consequences associated with decisions made in local courts, especially those decisions made by prosecutors, judges, and defense counsel.

We need to become smarter about how these decisions are made. We need to be more selective in who we decide should be incarcerated. Making smarter and more selective decisions requires changes in procedures, statutes, and culture. All of this will be covered in the following pages.

COMPREHENSIVE REFORM

Despite what some policy makers may wish, the criminal justice system as currently designed and operated does a horrible job of reducing crime and reoffending. We have spent the past fifty years trying to punish bad behavior out of criminal offenders. It has not worked and we have done a remarkable job of proving that.[63]

Unfortunately, criminal offenders often leave the justice system in worse shape than when they went in, reducing the likelihood that they can be productive members of society. In fact, current criminal justice policy has created a class of individuals who in all likelihood will be permanently dependent on public resources. That is not prudent public policy, nor is it a good use of public resources.

Again, many criminal offenders enter the justice system with complex, comorbid conditions. Poverty, addiction, and mental illness tend to co-occur. Many have experienced traumatic brain injuries leading to neuro-cognitive impairment such as executive dysfunction. Periodic homelessness is not unusual, nor are educational deficits and employment problems. That perpetuates the cycle of reoffending.

It is important to appreciate the scope and scale of the challenges that have been dumped on the criminal justice system. Because of a variety of policy decisions at all levels of government, the criminal justice system has become the default set of agencies and institutions that are responsible for managing the consequences of these decisions. That has resulted in a significant expansion of the criminal law to address these problems as well as the requisite expansion of the size and cost of the criminal justice system.

But in my mind, comprehensive criminal justice reform should go well beyond reducing recidivism. For example, monitoring or supervising individuals on probation or parole is intended to manage the risk of reoffending, primarily by attempting to reduce criminal opportunity by imposing conditions on individuals, rules they are expected to comply with, as well as direct supervision by a parole or probation officer. Probation and parole constitute the largest segment of the US correctional population. So, in terms of sheer numbers of criminal offenders, the bulk of our recidivism reduction efforts are devoted to those who have been conditionally released to the community under supervision.

Attempting to reduce reoffending through supervision and control is only part of the equation, the part that focuses on the "how" of criminality, the opportunity to commit crime. What is missing is the "why" of criminality, those situations, circumstances, disorders, and impairments that are fundamentally related to offending and that characterize much of the US criminal justice population.

Jeffrey Butts and Vincent Schiraldi, two keen observers of American criminal justice, have done an excellent job of articulating this point in their commentary "Recidivism Reconsidered."[64] They recommend a broader perspective:[65]

> Relying on recidivism defines the mission of community corrections in law enforcement terms, relieving agencies of their responsibility for other outcomes such as employment, education and housing . . . The justice system should monitor and assess how people are reintegrated into a community following system contact. Rather than asking only "What's the recidivism rate?" policymakers and the public should learn to ask "What's the graduation rate, what's the employment rate, and how many are now living independently?" If justice systems are to be truly correctional, whether in the community or not, policymakers should begin to hold them to more rigorous standards . . . If community corrections programs were designed to facilitate

desistance rather than simply combatting recidivism, they would naturally focus their efforts on maximizing skills, strengths and positive assets.

The point is well taken. The focus on reducing recidivism directs resources to managing risk and punishment, rather than those positive factors that enhance desistance from crime. This simple focus on recidivism got us to where we are today, a criminal justice system that still is primarily focused on trying to punish reoffending out of individuals. As we continue to use recidivism as the holy grail of criminal justice, our attention will remain on the bankrupt idea that punishment is key to reducing reoffending.

A primary focus on desistence forces us to think about the factors associated with criminality and, in turn, reducing the risk of criminal involvement. It expands the complexity from the reflexive crime and punishment model, to the more sophisticated and realistic approach of mitigating criminogenic circumstances and promoting those associated with desistence. The goal should be to return those who have been through the justice system back to the community in a position to remain crime free (obviously), as well as to be contributing, productive, taxpaying members of society, earning a living, supporting a family, and not being a burden on public resources. In order to accomplish that, we have to 1) effectively manage risk of criminality; 2) identify why particular offenders reoffend; 3) mitigate those circumstances; and 4) promote those factors that are associated with being economically productive, responsible adults. Moreover, this needs to be done on a case-by-case basis, where the interventions are tailored to the individual and his or her circumstances.

Many would argue that this should not be the responsibility of the criminal justice system. I could not agree more. But this is where we find ourselves. I have argued many times that criminal justice reform is not just about reforming the criminal justice system. Rather, it involves fundamental changes to collateral institutions such as public health, education, workforce training, and housing, among others.

Unfortunately, there seems little reason to be optimistic about the bigger picture of reform. I just do not see a political appetite for fundamental reinvention of public health, education, or housing. While it is clear from the efforts of interest groups and nonprofits that these institutions are flawed in fundamental ways, and in turn contributing to the dysfunctionality of the criminal justice system, creating sufficient, evidence-based public health capacity or appropriately funding public education or public housing do not show up on the political radar. I may be wrong. The current (summer of 2020) demand to defund local law enforcement and divert that money to public health and affordable housing may gain traction. If it does, then we may see some changes in local human services.

REFORM IS LOCAL

Nearly all of the calls for criminal justice reform place the responsibility at the state or federal level, calling on state legislatures and Congress to change sentencing and parole laws, decriminalize drug crimes and other public-order offenses, expand opportunities for probation, reduce the size of prisons, and a variety of other legislative and statutory changes. Such changes are fundamentally important and must be part of the bigger picture of criminal justice reform. However, my concern is that the attention focused on legislative decisions detracts from where I believe most of criminal justice reform must occur—at the local level of government.

Crime is local. It occurs in cities and counties, in neighborhoods, on streets, in parking lots and parking garages, in houses and businesses. As such, crime is considered an affront or harm to a community. Moreover, the Sixth Amendment prescribes that criminal offenders shall be adjudicated in the community in which it occurred.

> In all criminal prosecutions, the accused shall enjoy the right to a speedy and public trial, by an impartial jury of the State and district wherein the crime shall have been committed, which district shall have been previously ascertained by law.

The location where a criminal case shall be prosecuted in state prosecutions is the county (or county equivalent) in which the crime occurred. For federal prosecutions, the proper venue is the federal judicial district in which the crime occurred.

There are more than 3,100 counties or county equivalents in the United States. Each of these is subject to the laws put in place by state legislatures, laws that govern such things as criminal procedure, criminal offenses, sentencing, and parole release. Thus, legislatures set the stage for the administration of criminal justice, and it is in local jurisdictions where all of this plays out.

The bulk of the criminal justice system is local—police, prosecutors, judges, courts, pretrial officials, jails, and probation are all located in counties, and counties define the jurisdiction where they have authority. There is variation across states in terms of which level of government is responsible for paying for particular components of criminal justice. However, when it is aggregated and averaged across states, the majority of criminal justice expenditures are incurred by local government, that is, cities and counties.[66] Law enforcement is a large component of local expenditures (local police and sheriff), but the court system adds substantially to the overall spending by local government as well. Local government accounts for nearly two-thirds of total nonfederal criminal justice expenditures (63 percent). The states' responsibility is 37 percent and the bulk of that is expenditures on corrections (mainly prison and parole).

The court systems in this country are local entities, consisting of locally elected judges and District Attorneys (a few states appoint judges and District Attorneys), which are responsible for adjudicating criminal offenders who commit crimes in local jurisdictions. While the courts in a particular state are subject to the laws and procedures prescribed by that state's legislature, there is built-in flexibility in terms of how cases are resolved (for example, criminal prosecution versus deferred adjudication or other forms of pretrial diversion) and how offenders are punished (for example, prison or jail versus probation). Presumably, these differences across counties in case outcomes, for example, are a reflection of local beliefs, attitudes, and values.

So, the decisions made by local prosecutors, judges, and public defenders determine, within boundaries set by state laws, the outcomes of cases. In turn, it is my working premise that comprehensive, effective, cost-efficient criminal justice reform, defined as reducing crime and recidivism, should devote considerable effort and resources to changing the decision-making processes in local court systems.

There is one additional consideration that I believe supports local jurisdictions, especially urban areas, as the center of gravity for criminal justice reform. Most large metropolitan areas in the United States tend to be more liberal and, in many cases, more progressive, than their rural counterparts, and in many instances, than their state legislatures. For example, Hillary Clinton won eighty-eight of the one hundred largest counties in the 2016 election; and fifteen of the twenty largest cities in the United States have Democratic mayors.

There has been pushback from state legislatures in recent years to local progressive policies (for example, the transgender bathroom issue, minimum wage, taxes on soft drinks, and gun control, among others). Nevertheless, these larger metropolitan counties are politically conducive for meaningful criminal justice reform. In fact, the progressive prosecutors who have been elected in recent years represent the leading edge of rethinking criminal prosecution. Having said that, there certainly has been opposition to decisions not to prosecute low-level drug possession cases and minor theft cases, and changing standards for pretrial detention. That opposition originates from law enforcement and district attorney associations, and state legislatures, as well as the Attorney General of the United States, who recently declared in a speech before the Fraternal Order of Police that[67]

> the emergence in some of our large cities of district attorneys that style themselves as "social justice" reformers, who spend their time undercutting

the police, letting criminals off the hook and refusing to enforce the law, is demoralizing to law enforcement and dangerous to public safety.

There is no evidence that the policies of progressive prosecutors are dangerous to public safety, but, unfortunately, evidence and science are not always the standard.

Despite some resistance, these more progressive communities are serving as incubators of justice reform innovation, especially with regard to criminal prosecution. While this is all relatively new, it appears that there is ongoing, local political support for these progressive initiatives.

It is important to point out that within the rather highly structured system of laws and procedure, there is a considerable amount of discretion. The criminal code identifies all of the acts that are violations of the criminal law. The penal code dictates how sentencing will occur and the appropriate punishment upon conviction of a particular crime. The code of criminal procedure lays out the various due process protections and procedural rules that govern the processing of cases. Within that context, there is considerable opportunity for judgment or discretion, which permits variation in how criminal justice is administered locally.

A good example of this is Williamson County, Texas, historically a largely rural, conservative county just north of Travis County, home to Austin and the University of Texas. For decades, Williamson County branded itself the toughest county in Texas, which is, as many know, a decidedly tough-on-crime state. That agenda was spearheaded by Ken Anderson, the long-term District Attorney. Williamson County was known as being tough on crime, and the DA, the prosecutors, and the judges fulfilled this promise.

Among other things, Williamson County is where Michael Morton was prosecuted, convicted, and sentenced to prison for murdering his wife. It turns out, however, that he did not murder his wife. He spent nearly twenty-five years in prison due to the illegal acts of District Attorney Ken Anderson, who withheld exculpatory evidence from the defense, a violation of *Brady v. Maryland*. Apparently, the goal was tough on crime at any cost.

Fast forward to 2016 and the election of Shawn Dick, a progressive Republican who is now the Williamson County District Attorney. He, in collaboration with Judge Stacy Matthews and others, is in the process of developing and implementing a variety of innovative diversion programs in an effort to reduce reoffending and address criminogenic circumstances that are associated with criminal offending. Their goal is to rebrand criminal justice in Williamson County from being tough on crime to being smart on crime. This is the same county that was trying to be the toughest in Texas just a few years ago. This is possible because local officials can and do shape the administration of criminal justice in important ways.

While we are in the midst of an emerging national conversation about justice reform, high-profile advocacy from a variety of pundits and celebrities, and a wide range of national nonprofit organizations devoted to reforming everything from policing to reentry from prison, and especially the reduction of the prison population, the local justice system is in important ways an epicenter of fundamental reform. Evidence of this, which will be a central element of this book, is the trend of electing progressive, reform-oriented District Attorneys and judges in local elections.

REFORM IS LODGED IN THE COURT SYSTEM

As my thinking about criminal justice reform has evolved, my focus has narrowed, not because other aspects of criminal justice are unimportant, but because the reality of public policy is the need to leverage reform efforts. There is an increasing consensus that the decisions that are made in the pretrial phase, from the point of arrest through criminal conviction, as well as the sentencing phase, have the greatest impact on the performance of the criminal justice system. What Caleb Foote, the noted legal thinker and professor of law, declared six decades ago certainly holds true today—what is decided in the pretrial phase essentially determines everything else.

This focus on the court system is not intended to detract from other very important components of criminal justice reform. Sentencing needs to be fundamentally overhauled, beginning with eliminating most mandatory and mandatory minimum sentences. Discretion should be returned to judges so they can make individualized sentencing decisions, informed by what I propose in the following pages. Facilitating successful reentry from prison (including mitigating the criminogenic effects of incarceration, assistance with housing, employment, family circumstances, health care, mental health care, and substance-use disorders, etc.) must be a key element of fundamental reform. Parole is an opportunity to provide such reentry assistance. Unfortunately, underfunding and a tough-on-crime culture have seriously inhibited parole in fulfilling its intended function. In many jurisdictions, probation is a lost opportunity that unnecessarily results in the revocation of individuals to prison and jail, with little effort to reduce the likelihood of revocation through providing rehabilitative programs and services. Then there is law enforcement and the variety of problems that are routinely brought to the public's attention in media reports detailing excessive use of force, officer-involved shootings, responses to mental health crisis situations, and racial profiling, among others.

There is consensus among many observers that prosecutors are the most powerful, influential actors in the US criminal justice system. That is not to detract from the roles and responsibilities of judges, but when we consider the variety of decisions that prosecutors make, it becomes evident that these are the decisions that have the greatest consequences. Prosecutors occupy a pivotal position in the day-to-day administration of local criminal justice. As such, the role of the prosecutor in the court system warrants considerable attention in moving reform policy forward.

What should the courts of the future look like? How should the roles and responsibilities of judges, prosecutors, and the defense bar change, and how should the interactions of these key individuals in the court system transform to achieve the big-picture goals of criminal justice as I have outlined above? Answering these questions and more is what this book is about.

NOTES

1. Enns et al., "What Percentage of Americans Have Ever Had a Family Member Incarcerated?"
2. Elderbroom et al., "Every Second: The Impact of the Incarceration Crisis on America's Families."
3. Friedman, "Just Facts: As Many Americans Have Criminal Records as College Diplomas."
4. Gramlich, "America's Incarceration Rate Is at a Two-Decade Low."
5. Robertson, "Crime Is Down, Yet U.S. Incarceration Rates Are Still Among the Highest in the World."
6. The Sentencing Project, "People Serving Life Exceeds Entire Prison Population of 1970."
7. Justice Policy Institute, "Sentencing: Long Prison Terms."
8. Porporino, "Developments and Challenges in Probation Practice."
9. Committee on Causes and Consequences of High Rate of Incarceration, Jeremy Travis (Editor), Bruce Western (Editor), Steve Redburn (Editor), and Committee on Law and Justice, *The Growth of Incarceration in the United States.*
10. Jalbert et al., "A Multi-Site Evaluation of Reduced Probation Caseload Size in an Evidence-Based Practice Setting."
11. Bureau of Justice Statistics, "Sentencing and Time Served."
12. The Urban Institute, "A Matter of Time," http://apps.urban.org/features/long-prison-terms/demographics.html.
13. The Sentencing Project, "Fact Sheet: Trends in U.S. Corrections."
14. The Pew Center on the States, "Time Served: The High Cost, Low Return of Longer Prison Terms."
15. The Sentencing Project, "Fact Sheet: Trends in U.S. Corrections."

16. Wodahl, Ogle, and Heck, "Revocation Trends: A Threat to the Legitimacy of Community-Based Corrections."

17. ACLU Pennsylvania, ACLU of Pennsylvania Releases New Report Detailing Massive Expansion of Criminal Law, https://www.aclupa.org/en/press-releases/aclu-pennsylvania-releases-new-report-detailing-massive-expansion-criminal-law.

18. Copland and Mangual, "Overcriminalizing America," https://www.manhattan-institute.org/html/overcriminalizing-america-overview-and-model-legislation-states-11399.html#notes.

19. Weiss and MacKenzie, "A Global Perspective on Incarceration."

20. Raphael and Stoll, "Why Are So Many Americans in Prison?"

21. The White House Fact Sheet, Law and Justice, December 21, 2018. Retrieved from whitehouse.gov/briefings-statements/president-donald-j-trump-secures-landmark-legislation-to-make-our-federal-justice-system-fairer-and-our-communities-safer/.

22. Jones, "Van Jones Prison Reform Bill a Christmas Miracle." Retrieved from https://www.realclearpolitics.com/video/2018/12/19/van_jones_prison_reform_bill_a_christmas_miracle.html.

23. Jones, "Ten Reasons to Celebrate the First Step Act." Retrieved from https://www.cnn.com/2018/12/21/opinions/ten-reasons-to-celebrate-first-step-act-jones-and-jackson/index.html.

24. Keane, Judy. "Bishops' Conference Praises Senate for Passage of the First Step Act and Encourages Passage in the House."

25. Vogt, "In First Step's Wake, States Tinker with Mandatory Minimums."

26. Brennan Center for Justice, "Follow the Texas Model."

27. Glog, Texas Public Policy Foundation, "Texas Adult Corrections: A Model for the Rest of the Nation."

28. McCullough, "Three Texas Inmates Have Died at the Hands of Prison Officers as Use of Force Continues to Rise."

29. Graves, "Texas State Jails: Time for a Reboot?"; Smith, Texas Criminal Justice Coalition, "A Failure in the Fourth Degree."

30. Smith, Texas Criminal Justice Coalition, "A Failure in the Fourth Degree."

31. Texas Department of Criminal Justice, "FY 2018 Statistical Report."

32. Nichanian, "From Marijuana to the Death Penalty, States Led the Way in 2019."

33. Nichanian, "From Marijuana to the Death Penalty, States Led the Way in 2019."

34. The Sentencing Project, "U.S. Prison Population Trends."

35. Booker et al., Brennan Center for Justice, *Ending Mass Incarceration: Ideas from Today's Leaders*.

36. Astor, "Left and Right Agree on Criminal Justice: They Were Both Wrong Before."

37. Kelly, *The Future of Crime and Punishment*.

38. Jaffe, *Insane Consequences*, 19.

39. Kelly et al., *From Retribution to Public Safety*; Kelly, *The Future of Crime and Punishment*.

40. World Population Review, retrieved from http://worldpopulationreview .com/countries/best-healthcare-in-the-world/.

41. Khazan, "What's Actually Wrong with the U.S. Health System."

42. Krugman, "Opinion: Why Does America Hate Its Children?"

43. APM Research Lab Staff, "The Color of Coronavirus."

44. Quiñones et al., "Racial/Ethnic Differences in Multimorbidity Development and Chronic Disease Accumulation for Middle-Aged Adults."

45. The National Law Center for Homelessness and Poverty, "Housing, Not Handcuffs," 2019. Retrieved from http://nlchp.org/wp-content/uploads/ 2019/12/HOUSING-NOT-HANDCUFFS-2019-FINAL.pdf.

46. Jan, "America's Affordable-Housing Stock Dropped by 60 Percent from 2010 to 2016."

47. Babcock, "Tech Start-ups Look to Disrupt the Affordable Housing Industry."

48. Janosko, "Individual Homelessness: What Are the Trends?"

49. There is an extensive literature on the failure of the US criminal justice system. See, for example, Kelly, *The Future of Crime and Punishment*; Kelly and Pitman, *Confronting Underground Justice*; Barkow, *Prisoners of Politics*; Alexander, *The New Jim Crow*; Benforado, *Unfair: The New Science of Criminal Injustice*; and Bazelon, *Charged: The New Movement to Transform American Prosecution and End Mass Incarceration*, among others.

50. Alper, Durose, and Markman, "2018 Update on Prisoner Recidivism: A 9-Year Follow-up Period (2005–2014)."

51. American Action Forum, "The Economic Costs of the U.S. Criminal Justice System."

52. Miller et al., "Incidence and Costs of Personal and Property Crimes in the United States, 2017."

53. Kirk and Wakefield, "Collateral Consequences of Punishment."

54. Gifford et al., "Association of Parental Incarceration with Psychiatric and Functional Outcomes of Young Adults."

55. Gifford et al., "Association of Parental Incarceration with Psychiatric and Functional Outcomes of Young Adults," 1.

56. Weidner and Schultz, "Examining the Relationship between U.S. Incarceration Rates and Population Health at the County Level," 1.

57. Kirk and Wakefield, "Collateral Consequences of Punishment."

58. Vergano, "The Criminal Justice System Is Bad for Your Health," 2.

59. Kaiser, "Revealing the Hidden Sentence."

60. Kaiser, "Revealing the Hidden Sentence."

61. Kaiser, "Revealing the Hidden Sentence."

62. BBC, "How Norway Turns Criminals into Good Neighbours."

63. There is an extensive literature on the failure of the US criminal justice system. See for example Kelly, *The Future of Crime and Punishment*; Kelly and Pitman, *Confronting Underground Justice*; Barkow, *Prisoners of Politics*; Alexander, *The New Jim Crow*; Benforado, *Unfair: The New Science of Criminal Injustice*; and Bazelon, *Charged: The New Movement to Transform American Prosecution and End Mass Incarceration*, among others.

64. Butts and Schiraldi, "Recidivism Reconsidered: Preserving the Community Justice Mission of Community Corrections," 2018. Retrieved from https://www.hks.harvard.edu/sites/default/files/centers/wiener/programs/pcj/files/recidivism_reconsidered.pdf.

65. Butts and Schiraldi, "Recidivism Reconsidered," 1, 13.

66. Bureau of Justice Statistics, "Percent Distribution of Expenditures for the Justice System by Type of Government, Fiscal 2016," retrieved from https://www.bjs.gov/index.cfm?ty=dcdetail&iid=286.

67. NBC News, "Progressive DAs Are Shaking Up the Criminal Justice System. Pro-police Groups Aren't Happy," August 19, 2019, retrieved from https://www.nbcnews.com/politics/justice-department/these-reform-prosecutors-are-shaking-system-pro-police-groups-aren-n1033286.

1

The US Criminal Court System

The administration of criminal justice is divided into four segments: state legislatures and Congress, law enforcement, the courts, and corrections. State legislatures at the state level and Congress at the federal level 1) write the criminal code, which defines behaviors that are violations of the criminal law; 2) prescribe how sentencing shall be conducted and what the punishment is; and 3) establish the rules for the lawful operation of the criminal justice system (the code of criminal procedure).

As I discussed in the introduction, both state legislatures and Congress have expanded the criminal code dramatically over the past fifty years. The result is the broadening of criminal liability, in turn increasing the number of individuals who end up in the criminal justice system. State and federal sentencing laws have also changed in striking ways, especially in terms of the upsurge of mandatory sentences. The goal has been to enhance punishment for more people. Changes to the criminal and penal codes have clearly accomplished that objective.

The code of criminal procedure, as the name implies, stipulates how the government shall lawfully conduct the business of the criminal justice system. This includes constitutional protections and guarantees found largely in the Bill of Rights, such as the Fourth Amendment protection against unreasonable searches and seizures, the Fifth Amendment protection against self-incrimination and double jeopardy, the Sixth Amendment right to counsel and to trial, and the Eighth Amendment prohibition against cruel and unusual punishment, among others. The code of criminal procedure also reflects decades and decades of court decisions that clarify, modify, or change what these protections and guarantees mean.

Law enforcement controls the front door of the justice system, responding to suspected crimes, investigating and gathering evidence, and arresting suspects once probable cause has been established. Probable cause, or
the reasonable belief that a crime has been committed and that the suspect
probably committed the crime, is the necessary evidentiary standard for a
lawful arrest. Once an arrest is made, the police consider the case cleared,
meaning essentially the end of their involvement, with the exception of
things such as subsequent follow-up investigation or testifying at hearings and trials. After an arrest is made, the case is handed off to the court
system, in particular the prosecutor and individuals who work in what is
called the pretrial system.

Corrections consists of the sets of individuals, agencies, and institutions
that are responsible for imposing correctional control over individuals
who have been convicted of a crime. It includes jail, prison, probation,
and parole, as well as variations or modifications of each of these. Jail,
prison, and probation are forms of post-conviction sentences that are imposed on individuals. Jail and prison serve to physically separate offenders from the community. Probation is conditional supervised release to
the community and is a sentence imposed in lieu of incarceration. Parole
is also defined as conditional supervised release to the community, but
it is what is imposed on individuals who are released early from prison.

The criminal court system consists of everything from the point of arrest
to the carrying out of the sentence, everything between law enforcement
and corrections. It includes the very early phases of processing cases, such
as booking suspects into jail and the preliminary hearing where detention
decisions are made, to charging and prosecutorial decisions, indictment,
arraignment, pretrial hearings, plea deals and the occasional criminal
trial, and determining the sentence.

While criticism of US criminal justice spans across all of its components
from police to prison and parole and everything in between, the court
system is the primary focal point of this book. That is not to say that
the concerns or problems with other components of American criminal
justice are unimportant. The US correctional system, especially prison
and jail, have been the primary targets of criminal justice reform. Mass
incarceration, probably the most commonly voiced criticism of US criminal justice policy, goes directly to the extensive use of prison and jail for
punishing individuals convicted of crimes. The critiques of prison and jail
do not end with the sheer size. The racial and ethnic disparities surrounding who is incarcerated are also commonly voiced. There also has been a
good deal of criticism leveled at probation and parole systems, directed in
part on the failure to adequately address the criminogenic needs of those
under supervision and what is perceived to be an excessive use of revo-

cation. Law enforcement certainly has been under fire for use of force, officer-involved shootings, and racial profiling, among other things.

My decision to focus on the courts is driven by one crucial observation. The decisions made by the key actors in the court system—judges, prosecutors, and defense attorneys—have considerable downstream impacts, including the probability of criminal conviction, the nature and severity of the punishment, and ultimately the likelihood of recidivism, as well as effects on many other longer-term outcomes. The judicial decision to detain someone during the pretrial phase can be and often is highly criminogenic. Obviously, the sentence imposed by the judge has a substantial impact on the risk of future criminality as well as a variety of other circumstances such as employment and housing. Moreover, prosecutorial decisions such as what charges to bring, what to indict a defendant for, terms of plea negotiations, and sentence recommendations have profound implications for case outcomes.

The courts we are concerned with here are referred to as trial courts, the felony trial courts (called District Courts, Superior Courts, Circuit Courts), which are courts of original or general jurisdiction, and the misdemeanor courts, which are characterized by limited jurisdiction (called County Courts, Municipal Courts, Magistrate Courts, Justice of the Peace Courts). These trial courts, and the judges or magistrates who preside over them, are responsible for overseeing the processing of felony and misdemeanor cases. This typically begins with the first time a defendant appears in court after his or her arrest. The term for this hearing varies depending on the state, but the common label is magistration, or initial appearance. At this hearing, a suspect is informed of the charges and his/ her due process protections, is asked to enter a plea, and if the individual is in jail, which is routine for felonies and many misdemeanors, the court will make a determination regarding release, typically by setting a bail amount. The use of money bail and how decisions are made about release versus detention are very contentious issues at the moment and a topic that we will return to later.

The court will then oversee a variety of activities in the processing of felony and misdemeanor defendants, including appointment of counsel, formal charging, determination of probable cause, indictment where the formal charges are determined (either by a grand jury, which files an indictment, or by a prosecutor, who files a bill of information), arraignment, where the defendant is informed of the charges and enters a plea, pretrial hearings on a wide variety of matters, plea negotiation followed by a guilty plea, occasionally a criminal trial, sentencing hearings for those who enter a guilty plea or are convicted at trial, and probation revocations, where someone on conditional release has violated the conditions of supervision and is before the court to determine if he/she should be revoked to incarceration or permitted to remain on probation, among others.

THE STATE OF THE CRIMINAL COURTS

My purpose with this book is to examine the relationship between the administration of American criminal justice and the court system as broadly conceived (from arrest through sentencing). The guiding question is what is the role of the courts, the key players in the courts, and the decisions they make in understanding the dysfunction and ineffectiveness of the criminal justice system. The more important task is then to identify necessary changes to the court system in order to move comprehensive criminal justice reform forward. I begin by assessing the functioning of the American criminal courts, in particular, the demands on court resources.

A report recently issued by the American Bar Association Task Force on Preservation of the Justice System titled "Crisis in the Courts" declared:[1]

> The courts of our country are in crisis. The failure of state and local legislatures to provide adequate funding is effectively—at times literally—closing the doors of our justice system . . . There can be little doubt that the adverse impact of budget cuts on the courts' ability to resolve cases in a reasonably prompt manner degrades their traditional roles in maintaining societal order and public safety. Most obviously, many states have experienced delays in the resolution of criminal dockets to the point where judges and prosecutors are faced with the dilemma of warehousing untried defendants in local jails . . . Such delays are rapidly becoming the rule.

Margaret Marshall, the Massachusetts Chief Justice, described the underfunding and crowding in her state courts as at "the tipping point of dysfunction."[2] George Gascon, the former District Attorney of San Francisco County, California, describes the lack of judges, staff, and courtrooms in San Francisco as a "tremendous problem."[3] San Francisco Public Defender Jeff Adachi calls it a "crisis in the courtroom."[4] When asked about case backlogs and underfunding of courts, the presiding judge for the Santa Clara County (California) Superior Courts stated, "I'd say it's gotten worse [in the last ten years]. Because of the cumulative effect of years of underfunding is really taking its toll, even in some courts that were able to absorb some of the underfunding early on. The cumulative effects are really taking hold now."[5]

Unfortunately, this situation is not new. As Jerold Israel noted in 1996:[6]

Since the mid-1960s, no element of the criminal justice environment has received more attention and been accorded more importance, in both popular and professional commentary, than has the pressure of heavy caseloads. The lack of sufficient resources to deal with overbearing caseloads has been widely characterized as the most pervasive and most critical administrative challenge faced by police, prosecutors, public defenders and courts. National commissions have regularly complained that the criminal justice system is "overcrowded, overworked and undermanned" and must be given "substantially more money" to cure those ills if it is to perform all of the tasks assigned to it.

In some respects, this is a simple matter of increasing demand on the criminal justice system without proportional increases in capacity. Between 1960 and 2018, the US population increased from 179,323,175 to 327,167,434, an 82 percent increase. All else equal, the greater the size of the population, the greater the volume of crime. Over this same time period, the number of violent crimes increased by more than 330 percent, from 288,460 in 1960 to 1,245,065 in 2018. The number of property crimes increased substantially as well, by 132 percent. The pressure on the criminal courts was even more drastic than these long-term trends depict because crime in the United States declined significantly beginning in 2001. Focusing just on the period of dramatic growth in crime, between 1960 and 2000, shows an increase of 400 percent in the number of violent crimes and an increase of nearly 240 percent in property crimes.[7]

The evidence is clear that the expansion of the capacity of the court system—in particular, increases in the number of prosecutors, judges, and public defenders—was not, under any circumstances, nearly proportional to the increase in demand. A longer-term explanation for the lack of adequate funding of the court system is, in part, the massive expansion of corrections over the past forty-five years. There was a 400 percent increase in state spending for corrections between the early 1980s and today.[8] This clearly represented a striking shift in criminal justice spending at the state level. Since state general funds are not limitless, this likely required shifting funds from other areas to fund the increase in corrections. Funding for the courts was undoubtedly impacted by this.

The American Bar Association (ABA) traces the current problems in the courts to more recent events—the economic crisis and recession that began in 2007–2008 and the budget cuts that followed, budget cuts that the ABA argues were more severe than those imposed on other government agencies and entities. The underfunding of the court system has resulted in substantial backlogs of cases, delays in case resolution, and a variety of other collateral consequences.

Over the same approximate period of time, when the recession was creating significant consequences for case processing and disposition, and creating increasing backlogs, criminal case filings were declining. Between 2006 and 2016, the total number of criminal cases nationwide decreased by 17 percent.[9] This has been largely due to substantial declines in crime. Violent and property crimes began declining in the early 1990s. While the rate of violent and property crimes dropped by nearly 50 percent, the number of violent and property crimes declined a more modest 34 percent.[10]

It seems that there were two countervailing trends impacting court caseloads and workloads. Decreasing crime should have mitigated the caseload pressure, but reductions in funding of state courts appear to have resulted in increased pressure on the courts.

A closer look at court statistics reveals substantial variation in caseloads, clearance rates, and backlogs. For example, a compilation of 2016 data on twenty-three states shows differences in clearance rates (the ratio of outgoing or disposed cases divided by the number of incoming cases, expressed as a percentage) ranging from highs of 115 percent in New Mexico, 113 percent in Arizona, and 111 percent in Washington, to lows of 93 percent in Nevada, 88 percent in New Jersey, and 85 percent in California.[11] To be clear, these percentages do not measure the amount of backlog, which is the number of cases carried over from one year to the next. The clearance rates just show the relative ability of courts in a given year to manage the number of new cases compared to the number of disposed cases.

The age of cases disposed, another performance metric, measures the percent of resolved felony cases in a given year that were less than 90 days old, between 91 and 180 days, 181 to 356 days, and more than 365 days. This is an indication of how timely cases are disposed.

The data from the Texas Office of Court Administration on average age of cases at disposition indicate that statewide, 43 percent of felonies are disposed of within ninety days, 20 percent are resolved between three and six months, another 18 percent between six months and one year, and 20 percent require more than one year to resolve.[12] Comparable data for Pennsylvania show that the majority of felonies are disposed of within six months. Eleven percent require a year or more. Wisconsin criminal courts dispose of 55 percent of felony cases within six months and 85 percent within one year.[13,14] About 83 percent of felony cases in California are disposed of within one year.[15] Finally, the Oregon felony courts disposed of 51 percent of active cases within six months, and 71 percent within one year. Significantly, 17 percent took twenty-four months or more to resolve.[16]

So, what can we conclude from clearance rates and age of disposed cases? At first glance, it seems that these standard court performance statistics indicate that while there is variation across states and across counties within states, for the most part the criminal courts are holding their own. They appear to be disposing about as many cases as are coming in the front door, resolving most cases within a year.

However, these measures do not accurately reflect the ongoing pressure on the criminal courts. Two additional measures, the number of cases pending at the end of the year and a bit more formal backlog index, depict a situation that requires the courts to carry over cases from one year to the next.

By way of example, in 2018, the Texas District Courts, which have jurisdiction over felony criminal matters as well as a variety of civil and other matters, added 931,700 cases and disposed of 865,230. The bad news is that they started the year with 888,570 pending cases, a number that has only increased over time. The Texas County Courts, with jurisdiction over misdemeanor crimes and smaller civil matters, added 645,900 cases and disposed of 623,400, but also had 595,500 carried over from the prior year.[17]

The Texas Office of Court Administration collects court data for a metric called the backlog index.[18] The backlog index is the ratio of the number of active, pending cases at the beginning of a given year over the number of cases disposed during that year. An index value of 1.0 means the court disposed of the equivalent of the number of pending cases in a given year. Values of 1.0 or less show relative efficiency of a court. Values over 1.0 represent courts that are having difficulty keeping up.

For the period September 2017 through August 2018, the state-level felony court clearance rate for Texas was 98 percent and the backlog index was .5. The figures for the largest metropolitan areas in the state were comparable to the statewide statistics. However, there was substantial variation across counties. There were a number of typically smaller counties with clearance rates in the 40s, 50s, 60s, and 70s and backlog indexes of over 2, 3, and greater. The pattern for misdemeanor courts was similar, although there was a considerably larger number of counties with low clearance rates and high backlogs.

The Texas criminal courts are not an exception in terms of the necessity of carrying over cases from one year to the next. For example, in 2017, the Indiana criminal courts had 806,275 new felony and misdemeanor cases filed, disposed of 777,767, but began the year with 865,093 cases from the prior year. The courts ended the year with nearly 900,000 cases unresolved and thus carried over to 2018.[19] The Illinois felony courts in the first quarter of 2019 had 17,400 new cases filed, disposed of 18,580, but had 81,911 pending cases. The Illinois misdemeanor courts had 37,236 new cases filed, disposed of 26,400, but also faced 209,000 pending or carried-over cases.[20] In fiscal year 2018, the Missouri felony courts had 47,000 new filings, 46,150 dispositions, and nearly 30,000 felony cases carried over.

The misdemeanor courts had 97,000 new cases, 95,400 dispositions, and 119,000 pending cases. The Court of Common Pleas in Pennsylvania had 79,100 pending cases on January 1, 2017, and 80,171 pending cases on December 31, 2017.

Perhaps a more vivid description of this issue is accomplished by looking at the courts in a particular county. Travis County, Texas, where Austin is located, is a large metropolitan county of about 1,250,000 residents. The county provides a justice system profile that reports court statistics for both felony and misdemeanor courts. While a bit dated (2010 to 2014), the data reflect a persistent pattern in this particular county that is characteristic of many counties in the United States. Between 2010 and 2014, there were roughly 9,000 to 10,000 new felony cases indicted. While the courts were able to dispose of between 8,000 and 9,000 cases in a given year, the courts had to carry over 20,000 to 23,000 felony cases each year. By way of reference, there are eight felony court judges in the county.[21]

We see the same patterns in the misdemeanor courts. There were between 30,500 and 34,000 new misdemeanor cases filed each year and between 82,500 and 88,100 pending or carried over each year. There are eight misdemeanor judges in the county.[22]

The problem is not just that the number of cases carried over within a given year in the criminal courts in Texas, or Pennsylvania or Missouri or Indiana or Illinois, is large. The greater concern is that the criminal courts nationwide do not appear to be significantly reducing the numbers of pending cases over time. At best, they appear to be treading water, without gaining any ground.

The federal courts are no exception. Data for the United States District Courts, which combine criminal and civil cases, show a persistent number of civil and criminal cases pending over recent years. In 2014, there were 392,000 new case filings, 360,000 dispositions, and 423,000 cases pending. In 2019, there were 412,300 new filings, 418,600 dispositions, and 457,000 cases pending.[23] Looking just at criminal cases shows a similar trend. In 2014, there were 66,200 new federal felony cases filed, 67,600 terminated/disposed, and 74,100 pending. In 2019, there were 73,000 new filings, 66,300 terminations, and 84,700 pending.[24]

If we drill down one more layer and look at the day-to-day activities of state misdemeanor courts and felony courts, we can see how busy the criminal courts are from a slightly different vantage point. I have obtained a sampling of daily dockets from a typical metropolitan misdemeanor and felony court. I obtained the misdemeanor court dockets for four randomly selected days, with the only stipulation being that they were not trial days. When there are trials, all of the other business of the court stops, and I wanted to capture the variety and volume of activities in a typical metropolitan misdemeanor court on a typical day. Each docket lists the defendants, cause numbers, charges, purpose of the appearance, bond amount, and so on.

There are two ways to look at the number of items on a docket, either by the number of defendants or by the number of causes or charges (the number of charges represents the number of cases). The difference between the number of defendants and number of cases is defendants can and often do have multiple charges or cases. Each is given a different cause number and is thus a separate item on the docket. The number of defendants scheduled for appearances on each of the four days ranged from 105 to 149. The number of cases varied from 130 to 181. These are all separate hearings on a variety of different matters, including, among other things, motions to revoke probation, plea negotiation hearings, pretrial conferences, sentencing hearings, and settings. These all involve the judge and court staff, prosecutors, and defense lawyers as well as defendants.

A typical felony docket is just as crowded as a misdemeanor docket. I obtained several felony dockets from three different days. The number of cases on these dockets ranged from 120 to 155. Common activities included motions to revoke probation, plea negotiation hearings, pretrial hearings, sentencing hearings, and settings. One of the dockets included two capital murder sentence hearings, which required that the court begin thirty minutes early to accommodate these two cases!

The caseload pressure on prosecutors is equally challenging. While the statistical evidence is scattered and there are no widely accepted national standards for what is a reasonable caseload, most experts agree that prosecutors are dealing with unmanageable numbers of cases on a daily basis. Duffie Stone, the president of the National Association of District Attorneys, stated that the problem of overburdened prosecutors "is very common. A lot of counties that I have seen equate public safety exclusively with the sheriff's office and they leave out the component that prosecutors are part of the public safety equation."[25]

The trends over time in the number of local prosecutors and the number of felony case filings are indicative of increasing caseload pressure on prosecutors. Between 1974 and 2005, the number of prosecutors in the United States increased by nearly 60 percent, from roughly 17,000 to 27,000. Over that same time period, the number of felony filings increased by 233 percent, from 300,000 to 1 million.[26]

Data from 2006 show considerable variation in caseloads across large metropolitan District Attorneys' offices. The total number of felony and misdemeanor filings per prosecutor ranged from lows of 90, 132, 150, and 158 to highs of 406, 408, 433, and 457.[27] Other data based on the number of cases filed and the number of prosecutors show even higher caseloads. For example, in Oklahoma, prosecutors handle on average 340 cases.[28] In

Harris County (Houston), Texas, the average caseload is 489. In Guilford County, North Carolina, it is 565, and Maricopa County (Phoenix), Arizona, 718.[29] It is important to note that these estimates are low because not all prosecutors in a District Attorney's office prosecute cases.

The American Bar Association has set standards for manageable public defender caseloads—150 felony cases or 400 misdemeanor cases per year. Despite these standards, public defenders' caseloads far exceed the guidelines on a routine basis. There is no shortage of reports detailing excessive caseloads for public defender offices across the country. For example, public defenders in Chicago and Atlanta have had to handle more than 2,000 misdemeanors each per year. Recently, due to funding cuts, public defenders in New Orleans were forced to handle nearly 19,000 misdemeanors. Their counterparts in Miami were responsible for more than 700 felonies each.[30] A good overall state of public defense in the United States is provided by a relatively recent survey conducted by the Bureau of Justice Statistics. They found that approximately one-quarter of public defense systems had enough attorneys to adequately manage their caseloads.[31] More about this in chapter 5.

The American Bar Association, among many other observers, has declared that the US court system is in a state of crisis. The common denominator among most observers is lack of funding for courts, prosecutors, and public defenders, resulting in unmanageable caseloads and workloads.

I will discuss the critical and far-reaching consequences of excessive court dockets, excessive prosecutor caseloads, and excessive public defense caseloads later. The point at the moment is that from the perspective of the very simple metric of numbers of cases, the US criminal justice system is facing massive challenges.

WHAT THE CRIMINAL COURT SYSTEM LOOKS LIKE TODAY

What we have today, which is in part a result of underfunding and very heavy caseloads and dockets, is a court system that prioritizes case processing and expediency, and does so by an extraordinary reliance on deals and procedural shortcuts.

Plea deals were originally developed for cases in which there was nothing to litigate, where both the government and the defendant agreed on the evidence and thus there was no reason to hold a criminal trial. Today, plea negotiation is not the exception, it is the rule that defines the day-to-day business of the American criminal courts. In both state and federal courts, 95 to 98 percent of criminal convictions for both felonies and misdemeanors are arrived at through a plea bargain.

Plea bargaining, the agreement between the state and the defendant to waive trial typically in exchange for lesser punishment, has made it possible for the courts to keep the doors open. Plea deals allow the expedited processing of larger and larger numbers of criminal defendants. It is the primary mechanism for managing extraordinarily crowded court dockets and otherwise unmanageable prosecutor and public defender caseloads.

Plea dealing can be accomplished in three ways. Charge bargaining involves modifying the charge(s) to which a defendant pleads guilty, typically by reducing the severity and/or dismissing charges in cases where a defendant is accused of multiple crimes. Sentence bargaining is an agreement to a stipulated sentence in exchange for a plea of guilty. Fact bargaining is, as the name implies, the negotiation of particular evidence in a case. For example, a defendant may have been in possession of a weapon when committing a crime, but the prosecutor agrees to ignore this evidence in exchange for a guilty plea. The bottom line for all of this is lesser punishment in exchange for waiving the right to trial, resulting in expedited processing of cases.

Presumably, no one would design a plea system like the one we have as the best way to achieve justice, whatever that means. Rather, where we are today is purely a matter of economics. We have obviously made policy decisions that blatantly favor this form of case disposition over the expansion of resources for the courts. As a result, the reality is that there is no choice to be made regarding the reliance on plea negotiation absent fundamental changes to the funding of the court system.

Plea bargaining also exists because it serves the interests of the key players in the process. As discussed earlier, judges, prosecutors, and public defenders all share the burdens of heavy dockets and caseloads. They also share the common interest of moving as many cases as quickly as possible. Plea bargaining allows them to do just that.

Christopher Murell, a civil rights lawyer and executive director of the Promise of Justice Initiative, puts it in context.[32]

> It is about courtroom culture—on the part of judges, DAs, and public defenders alike—of trying to get all the cases processed expediently, without friction. The judges and DAs get angry at you for not giving them a heads up that you're going to file a motion, because that will mess up their schedule. A fair trial is considered an interruption.

But plea bargaining on such a massive scale has costs. Even though it is an absolutely essential component of the US criminal justice system as currently configured, it is not without its critics, especially regarding a large number of due process and justice concerns. One is the potential for coercion in persuading a defendant to plead guilty. A plea deal is based on a confession, which, in order to be lawful, needs to be knowing and voluntary. Things like threats of greater punishment, known as the trial penalty, are explicitly or implicitly used as a way to persuade a defendant to accept a plea deal. Pretrial detention is often a motivator for a defendant to accept a plea deal. For example, a plea deal may stipulate that in exchange for a guilty plea and release from jail, the defendant will be sentenced to time served. While there is reason to believe that coercion in some form and to some degree plays a significant role in the plea process, it is difficult to measure its frequency. The best evidence available that innocent defendants will utter false confessions is based on data on exonerations. The National Registry of Exonerations has recorded 2,372 exonerations as of end-of-year 2018. These are cases where individuals have been convicted and incarcerated, but subsequent evidence such as DNA is used to prove their innocence. The startling fact is that nearly 20 percent of these exonerations involved convictions based on defendants' confessions, confessions that were clearly false.[33]

Whether a defendant knowingly confesses, the second criterion for a lawful confession depends in part on access to and adequacy of defense counsel. Given the underfunding and caseload pressures on public defenders, this seems like a reasonable concern.

There are many other due process and procedural issues surrounding the practice of plea negotiation. These are articulated elsewhere, so there is no reason to go into depth here.[34] But it is important to point out that there is a concerning lack of judicial and legislative oversight and regulation. In fact, the US Supreme Court has upheld a variety of practices that lead others to question the fairness and accuracy of plea negotiation. For example, the court in *Brady v. United States* held that the threat of more severe punishment, including the death penalty, is not sufficiently coercive to nullify a plea deal.[35] The Supreme Court has also spoken to the issue of a lawful confession being knowing. In *United States v. Ruiz*, the Court held that the government is not required to provide material evidence to a defendant prior to entering into a plea deal.[36] Moreover, most plea deals require waiver of a variety of rights, such as right to trial and right to confront and cross-examine witnesses. Importantly, these waivers also typically include the right to appeal the conviction and the sentence.

While there is a role for the trial court judge in the plea process, it is after the fact in an often cursory, pro forma manner. As Jenia Turner, a leading plea negotiation legal expert, concludes:[37]

> The Supreme Court has also done little to ensure the transparency and reviewability of negotiated judgments. . . . Plea negotiations thus remain opaque and largely immune from review in most US jurisdictions.

American jurisprudence requires *in theory* that an individual cannot be convicted of a crime unless the government proves two things—actus reus, or the criminal act and all of its elements, and mens rea, or criminal intent. The theory is that intent is not only necessary for proving culpability and thus criminal liability, it is also a necessary element of determining punishment. The argument is that punishment should be proportional to culpability. As legal expert Darryl Brown puts it:[38]

> On both the American and English accounts, the effect of mens rea requirements for each offense element provides its normative appeal: the degree of liability and punishment will be proportionate to culpability and limited by it . . . This debate over culpability requirements matters for broader reasons of political legitimacy . . . it ensures that one is punished only for choices one has made, not for events one did not will or anticipate.

Crystal Mason was recently convicted in Texas of illegally voting. She was sentenced to five years in prison. Mason was convicted because she voted in the 2016 election, which is prohibited by Texas law since she had been convicted of a felony and was still on supervised release at the time she voted. Texas law prohibits voting in these circumstances until the entire sentence is completed, and since supervised release was a part of the sentence, her voting violated the law.

The problem in this case is that Ms. Mason did not know that she was ineligible to vote and no one in the justice system informed her of her ineligibility. The appellate court held:[39]

> Contrary to Mason's assertion, the fact that she did not know she was legally ineligible to vote was irrelevant to her prosecution, Justice Wade Birdwell wrote for a three-judge panel on Texas' second court of appeals.

The obvious question this raises is if Mason did not know she was ineligible, how can she have had the necessary criminal intent to vote illegally? The government could argue that being ignorant of this provision in the law is not a defense. However, because states and the Congress have expanded the criminal codes in unprecedented ways, the old "ignorance of the law is no excuse" has become increasingly problematic. Regardless of that, the ignorance issue goes directly to the heart of the criminal intent issue—without awareness or knowledge, how can there be intent?

Mens rea has taken a back seat over the past fifty years in the prosecution, conviction, and punishment of criminal defendants.[40] I suggest there are three primary reasons for that. One, in the day-to-day reality of plea negotiation, all that generally is required for conviction is the admission of guilt by the defendant for the criminal act. In effect, mens rea does not really play an important role in a plea deal. If anything, since it is an additional item to prove, it may slow the process down, something that the court system can ill afford.[41]

The second reason is simply poor drafting of laws by state legislatures leading to uncertainty regarding when and if culpability standards apply for certain offenses and, in particular, whether mens rea applies to various elements of crimes. Moreover, in some states, legislatures have explicitly relaxed mens rea requirements.[42]

> The evidence allows this conclusion: even after the enactment of express culpability presumptions, courts and legislatures in those states remain uncommitted to the correspondence [mens rea] principle as a core premise of criminal law. State adoption of [mens rea] reforms should not be taken as a signal that states thereby committed their criminal justice systems to the premise that punishment is justified only in proportion to liability . . . The principle is the idea that no proof of culpability is required beyond that needed to ensure that an actor is not convicted for purely innocent conduct. This view describes much of what legislatures and courts widely take as the normatively acceptable, and preferable, relationship of punishment to culpability. The purpose of culpability is primarily, and often exclusively, to distinguish innocent actors from guilty ones . . . Once proof of culpability reveals that a defendant is not an innocent actor, the essential work of mental state requirements is done.

It is important to point out, as I indicated above regarding plea negotiation, that the decisions about mental states of defendants are not made by juries in open court. They are most typically made by prosecutors.

There is another factor that has played a significant role in the decline of criminal intent in decision-making in the US court system. Tough-on-crime policies, where the goal has been more punishment for more people, have been based on instrumental principles of incapacitation, deterrence, and enhancement of public safety. Those goals have often superseded questions about culpability and liability, especially for offense characteristics that serve as punishment enhancements. In those circumstances, the proportionality of punishment is a function of the seriousness of the criminal act, and less so on responsibility or culpability.

The criminal courts in most jurisdictions today are crowded, overloaded places where the goal is to move as many people as quickly as possible. The reality is docket control and caseload management, which are facilitated by a variety of procedural shortcuts and mechanisms for expediting processing of cases.

However, as the courts have become more efficient in processing criminal cases, law professor Darryl Brown proposes there may be perverse effects on the criminal courts. Brown[43] suggests:

Plea bargaining and a range of related, doctrinally authorized practices for making the criminal process more efficient can perversely increase demand for criminal prosecutions, rather than serving as a means to meet demand for enforcement that is driven by crime rates . . . Do we plea bargain because we have more cases or do we have more cases because we plea bargain?

Brown's argument is provocative. A consequence of efficiency of criminal adjudication is the expansion of the criminal law, what some call overcriminalization. The lower the price of criminal adjudication, due to increasing reliance on such procedural alternatives as plea negotiation, the more legislators may be persuaded to rely on the criminal justice system over other policy options for regulating behavior. The significant incentive to legislators is the relative cheaper cost of prosecution and conviction. Brown notes:

That amounts to an incentive for legislatures to expand the types of conduct or social harms that they criminalize; it incrementally makes criminal law enforcement more appealing as a policy response to social problems.[44]

Consider the prosecution and conviction of individuals with substance-use disorders (upwards of 80 percent of justice-involved individuals) or mental illness (roughly 50 percent of those in the justice system). A persistent question that plagues US criminal justice policy is why are disordered individuals so over-represented in the justice system. A quick answer places the blame on a significantly underfunded public health system. If we consider what Brown is suggesting, this makes sense. The criminal justice response to problems associated with substance abuse and/or mental illness may very well be perceived as cost effective, considering how the court system has been able to accommodate increasing caseloads by enhancing efficiency. The management of substance-use disorders and mental illness via the criminal justice system may be perceived by legislators to be cheaper than funding adequate capacity and expertise for public health. What that logic fails to appreciate is the extraordinarily high rate of reoffending. Every time someone enters the criminal justice system, a variety of costs are incurred from a variety of agencies and organizations, including law enforcement, the jail, prosecutors, court staff, judges, pretrial services, and public defense, not to mention corrections.

The increased efficiency of the courts has significant due process concerns. One of the distinguishing features of American jurisprudence is the Bill of Rights, in particular the Fifth Amendment protection against coerced confession and the Sixth Amendment right to counsel, right to a trial by jury, and right to confront and cross-examine witnesses. In very significant ways, these constitutional protections and guarantees are absent in the American criminal court today. A primary reason is that many of these protections are routinely waived in the course of plea negotiation. Plea deals also often require a defendant to waive the right to appeal the conviction. Waiving the right to appeal further reduces the cost of criminal prosecution by avoiding the prosecutorial (and other) costs of appeal.

It is important to underscore that the increased efficiency and lower cost of criminal adjudication has not, in all likelihood, reduced the caseloads and workloads of prosecutors, public defenders, and judges. Rather, those caseloads and workloads may very well have increased, due in part to the expansion of the criminal law, as well as long-term increases in felony filings in criminal courts. Again, both of these trends have been facilitated by the relative increase in processing efficiency and decline in the cost of criminal prosecution.

The title of this book is *The Crisis in America's Criminal Courts*. The crisis I refer to is not per se the overburdened courts or the procedural shortcuts and slighting of a variety of constitutional protections. These certainly contribute to and exacerbate the bigger-picture problem that I see as the true crisis in the courts.

I presume most would agree that the American criminal justice system is dysfunctional. While there are many ways of characterizing that dysfunction, I would offer the profound failure to reduce crime and recidivism as the prime candidate. As I mentioned in the introduction, at best, criminal justice policy accounts for 10 to 15 percent of the crime decline in this country over the past twenty-five to thirty years. Coupled with a recidivism rate of 85 percent, one would be hard-pressed to conclude that this has been a good return on investment. In addition to that is the fact that most offenders who leave the justice system after a period of incarceration or community supervision find themselves in quite problematic circumstances and are at a higher risk of reoffending than when they went in. So, not only does the criminal justice system fail to effectively reduce crime and recidivism, it is actually counterproductive. The price tag in terms of direct criminal justice costs is tremendous.

The obvious question is where do we go for solutions to correct the ineffectiveness and cost inefficiency of the justice system? Comprehensive criminal justice reform includes extensive changes to essentially all aspects of the system. Law enforcement faces many profound challenges. Sentencing laws are in dire need of reform. How we run prisons and jails has been the subject of considerable criticism, and rightly so. We just have to look at how Norway and Germany manage their prisons to realize that there are viable alternatives that avoid many of the negative consequences associated with US prisons. We would also have to change how we address reentry to the community from prison, reducing the many barriers that exist to successful reintegration and economic productivity. Moreover, as we administer it today, probation fails to live up to the intention of providing offenders with programs and services that mitigate their criminogenic circumstances and in turn reduce reoffending and revocation to prison or jail. Then there are the racial and ethnic disparities we find in the American criminal justice system, most commonly noted in terms of the race/ethnic composition of the prison system.

In addition to all of this is the role played by state legislatures and Congress in reforming the criminal justice system. The legislative branch of government has a fundamental part in terms of changes to statutes, policies, procedures, and funding in support of fundamental criminal justice reform. Ending mass incarceration, the rallying cry for many criminal justice reform advocates, requires a variety of changes to sentencing laws, parole eligibility and parole release procedures, revocation procedures for parole and probation, laws governing diversion from incarceration, and policies regarding implementation of diversion programs and standards for operation, just to name a few. There are many ways that state legislatures and Congress can help drive and support fundamental criminal justice reform.

While there is no shortage of targets of criminal justice reform, the key question in my mind is how do we most effectively leverage our effort and resources to turn around a system that for the past forty-five years or so has focused nearly exclusively on trying to punish bad behavior out of criminal offenders, presumably in an effort to reduce crime and recidivism. I believe a case can be made that the best place to target much of our effort is on the court system. There are two key reasons that I believe justify this focus. One is what I discussed in the introduction, which is that most criminal justice reform is local.

The key actors in the US court system—particularly prosecutors, judges, and defense counsel—are routinely charged with making the key decisions that have profound, lasting, downstream effects, decisions that set the stage for everything else. Prosecutors decide what cases to prosecute, what charges to file and indict, what evidence to use, what terms to negotiate in a plea deal, what sentence to attach to a plea deal, or what sentencing recommendation to make. Public defenders, who represent the vast majority of criminal defendants since the vast majority are indigent, decide how to defend a particular client, how much time to allocate to a case, what, if any, investigation should be conducted, what due process issues to pursue, what to advise the defendant in terms of the risk of conviction and punishment, what to negotiate and recommend to the defendant regarding a plea deal, and so on. Judges oversee the process, presiding over a multitude of activities, such as detention hearings, pretrial motions and hearings, a variety of defendant appearances, and plea negotiation hearings and sentencing hearings, among others.

One of the most important characteristics of all of these individuals who are involved in the court system is the use of discretion. Within the context of an explicit set of rules established by the Constitution, statute, case law, regulations, and rules of criminal procedure, at the end of the day, it is individuals who exercise judgment and make decisions that have profound impacts on case outcomes and thus ultimately the functioning of the criminal justice system. That is not to say that the correctional system is absolved of blame or responsibility. Clearly our correctional systems are largely criminogenic, increasing the risk of reoffending. So, yes, we do need to drastically reform corrections. But the decisions that are made on a daily basis in the court system determine, among other things, who goes to prison or jail and for how long.

Thus, the critical starting point for fundamental criminal justice reform is to stem the flow of individuals into prison and jail. A compelling argument can be made that most individuals who are in prison and jail today do not, in the interest of public safety, need to be there. In fact, the evidence is clear that in many, many cases, incarceration is counterproductive, aggravating individuals' circumstances and making it much more difficult to remain crime free down the road.

It is well established that most offenders who enter the criminal justice system today arrive with often complex circumstances. The majority come from backgrounds of poverty and disadvantage, with educational and employment deficits, psychological and psychiatric problems often resulting from or exacerbated by environmental and physical trauma, neurodevelopmental impairments, and substance abuse, among others. Moreover, these circumstances and disorders tend to co-occur, adding to the complexity of offenders' situations.[45] It is no wonder that punishment has failed to reduce crime and recidivism. Punishment does nothing to change offenders' circumstances. Indeed, frequently punishment exacerbates those circumstances.

If crime were simply a matter of making a bad decision by individuals who were not otherwise disordered or disadvantaged, the situation would be substantially different. But that is not the reality. So, we find ourselves in a criminal court system today where the key decision makers are lawyers. That would not be of as much concern if those lawyers were only dealing with legal and procedural issues. But, ultimately, they are tasked with so much more, routinely making decisions about offenders' complex, comorbid conditions, without appropriate expertise or experience in such matters.

Imagine walking into a hospital emergency department with severe abdominal pain and the person who diagnoses and treats you is a podiatrist, someone not really qualified to diagnose and treat a gastrointestinal disorder. While this scenario is unlikely, if it did occur, it would probably be considered medical malpractice. Unfortunately, something very similar to this happens routinely in the American court system.

The primary question addressed in this book is how do the key players in the criminal court system make decisions, in what ways is the decision-making process compromised, how do the decisions that are made affect long-term outcomes, and how do we ultimately rectify the situation. This is, in fact, the crisis I refer to in the book's title—the seriously compromised decision-making process in the courts that I believe is the prime contributor to the dysfunctionality of American criminal justice.

NOTES

1. American Bar Association Task Force on Preservation of the Justice System Report to the House of Delegates, 1, 4

2. Schauffler and Kleiman, "State Courts and the Budget Crisis," 1.

3. Stock, Witte, and Horn, "Budget Cuts to Courts Now Affecting Criminal Cases."

4. Stock, Witte, and Horn, "Budget Cuts to Courts Now Affecting Criminal Cases."

5. Stock, Witte, and Horn, "Budget Cuts to Courts Now Affecting Criminal Cases."

6. Israel, "Excessive Criminal Justice Caseloads: Challenging the Conventional Wisdom," 761.

7. The Disaster Center, "United States Crime Rates 1960–2018."

8. National Association of State Budget Officers, "State Spending for Corrections."

9. Schauffler, National Center for State Courts, "The Rise and Fall of State Court Caseloads."

10. Federal Bureau of Investigation, Uniform Crime Reporting Statistics, "State Level Crime Estimates."

11. National Center for State Courts, "Criminal Caseload Clearance Rates in 23 States, 2016."

12. Texas Office of Court Administration, "District Courts: Age of Cases Disposed."

13. Darr, Supreme Court of Pennsylvania.

14. Wisconsin Court System, *Publications, Reports, and Addresses Circuit Court Statistics*, 2017 reports.

15. Judicial Council of California, "2018 Court Statistical Report Statewide Caseload Trends 2007–2008 through 2016–2017."

16. Oregon Judicial Branch, *Reports, Statistics, and Performance Measures*.

17. Texas Office of Court Administration, "Annual Statistical Report for the Texas Judiciary."

18. The following data were obtained from the Texas Office of Court Administration, "Constitutional County Court Performance Measures," "Statutory Performance Measures," "District Court Performance Measures," "Constitutional

County Court Age of Cases Disposed," "Statutory County Court Age of Cases Disposed," and "District Court Age of Cases Disposed."

19. Indiana Office of Judicial Administration, Indiana Supreme Court, "The Judicial Year in Review."

20. Illinois Circuit Court, *Illinois Circuit Court Statistics 2019*.

21. Travis County, Texas, "Justice System Profile, Fiscal Years 2010–2014."

22. Travis County, Texas, "Justice System Profile, Fiscal Years 2010–2014, 2006–2010."

23. United States Courts, "National Judicial Caseload Profile."

24. United States Courts, "Criminal Cases Commences, Terminated, and Pending (including Transfers), during the 12-Month Periods Ending June 30, 2018 and 2019"; United States Courts, "Criminal Cases Commences, Terminated, and Pending (including Transfers), during the 12-Month Periods Ending March 31, 2014 and 2015."

25. Cueto, "Why Prosecutorial Overload Can Spark More Problems," 1–2.

26. Brown, "The Perverse Effects of Efficiency in Criminal Process."

27. Gershowitz and Killinger, "The State (Never) Rests."

28. Adcock, "'Staggering' Caseloads for Prosecutors."

29. Texas Southern University, Barbara Jordan-Mickey Leland School of Public Affairs, "An Examination of Prosecutorial Staff, Budgets, Caseloads and the Need for Change"; Sanderlin, High Point Enterprise, "Prosecutors Handling More Cases than Recommended."

30. Primus, "Defense Counsel and Public Defense."

31. Furst, Brennan Center for Justice, "A Fair Fight."

32. Hager, The Marshall Project, "When There's Only One Public Defender in Town."

33. National Registry of Exonerations, 2018.

34. See, for example, Kelly and Pitman, *Confronting Underground Justice*; Turner, "Plea Bargaining"; Turner, *Plea Bargaining Across Borders*.

35. Brady v. United States, 397 U.S. (1970).

36. United States v. Ruiz, 536 U.S. 622,122 (2002).

37. Turner, "Transparency in Plea Bargaining," 221.

38. Brown, "Criminal Law Reform and the Persistence of Strict Liability," 291–92.

39. Levine, "Texas Upholds Sentence for Woman Who Didn't Know She Was Ineligible to Vote."

40. Kelly and Pitman, *Confronting Underground Justice*.

41. See Kelly and Pitman, *Confronting Underground Justice* for a detailed discussion of mens rea and plea negotiation.

42. Brown, "Criminal Law Reform and the Persistence of Strict Liability," 324–25.

43. Brown, "The Perverse Effects of Efficiency on Criminal Process," 186, 195.

44. Brown, "The Perverse Effects of Efficiency on Criminal Process," 200–201.

45. See Kelly, Pitman, and Streusand, *From Retribution to Public Safety* for an extended discussion of the circumstances, deficits, and impairments that the majority of criminal offenders present with when they enter the criminal justice system.

2

✢

Decision-Making
in the Criminal Courts

As I stated in the introduction and in chapter 1, in my mind, the primary focus of criminal justice reform must be on decision-making, and in particular, the decision-making of the key individuals in the criminal court system. I have tried to make the case that the decisions made in the courts determine essentially everything else. That is, the discretion exercised by prosecutors, judges, and public defenders drive the important outcomes of the criminal justice system. Decisions such as charges, pretrial detention versus release, the type and quality of criminal defense, diversion versus criminal prosecution, the plea negotiation process and the plea outcome, and the sentence are all fundamentally related to the probability of reoffending. Thus, the decisions that are made by prosecutors, judges, and public defenders are very important or the most important determinants of the success or failure of the US criminal justice system.

Assuming there is merit to this argument, then it makes sense to spend some time taking a look at decision-making. I first focus on what cognitive psychology tells us about decision-making in general, and then what evidence there is regarding decision-making of judges, prosecutors, and public defenders.

THE COGNITIVE PSYCHOLOGY OF DECISION-MAKING

Understanding decision-making historically was largely the purview of economics and based on the presumption of human rationality and optimization of utility. Then in the 1970s, cognitive psychologists introduced a variety of concepts that more realistically reflected human decisions. Since then, there has been a considerable amount of theoretical development and research on the cognitive psychology of choice or decision-making.

The decisions we make and how we make them depend on a number of circumstances, such as how much information is available, how important the issues are and what the consequences are, how many alternatives there are and how they are framed, or how much time one has to make a decision. Clearly, not all decisions are equal. What to have for dinner versus how much to invest in retirement or whom to marry are quite different, especially in terms of importance and consequences.

Psychologists have identified two different models of decision-making, often referred to as System 1 and System 2. System 1 decision-making is quicker, generally unconscious and emotionally driven, described as more gut-level and based on the use of cognitive shortcuts. System 1 is also typically automatic. System 2 is slower, more analytical and deliberative, invoking tools such as cost/benefit analyses and considering and weighing all alternatives.

As Daniel Kahneman, who has written extensively about these two systems, describes it, System 1 and System 2 do not represent an either-or decision-making process. Rather, they interact on an ongoing basis. Both are continuously active, but System 1 runs automatically and System 2 is on sort of a low-effort idle speed. Kahneman describes the interaction in the following way.[1]

> The division of labor between System 1 and System 2 is highly efficient: it minimizes effort and optimizes performance. The arrangement works well most of the time because System 1 is generally very good at what it does: its models of familiar situations are accurate, its short term predictions are usually accurate as well, and its initial reactions to challenges are swift and generally appropriate.

Kahneman warns, however, that System 1 is error prone.[2]

> System 1 has biases, however, systematic errors that it is prone to make in specified circumstances. It sometimes answers easier questions than the one it was asked, and it has little understanding of logic and statistics. One further limitation of System 1 is that it cannot be turned off.

One useful illustration of System 2 is what is called the weighted additive rule, known as "the traditional gold standard for rational preferences."[3] The weighted additive rule requires the user to focus effort on five activities: identifying all relevant information necessary for making the decision; having access to the value of the different pieces of information; determining the importance or weights of each of the pieces of information; summing the weighted pieces of information to get an overall "score" for all of the alternatives; and finally comparing the alternatives to determine the one with the highest score or value, which then is the alternative that should be selected.

The weighted additive rule is an intensive, resource-heavy, deliberative analytical tool that may under certain circumstances be appropriate for decision-making. For example, assume that a large industry-leading company is considering acquiring some smaller, competitive companies. The weighted additive rule might be a very useful analytic framework for assisting in the decision regarding which companies to acquire. However, it probably is not appropriate for many day-to-day decisions we all make, in part because the analytic approach may not be necessary and because it requires more time and effort, resources that are typically in limited supply.

So, how do we manage the real constraints we all experience in routine decision-making? As Anuj Shah and Daniel Oppenheimer argue, that is where heuristics come in:[4]

> Clearly, such an algorithm requires great mental effort; however, people do not have unlimited processing capacity. People must operate within the constraints imposed by both their cognitive resources and the task environment—a concept known as bounded rationality. As the demands on limited cognitive resources increased, people may employ methods or strategies that reduce the effort they expend on computation. We will therefore refer to heuristics as methods that use principles of effort-reduction and simplification. By definition, heuristics must allow decision makers to process information in a less effortful manner than one would expect from an optimal decision rule.

Heuristics are cognitive shortcuts that allow decisions to be made more quickly and more easily compared to complex, analytical decision rules. As such, they are tools for System 1 decision-making. Psychologists have identified dozens of these that serve to significantly lessen effort and enhance the economy of decision-making. For example, the *recognizable* heuristic refers to a situation where one of the alternatives being considered is something recognizable. In that situation there is a tendency to choose the recognized option, thus reducing the amount of effort, information, and time needed to make the decision. Another common example is the *representativeness* heuristic, where the decision maker tends to dismiss statistics and rely on stereotypes. Another is the *affect* heuristic, where individuals assess likelihoods based on how they feel about particular options. If they feel positively about one, they consider it less risky than an option for which they feel negatively. The *availability* heuristic involves relying on information that is readily accessible for making a decision. For example, a psychiatrist is evaluating a patient who reports depression. A former patient of this psychiatrist committed suicide due to his depression. Because of the availability or salience of that event, the doctor may incorrectly assume the patient is suicidal. A final example is *confirmation bias*, which is seeking information that is consistent with an individual's prior beliefs.

TESTING SYSTEM 1 AND SYSTEM 2 DECISION-MAKING

A reasonable question is how often are decisions based on System 1 or System 2 processes, the quick, easy, intuitive, gut-level response, compared to the more time-consuming, methodical, and deliberative approach. The Cognitive Reflection Test (CRT) was designed to answer that question. The CRT is a series of three questions/problems, each of which has an intuitive (but incorrect) answer and an analytical (and correct) answer. The questions are:

1. A bat and ball cost $1.10 in total. The bat costs $1.00 more than the ball. How much does the ball cost?
2. If it takes 5 machines 5 minutes to make 5 widgets, how long would it take 100 machines to make 100 widgets?
3. In a lake, there is a patch of lily pads. Every day, the patch doubles in size. If it takes forty-eight days for the patch to cover the entire lake, how long would it take for the patch to cover half the lake?

The intuitive answer for question #1 is 10 cents. But with a bit of deliberation and analysis, it is evident that answer is wrong. If the ball costs 10 cents and the bat costs a dollar more than that, then the total cost is $1.20. The correct answer is that the ball costs 5 cents and the bat costs $1.05.

The CRT was designed to invoke activation of System 1 so it evaluates how often respondents use System 1 versus System 2 processes, indicated by the frequency of correct and incorrect answers. Several studies have estimated the frequency of correct and incorrect answers on various populations. The average across studies is that more than one-half answer all three questions incorrectly.[5]

Now more to the point—What do we know about how the key decision makers in the US court system make decisions? The short answer is quite a bit about judges, a fair amount about prosecutors, and not much about public defenders.

JUDICIAL DECISION-MAKING

Historically, there have been two prevailing views of judicial decision-making—the formalist and realist approaches. The formalist presumes that judges decide things in a deliberative, analytical, mechanical manner, applying legal rules and procedure in a structured manner. Realists, on the other hand, view judicial decision-making as intuitive, based on feelings or hunches. The formalist and realist dichotomy corresponds to System 1 and System 2 approaches to decision-making. Just as System 1 and 2 interact and complement each other, so too, it is argued, do the formalist and realist models of judging.[6] Chris Guthrie and colleagues call the hybrid model "intuitive-override," which posits that judges generally make intuitive, System 1 decisions but sometimes override those decisions with analysis and deliberation (System 2).

Research on how judges decide is compelling—they make decisions like most adults do, in a nondeliberative, intuitive manner. This is despite the fact that much of what judges do requires that they suppress intuition and carefully deliberate.[7] However, the research also showed that judges can override intuitive processes with more deliberative analysis and decision-making. This evidence is based on several hundred judges taking the CRT.

Several other studies evaluated judges' decisions in hypothetical legal cases and confirm what the CRT results show.[8]

> Overall, the research shows that, at least in the evaluation of hypothetical legal cases, judges rely heavily on intuitive mental shortcuts in a wide range of contexts. Viscusi (1999) also reached similar conclusions in his study of judges. He found that judges relied on many simple, misleading heuristics in evaluating legal fact patterns. Whether judges use the same heuristics in actual cases is less certain, but experimental studies show heavy reliance on heuristics by judges.

Moving from the experimental to actual cases reveals similar use of simple, intuitive decision rules in situations involving a complex array of evidence. For example, in a study of judicial bail decisions, where judges reported considering seriousness of the instant offense, prior criminal history, ties to the community, employment history, public safety risk and flight risk, they inevitably relied on the prosecutor's recommendation for bail.[9] Other research on trademark cases, immigration, awarding of attorneys' fees, and other situations show that judges are largely intuitive thinkers who routinely rely on shortcuts.

Anchoring is a heuristic that refers to the use of numeric anchors or reference points in making quantitative judgments. The use of anchoring is particularly evident in judges' sentencing decisions. Sentencing is

driven in part by statute, which determines how much latitude or discretion a judge has in reaching a decision. In states that have indeterminate
sentencing, which provides considerable discretion within statutory
minimum and maximum sentences, the judge can consider a broad array
of factors in a manner he or she sees fit. However, a common anchor in
sentencing is the prosecutor's recommendation or the recommendation
provided by a probation officer in the presentence investigation report.[10]
In their *Annual Review of Law and Social Science* article, Jeffrey Rachlinski
and Andrew Wistrich conclude:[11]

> Research on judges strongly points to the conclusion that judges rely heav-
> ily on intuitive reasoning to evaluate legal disputes . . . Doubtless, judges
> can and do engage in more deliberative, complicated analysis at times, but
> the evidence suggests that their reliance on intuitive reasoning leaves them
> vulnerable to errors in judgment.

Not only can intuitive decision-making lead to errors in judgment, it
also opens the door for emotion and other problematic influences such as
race and gender. At least in hypothetical cases, emotion influences how
judges decide cases. Rachlinski and Wistrich report a number of studies that demonstrate the role of judges' emotional reactions to litigants
in deciding hypothetical cases. In some experimental situations, judges
essentially ignored rather complex legal matters in favor of emotional
reactions to the facts in the case. There is also a considerable amount of
evidence that judges are influenced by gender, especially in matters such
as criminal sentencing, where judges sentence women more leniently,
controlling for other relevant factors.[12] And then there is race. Perhaps
the most compelling research on judicial decision-making in the criminal
courts underscores the influence of race on bail decisions and sentencing.
Rachlinski and Wistrich conclude:[13]

> Overall, the body of research on the potential for invidious biases in judges
> arising from reliance on emotion or implicit stereotypes supports a troubling
> conclusion: Judges do not easily set such extralegal matters aside. The feel-
> ings and biases that influence most adults seem to also affect judges.

Again, a primary facilitator of the use of emotion and extralegal considerations in judicial decision-making is System 1 processes, or the quick,
intuitive decisions that rely on a variety of heuristics or cognitive shortcuts,
including beliefs and attitudes, hunches, and stereotypes. This is in part
due to the fact that judges are human, and humans are intuitive thinkers.
Consider the following sentencing situation, assuming that the case is
in an indeterminate sentencing jurisdiction (again, where the judge has
wide latitude and may consider a broad array of evidence). The indi-

vidual to be sentenced was convicted of a first-degree felony, which in my state of Texas (which is largely indeterminate) has a punishment range of probation to ninety-nine years in prison. At the sentencing hearing, the prosecutor presents a long list of aggravating circumstances, designed to persuade the judge to impose a more severe sentence. These could include such things as seriousness of the instant offense, prior criminal justice involvement, overall dangerousness and risk of reoffending, impact on the victim, prior drug abuse, and other negative evidence about the offender. Then the defendant will present mitigating evidence, perhaps explaining or downplaying prior criminal involvement as a result of peer pressure, poor parenting, abuse as a child, exposure to trauma and violence, addiction problems, mental health problems, intellectual and educational deficits and disabilities, and any number of other considerations.

Now, add to the problem at hand that the judge is able to consider none, any, or all of this evidence, weigh and evaluate the evidence as he or she sees fit, put some items at the top of the list as being most important and others at the bottom as being less important or irrelevant, and somehow add it all up and arrive at a number, either years on probation or years in prison. The "model" that the judge uses is up to him or her to develop. It may be ad hoc, based on the evidence in this case, or it could be how the judge considers evidence in every case he or she sentences.

Moreover, the judge is able to consider various goals of sentencing and determine which is appropriate for the case at hand. For example, the judge could sentence this individual to deter him from future criminality. Or the goal might be to incapacitate him (prevent him from committing crime by reducing criminal opportunity by incarcerating him or putting him on intensive probation supervision). Or the sentence could be designed to allow rehabilitation, by placing the offender on probation, where he can remain in the community, work and support his family, and receive programs and services designed to mitigate his criminality. Or, the judge could determine that the primary purpose of this sentence is revenge or retribution.

That is a lot to consider and perhaps more daunting still since there is no formula or even framework (like the weighted additive rule) for arriving at the appropriate answer. Each judge is expected to devise a sentence considering the evidence as he or she sees fit and attempt to accomplish whatever sentencing goal that seems suitable.

Then there is the pretrial detention versus release decision, which is presumably based on some consideration of public safety risk and flight risk. The former might be based on seriousness of the arrest charge, criminal history, and behavior on prior supervised release. Flight risk might be based on ties to the community reflected in things such as family in the area, length of residence and employment in the area, and ownership of a house, among others. The point of this deliberation is to use current characteristics and prior behavior of an offender to predict future risk. I will discuss this in more detail when I consider the use of risk-assessment instruments.

The point is that both the sentencing decision and pretrial detention decision, as well as many others that judges make, are complex matters, often involving a considerable amount of information. If and how judges use the evidence presented in a sentencing hearing or detention hearing is often unknown. What is known from research is that while judges report using a variety of evidence in arriving at a very specific conclusion (detention/release or a particular length of time in prison or on probation), the reality is that in these detention and sentencing situations, judges rely heavily on the prosecutor's recommendation.[14]

The substantial constraints on time and cognitive bandwidth due to extraordinary caseloads and workloads commonly result in judicial decision-making based on intuitive thinking, emotional reactions, and the use of a variety of stereotypes and cognitive shortcuts in getting the business of the court done.[15] This certainly makes sense considering the docket and caseload data I presented in chapter 1. Think of a criminal court judge who has say 150 or 175 different cases in a day and the necessity of relentlessly focusing on case processing. Routine reliance on System 1 decision-making is absolutely essential to keeping the doors to the courtroom open.

IMPLICIT BIAS

There is another very important issue regarding judicial decision-making to consider before we turn to how prosecutors make decisions. That is the matter of implicit bias.

It should come as no surprise that the US criminal justice system has an extensive history of explicit or conscious bias. This has been most notable in terms of race and ethnicity. Whether we go back to the Jim Crow days and the birth of the modern criminal justice system, or more recently to the New Jim Crow,[16] the reality is that the justice system is racist. Much of that has been accomplished through conscious, explicit, observable racial bias, exemplified by segregation and all-White juries, judges, and prosecutors. Other racial disparities are perhaps more subtle but still explicit, like the differential in the Federal Sentencing Guidelines between crack cocaine and powder cocaine (until recently, one-tenth of a gram of crack had the same punishment as one gram of powder cocaine). The bottom line is that the decisions made at all stages of processing individuals disadvantage Blacks. Blacks are more likely to be stopped by law enforcement, detained in jail awaiting disposition of the case, charged with more serious crimes, and receive harsher punishment than Whites.[17] While evidence indicates that explicit bias has declined over time, the disparities persist.[18]

Implicit bias, a well-established concept in cognitive psychology, has only recently entered the realm of the American criminal justice system and the courts in particular. Implicit bias is defined as follows:[19]

> Also known as implicit social cognition, implicit bias refers to the attitudes or stereotypes that affect our understanding, actions, and decisions in an unconscious manner. These biases, which encompass both favorable and unfavorable assessments, are activated involuntarily and without an individual's awareness or intentional control. Residing deep in the subconscious, these biases are different from known biases that individuals may choose to conceal for the purposes of social and/or political correctness. Rather, implicit biases are not accessible through introspection.

These mental processes include implicit memory, stereotypes, attitudes, and perceptions, among others. Implicit biases can unintentionally and unconsciously cause one to have feelings and beliefs about others based on such characteristics as age, race, and appearance—"actors do not always have conscious, intentional control over the processes of social perception, impression formation, and judgment that motivate their actions."[20]

Research shows that implicit bias is quite common (three-quarters of those who took a common implicit bias test show bias according to disabilities, age, race, and socioeconomic status),[21] is distinct from but related to explicit bias, and may contradict our publicly declared beliefs. Importantly, implicit bias has been empirically linked to behavior in a variety of settings, including work, school, and the legal system.[22]

So, what do we know about judges, judicial decision-making, and implicit bias? Quite a bit.

We think of judges as impartial, neutral overseers of the processing of criminal defendants. However, research indicates that when it comes to implicit racial bias, judges are no different than the general population. The Implicit Association Test (IAT) is a well-established, validated measure of the presence of implicit bias. Research conducted on judges confirms that implicit racial bias is widespread and can influence their judgment and decisions.[23] For example, a statewide study of the majority of judges in Illinois, conducted by the Illinois Supreme Court and the American Bar Foundation, found that judges were just like everyone else in terms of the presence of implicit bias. Bias towards race, gender, poverty, and attorneys was not only common but also affected decisions and outcomes.[24]

Research also confirms that judges have the cognitive skills to mitigate the influence of implicit racial bias. However, such control requires awareness of implicit bias, active and conscious control of it, and the time to do so. Implicit bias is taken very seriously in the federal court system. Federal trial judges (Federal District Judges and Magistrate Judges) are provided implicit bias training, including actually taking the IAT.

A strong case can be made for asserting that the caseload and workload pressures in most metropolitan criminal courts in the United States encourage quick, intuitive, emotional decision-making, an environment that may facilitate the introduction of negative stereotypes and other invidious influences (implicit biases), in turn enhancing the role of such factors in decisions.[25]

While much of the research on implicit bias in general and for judges in particular focuses on race and ethnicity (the IAT is tailored to specific targets of bias), some experts have suggested that there is good reason to believe that judicial implicit bias can affect decisions regarding a wide range of groups such as the disabled, the mentally ill, those with substance-use disorders, immigrants, the elderly, and many others.[26]

PROSECUTORIAL DECISION-MAKING

Compared to the work on judges, there has been little direct research on prosecutors regarding the prevalence of intuitive, emotional, System 1 decision-making versus deliberate, analytical System 2 decision-making. I have not found any research that applies the Cognitive Reflection Test on prosecutors. However, that does not prevent drawing conclusions about prosecutorial decision-making.

The writing about prosecutorial decision-making has focused on a variety of cognitive biases and heuristics that likely promote or facilitate intuitive, emotional, shortcut decisions. Researchers have argued that many cognitive heuristics or shortcuts influence prosecutorial decisions since they influence decisions of humans in general and judges in particular.[27]

> Drawing on the cognitive literature, the growing literature of behavioral law and economics explores the limitations of cost-benefit rationality, challenging the assumption of traditional economists that people are perfect wealth maximizers. From both the cognitive and behavioral economics literature emerges a theory of bounded rationality that seeks to explain how cognitive biases and limitations in our cognitive abilities distort perfect information processing in nonrandom, predictable ways.

The logic in generalizing these arguments to prosecutors is based on the convincing assertion that there is no reason to think that prosecutors are any different than the general public or judges.[28] An example of cognitive bias that likely influences prosecutors' decisions is confirmation bias or selective information processing (the tendency to pursue and positively interpret evidence that supports preconceived hypotheses or conclusions). Confirmation bias may be a substantial factor in the selective viewing of news, such as Fox versus MSNBC or CNN. We tend to seek information that supports how we think about things, as well as our beliefs and expectations, and reject information that is inconsistent with or contradicts what we believe. Belief perseverance is another cognitive bias that functions to support our existing assumptions and conclusions, making us resistant to change in the face of new evidence. Both confirmation bias and belief perseverance cause us to more heavily weigh information or evidence that is consistent with our beliefs and hypotheses and discount contradictory evidence.[29] It is not difficult to see how these biases can lead to wrongful conviction (for example, by undervaluing exculpatory evidence) as well as prosecutors' ignoring or dismissing mitigating evidence in the sentencing decision.

It is reasonable to expect that anchoring is a cognitive bias that is commonly an element in plea bargaining. For example, a prosecutor initially offers a deal with a very high sentence or threatens the "trial penalty" sentence if a defendant seems unwilling to engage in a plea deal. This high anchor renders a subsequent, lower offer that is more reasonable from the defendant's perspective.

There are a good number of experts who have written about the problem of implicit bias in prosecutorial decision-making. While there is no evidence of application of the IAT to prosecutors, many have made the plausible argument that prosecutors are not immune to the influences of implicit bias that are so common in the general population.[30]

The US Department of Justice (DOJ) in June of 2016 announced that all DOJ law enforcement and federal prosecutors will undergo implicit bias training.

> The Department of Justice has a responsibility to do everything we can to assure that our criminal justice system is fair and impartial. Given that the research is clear that most people experience some degree of unconscious bias and that the effects of that bias can be countered by acknowledging its existence and utilizing response strategies, it is essential that we provide implicit bias training to our prosecutors and law enforcement agents.

Another example comes from San Francisco. George Gascon, the former District Attorney of San Francisco County, announced in June of 2019 that the DA's office was implementing a plan to remove implicit racial bias in prosecutorial decision-making.[31]

The broad discretion that prosecutors have, including charging, release or detention, indictment, plea deals and sentencing, in combination with extraordinary heavy caseloads and workloads, heightens the likelihood that prosecutors use cognitive shortcuts and emotional decision-making.[32] Again, the caseload data discussed in chapter 1 support the obvious conclusion that prosecutors, just like judges and public defenders, are typically consumed with case processing. Efficiently moving cases is certainly facilitated by System 1 decision-making.

The nature of prosecutorial discretion is also an important risk factor regarding the influence of implicit bias.[33]

> The subjectivity inherent to prosecutorial decision making leaves it far more vulnerable to the influences of implicit bias, affecting how prosecutors initially assess case files, interpret information about defendants, and recall their assessments at decision-making points.

It is important to emphasize that while racial disparity and discrimination are the most often tested and discussed consequences of implicit bias, research has shown that many other characteristics are subject to such bias. In fact, one of the strongest implicit biases is disability. Over three-quarters of individuals who were tested with the disability IAT exhibited an implicit preference of people without disabilities.[34]

PUBLIC DEFENDERS' DECISION-MAKING

There is little research on decision-making of indigent defense counsel. No one that I am aware of has used the CRT to test public defenders for the prevalence of System 1 versus System 2 decision-making, and I am aware of only one study that systematically applied the IAT to test for implicit bias among criminal defense lawyers.[35] Nevertheless, there is sufficient evidence on emotional, intuitive decision-making and implicit bias to justify generalization to indigent defense counsel. Moreover, the conditions under which public defenders work (lack of resources, caseload and time pressure, considerable discretion) provide an environment that increases the likelihood or requires the use of shortcut, intuitive decision-making, as well as enhancing the influence of implicit bias.[36]

The logic of attributing emotional, intuitive decision-making and the influence of implicit bias to public defenders is the observation that public defenders are essentially like everyone else. There is no reason to presume they have some immunity from these cognitive processes.

CONCLUSIONS

I argued in chapter 1 that, at a very basic level, much of the dysfunction of the US criminal justice system is a result of compromised or deficient decision-making by key individuals in the court system. Daniel Mears and Sarah Bacon made a very compelling case a decade ago regarding how caseload pressures compromise decision-making.[37]

> Larger caseloads, for example, increase the likelihood that different types of "cognitive errors" occur, accumulating with or amplifying the effects of one another and potentially causing ripple effects that ultimately lead to inefficiencies and poor outcomes.

The evidence presented in this chapter about decision-making by key court officials is troubling in a number of very important respects. First, it is well documented that there are extraordinary racial and ethnic disparities in the American criminal justice system. These disparities are quite evident in incarceration data but are evident upstream as well, such as who is stopped and searched, arrested, charged, indicted, prosecuted, convicted, and sentenced.[38] This clearly involves law enforcement, and the courts, including prosecution, defense, and judges. A recent study concludes that implicit bias is systemic, that it permeates the American criminal justice system and has perpetuated tough-on-crime policies and harsher, retributive punishment, especially for African Americans. The logic of this argument implicates implicit bias in lawmaking and policy development, as well as in the administration of criminal justice.[39]

> We posit that systemic implicit bias that pervades the criminal justice system even at the point when policymakers and citizens consider how to respond to perceived social problems. Most of the discussion about implicit bias is about what happens at trial or during the investigative stop—what happens to a policy in the real world. Yet, before a decision-maker thinks about the specifics of a policy—and long before that policy is put into practice—implicit bias shapes how people intuitively understand what makes a good punishment, how much of that punishment is necessary, and whether human beings deserve that punishment or not. Thus, implicit bias affects people's implicit theories of human nature as they begin to apply those theories to real policy decisions.

Implicit bias helps us understand the bigger picture of criminal justice policy and, in particular, our presumption of the culpability of criminal offenders, our sentencing models of just deserts and retribution, our relentless focus on more punishment for more people, and our simplistic thinking that punishment will reduce reoffending.

Moreover, the research on implicit bias explains to a significant degree the race/ethnic disparities in an era when explicit racial bias is less prevalent. These racial and ethnic disparities directly challenge our conceptions of impartiality, fairness, justice, and, ultimately, the legitimacy of the criminal justice system.

Equally disconcerting is the role of emotional, intuitive decision-making in lieu of more deliberate, analytical processes. Best we can tell from the evidence, System 1 processes and the reliance on cognitive shortcuts are quite common among the general public as well as among judges. We can extrapolate that conclusion to many prosecutors and public defenders as there is no reason to think they are somehow immune to emotional, intuitive decision-making. Moreover, the fact that judges, prosecutors, and public defenders are often extraordinarily busy increases the need for quick decision-making.

The image of judges that we embrace portrays them as dispassionate decision makers, applying the law based on evidence not emotion. The reality is quite different as judges are human. Take, for example, the role of emotions in criminal sentencing. Hon. Ray Price, Missouri Chief Justice, put it like this.[40]

> There is a better way. We need to move from anger-based sentencing that ignores cost and effectiveness to evidence-based sentencing that focuses on results—sentencing that assesses each offender's risk and then fits that offender with the cheapest and most effective rehabilitation that he or she needs.

Justice Price is not alone in protesting anger-based decision-making, including sentencing, pretrial detention/bail, and pretrial motions. Whether it is anger or distaste or fear or empathy or some other emotion, it is naive to think that judges can simply turn it off when making decisions on the bench. Research supports the prominent role that emotions play in judicial decision-making.[41]

> when the law is unclear, the facts are disputed, or judges possess wide discretion, their decisions can be influenced by their feelings about litigants. This may occur without their conscious awareness and despite their best efforts to resist it.

The role of emotion in the decision-making of judges and prosecutors is indisputable. And it can cut both ways with a sympathetic, empathetic prosecutor or judge, or any angry, fearful prosecutor or judge. Thus, emotional reactions by key decision makers can lead to a more lenient or more punitive outcome. Invariably, it leads to greater disparity in outcomes.

There is another issue related to emotion and intuition in decision-making, which gets to the heart of one of the most problematic aspects of the criminal justice system. The majority of criminal offenders enter the justice system with often complex, comorbid circumstances, disorders, impairment, and deficits. These circumstances require careful, analytical decision-making regarding assessment/diagnosis and evidence-based remedies, not emotional, intuitive, time-pressured decisions. Crime is often more complicated than a criminal offender simply making a bad decision, and the appropriate remedy is often way beyond simply punishing someone.

We know that mental illness and substance-use disorders are quite common among those in the criminal justice system and are fundamentally tied to the extraordinarily high recidivism rates in the United States. A decidedly relevant question is what do we know about decision-making in the court system regarding offenders with mental illness and substance-use disorders (among other criminogenic factors), and how is that decision-making implicated in the dysfunctionality of the criminal justice system? I begin by reviewing how the general public thinks about mental illness and substance abuse, then I turn to research on judges and prosecutors.

The extent to which mental illness and substance abuse are stigmatized in American society has been the subject of considerable research. The evidence is clear that such stigma is widespread and substantial, with serious negative impacts.[42] As a recent review of the evidence concludes, "Along with homelessness and substance abuse, which themselves are highly linked with mental disorder, mental illness receives extreme castigation."[43]

Stigmatizing beliefs among the general public about those with mental illness and substance-use disorders include perceptions of dangerousness, violence, and criminality. Perceptions of dangerousness and violence have increased over time and are widespread. Beliefs about the criminality of people with mental illness are prevalent. The most commonly stigmatized disorder is substance abuse.[44] The fact that substance abuse is criminalized (as is mental illness to a lesser extent) reinforces stigma and further marginalizes those with these disorders.[45]

Stigma regarding mental illness is alive and well among law school students. The study Suffering in Silence found that nearly half of law school students reported that they would be deterred from seeking help for a mental health problem because doing so would jeopardize their admission to the bar.[46]

Research evidence shows that prosecutors and judges hold less favorable and less compassionate attitudes toward defendants with mental illness and substance-abuse disorders.[47] The attitudes of judges and prosecutors are consistent with the attitudes of the general public, which is to be expected, as there is really no reason to think that the attitudes of prosecutors and judges should be that different from those of the general population.

Decision-making regarding mental illness and substance abuse becomes more problematic when we consider the role of implicit bias. There is considerable evidence that implicit bias toward those with mental illness and substance-use disorders is robust and pervasive.[48]

> Research on implicit bias against mental illness has demonstrated that laypeople possess strong negative biases against mental illness. Studies show that people possess both negative explicit and implicit attitudes and beliefs about people with mental illnesses and laypeople tend to associate the concepts of "bad," "blameworthy," and "helpless" with mental illness.

Again, there is no evidence and little reason to believe that judges and prosecutors differ in significant ways from laypeople in terms of implicit bias against individuals with mental illness and substance-use disorders.

Another survey of judges shows that a majority do not consider testimony of a clinical diagnosis of mental illness to be "science." Rather, they think of such evidence as "technical knowledge." Importantly, those who do not consider it scientific evidence think of clinical testimony as "overly subjective" and "not true science."[49]

After discussing the limited role that mental health testimony has traditionally played in criminal sentencing, Richard Redding and Daniel Murrie conclude:[50]

> A decade later, little has changed. If anything, forensic opinion is even less influential on sentencing decisions in an era of offense-based determinate sentencing as well as punitive "get tough" policies toward offenders.

The point of this discussion is whether the decision-making systems and processes in place in the US criminal court system are sufficient and appropriate for making evidence-informed judgments that are designed to enhance public safety and reduce recidivism. I believe that there is compelling evidence to support the conclusion that suboptimal decision-making is responsible for much of the ineffectiveness and cost inefficiency of the criminal justice system. One of the key causes of this are the unmanageable caseloads and workloads that the key officials in the court system face every day. I will propose a strategy in the last chapter that may help improve the decision-making process as well as the outcomes of those decisions.

NOTES

1. Kahneman, *Of 2 Minds: How Fast and Slow Thinking Shape Perception and Choice*, 12.

2. Kahneman, *Of 2 Minds: How Fast and Slow Thinking Shape Perception and Choice*, 12.

3. Shah and Oppenheimer, "Heuristics Made Easy: An Effort Reduction Framework," 208.

4. Shah and Oppenheimer, "Heuristics Made Easy: An Effort Reduction Framework," 207.

5. Sinayev and Peters, "Cognitive Reflection vs. Calculation in Decision Making."

6. Guthrie, Rachlinski, and Wistrich, "Blinking on the Bench: How Judges Decide Cases."

7. Rachlinski and Wistrich, "Judging the Judiciary by the Numbers: Empirical Research on Judges."

8. Rachlinski and Wistrich, "Judging the Judiciary by the Numbers: Empirical Research on Judges," 213.

9. Ebbesen and Konecni, "Decision Making and Information Integration in the Courts."

10. Rachlinski and Wistrich, "Judging the Judiciary by the Numbers: Empirical Research on Judges."

11. Rachlinski and Wistrich, "Judging the Judiciary by the Numbers: Empirical Research on Judges," 216.

12. Rachlinski and Wistrich, "Judging the Judiciary by the Numbers: Empirical Research on Judges."

13. Rachlinski and Wistrich, "Judging the Judiciary by the Numbers: Empirical Research on Judges," 222.

14. Ebbesen and Konecni, "Decision Making and Information Integration in the Courts"; Ebbesen and Konecni, "An Analysis of the Sentencing System"; Dahmi, "Psychological Models of Professional Decision Making"; Farina, Arce, and Novo, "Anchoring in Judicial Decision-Making"; Worden, "The Judges Role in Plea Bargaining."

15. Rachlinski and Wistrich, "Judging the Judiciary by the Numbers: Empirical Research on Judges"; Guthrie, Rachlinski, and Wistrich, "Blinking on the Bench: How Judges Decide Cases"; Rachlinski, Wistrich, and Guthrie, "Can Judges Make Reliable Numeric Judgments? Distorted Damages and Skewed Sentences"; Gilbert, "Inferential Correction."

16. Alexander, *The New Jim Crow*.

17. Hinton, Vera Institute of Justice, "Research Confirms that Entrenched Racism Manifests in Disparate Treatment of Black Americans in Criminal Justice System."

18. Rachlinski, Johnson, Wistrich, and Guthrie, "Does Unconscious Racial Bias Affect Trial Judges?"

19. Kirwan Institute for the Study of Race and Ethnicity, "Understanding Implicit Bias."

20. Greenwald and Krieger, "Implicit Bias: Scientific Foundations," 945–46.

21. Irwin and Real, "Unconscious Influences on Judicial Decision-Making: The Illusion of Objectivity."

22. Pyun, "When Neurogenetics Hurts: Examining the Use of Neuroscience and Genetic Evidence in Sentencing Decisions Through Implicit Bias."

23. Rachlinski, Johnson, Wistrich, and Guthrie, "Does Unconscious Racial Bias Affect Trial Judges?"

24. Anderson, "Statewide Judicial Decision-Making Study Results Announced."

25. Wistrich and Rachlinski, "Implicit Bias in Judicial Making"; Bennett, "The Implicit Racial Bias in Sentencing."

26. Levinson, Bennett, and Hioki, "Judging Implicit Bias: A National Empirical Study of Judicial Stereotypes."

27. Burke, "Improving Prosecutorial Decision Making," 1591.

28. Burke, "Improving Prosecutorial Decision Making"; Burke, "Neutralizing Cognitive Bias"; Burke, "Prosecutorial Passion, Cognitive Bias, and Plea Bargaining"; Findley, "Tunnel Vision"; Godsil and Jiang, "Prosecuting Fairly: Addressing the Challenges of Implicit Bias, Racial Anxiety, and Stereotype Threat"; Kang et al., "Implicit Bias in the Courtroom"; Babikian, "Cleaving the Gordian Knot."

29. Findley, "Tunnel Vision."

30. Godsil and Jiang, "Prosecuting Fairly: Addressing the Challenges of Implicit Bias, Racial Anxiety, and Stereotype Threat"; Kang et al., "Implicit Bias in the Courtroom"; Babikian, "Cleaving the Gordian Knot."

31. Queally, "San Francisco DA Unveils Plan Aimed at Removing Implicit Bias from Prosecutors."

32. Kang et al., "Implicit Bias in the Courtroom."

33. Babikian, "Cleaving the Gordian Knot," 149.

34. American Bar Association Commissions on Disability Rights, "Implicit Biases and People with Disabilities."

35. Eisenberg and Johnson, "Implicit Racial Attitudes of Death Penalty Lawyers."

36. Richardson and Goff, "Implicit Racial Bias in Public Defender Triage"; Lyon, "Race Bias and the Importance of Consciousness for Criminal Defense Attorneys."

37. Mears and Bacon, "Improving Criminal Justice Through Better Decision-Making," 151.

38. Smith, Levinson, and Robinson, "Implicit White Favoritism in the Criminal Justice System."

39. Levinson and Smith, "Forum: Systemic Implicit Bias," 414.

40. Hon. Ray Price, Missouri Chief Justice, "State of the Judiciary."

41. Anleu, Rottman, and Mack, "The Emotional Dimension of Judging: Issues, Evidence and Insights"; Guthrie, Rachlinski, and Wistrich, "Blinking on the Bench: How Judges Decide Cases"; Wistrich, Rachlinski, and Guthrie, "Heart versus Head: Do Judges Follow the Law or Follow Their Feelings?" 911.

42. Hinshaw and Stier, "Stigma as Related to Mental Disorders"; Parcesepe and Cabassa, "Public Stigma of Mental Illness in the United States"; Tsai et al., "Stigma as a Fundamental Hindrance to the United States Opioid Overdose Crisis Response."

43. Hinshaw and Stier, "Stigma as Related to Mental Disorders," 368.

44. Parcesepe and Cabassa, "Public Stigma of Mental Illness in the United States."

45. Livingston et al., "The Effectiveness of Interventions for Reducing Stigma Related to Substance Use Disorders."

46. Holcombe, "Law Students Say They Don't Get Mental Health Treatment for Fear It Will Keep Them from Becoming Lawyers."

47. Batastini, Lester, and Thompson, "Mental Illness in the Eyes of the Law: Examining Perceptions of Stigma among Judges and Attorneys"; Lowder, Ray, and Gruenewald, "Criminal Justice Professionals' Attitudes toward Mental Illness and Substance Use."

48. Teachman, Wilson, and Komarovskaya, "Implicit and Explicit Stigma of Mental Illness in Diagnosed and Healthy Samples"; Pyun, "When Neurogenetics Hurts: Examining the Use of Neuroscience and Genetic Evidence in Sentencing Decisions through Implicit Bias," 1032.

49. Gatowski et al., "Asking the Gatekeepers: A National Survey of Judges on Judging Expert Evidence in a Post-*Daubert* World"; Redding and Murrie, "Judicial Decision Making about Forensic Mental Health Evidence."

50. Redding and Murrie, "Judicial Decision Making about Forensic Mental Health Evidence," 691.

3

The Front End
of the Pretrial System

Arrest, Detention, and Bail

OVERVIEW OF THE PROCESS

Someone is arrested in the United States every three seconds. What follows has substantial consequences for the individual as well as the criminal justice system, and public safety more broadly. It is also a process that has a variety of critical decision points where discretion rules the day.

Discretion begins with the police in the decision to arrest someone. The most common way in which people are arrested is simply if law enforcement has sufficient evidence. The standard is probable cause, a belief by a reasonable person that a crime has been committed and this individual probably committed that crime. Arrests are also made with an arrest warrant, which is supported by probable cause and issued by a judge. Finally, a law enforcement officer may arrest someone if he or she witnesses the commission of a crime. Examples include an officer sees someone intoxicated in public, sees someone assaulting someone else, or witnesses a drug transaction.

There were more than ten million arrests of adults and juveniles in 2018. The most common categories of arrests are drug-abuse violations (1.65 million), simple assault (1.06 million), and driving under the influence (1.00 million). Interestingly, 30 percent of all arrests are due to drug and alcohol violations. Violent crimes constitute only about 5 percent of arrests (murder, rape, robbery, and aggravated assault), or 15 percent adding in simple assault.[1]

Arrest generally means taking someone into custody, resulting in the individual being admitted or booked into jail. Another option when police suspect an individual of committing a crime is what is called cite and release or field release. In effect, the police issue a ticket to the individual, much like a traffic ticket, that serves as a promise to appear in court on a particular date and time. This is in lieu of jail detention. Roughly speaking, about one-half of the 10.3 million arrests each year result in the individual being transported to and booked into jail. The majority of the remainder are issued a citation.

A relative handful of those who are neither booked into jail nor issued a citation are diverted to some alternative for addressing underlying problems like mental illness or problematic behavior. The point is to utilize noncriminal or deescalated criminal justice responses in lieu of traditional criminal prosecution, conviction, and punishment. I have not found reliable estimates of how common diversion is in the United States, however, survey data indicate that despite increasing interest in such diversion programs, it is still uncommon. A recent (2014) survey of local law enforcement agencies showed that only one-third had police-initiated diversion programs. About one-quarter of those were pre-arrest, about one-quarter were at the point of arrest, and half were post-booking or at some later point after booking.[2]

Issuing a citation instead of arresting and booking into jail is premised on the idea that some, less serious offenses do not warrant detention in jail. It is clear from existing state laws that issuing citations is largely reserved for lesser crimes (misdemeanors). Forty-eight states permit citations for at least some misdemeanor crimes; twelve extend that to a limited number of felony cases.

The majority of states (twenty-eight) provide that the determination of when to issue a ticket for eligible offenses is up to the discretion of individual police or sheriff officers. That discretion is restricted in fourteen states depending on the circumstances, and nine states make citations mandatory for eligible offenses.[3] On balance, while state legislatures set various parameters around the use of citations, it still often falls on individual law enforcement officers to issue a ticket or arrest and book into jail for large numbers of crime situations. In some circumstances, the law requires an officer to assess characteristics of the offender rather than the criminal conduct, such as prior criminal history, ability to provide identification, intoxication, ties to the community, and risk of ongoing crime, among others. How those circumstances are assessed and evaluated by police on the street is unknown. I do not believe that we have any reliable research on the decision to arrest and book versus cite and release, which is unfortunate given its policy importance. We do know that judges typically analyze this kind of information in making release and detention decisions, and those decisions have been the subject of considerable research and policy discussion (the topic of bail reform), a subject I will turn to later.

The decision to cite or arrest/book into jail is of considerable importance. We will see later that pretrial detention has a variety of quite serious consequences for the individual being jailed. Pretrial detention also incurs financial costs on the local jurisdiction (jails are typically funded locally by city and/or county tax revenue).

Jails have two primary functions—pretrial detention and incarceration for individuals convicted of a misdemeanor and sentenced to incarceration. The majority (between two-thirds and three-quarters) of individuals in jail are there for pretrial detention. The percentage varies by jurisdiction, depending on such things as jail capacity, how decisions are made by prosecutors and judges regarding pretrial detention, and use of pretrial diversion, among others.

A recent 2019 analysis of jail bookings in Texas assessed data for twelve of the state's twenty-five largest counties, representing 40 percent of the population.[4] The results show that in the vast majority of the counties examined, misdemeanor jail bookings outnumbered felony bookings by a considerable margin. On average, misdemeanors represented nearly 60 percent of jail bookings. The most common crimes represented in the bookings are nonviolent alcohol and drug offenses (the top three are driving while intoxicated, possession of marijuana, and possession of a controlled substance). Nearly 20 percent of misdemeanor bookings were for Class C misdemeanor offenses, the lowest-level crime in Texas, which is defined as a fine-only offense (i.e., no jail time).

Once a suspect is arrested and booked into jail, within a limited amount of time, the individual will go before a judge or magistrate for what is generally called a detention hearing, a pretrial release hearing, or a bail hearing. The point of this hearing is for the court to determine what to do with the individual while the case is being processed. The government's interest at this point is to preserve public safety and assure that the individual does not simply ignore court instruction for subsequent proceedings or flee the jurisdiction. The options are release on recognizance (a promise to appear by the defendant), release on pretrial supervision (where the court can impose conditions of supervision such as electronic monitoring), release on bail (a financial condition of release), and outright denial of release, where the defendant is detained in jail pending subsequent adjudication of the case.

If bail is set, there are generally three ways the defendant can meet that condition: cash bond, where the defendant posts the full money amount with the court, a deposit bond, where the defendant posts typically 10 percent with the court and is liable for the balance if he or she fails to appear in court, and a commercial bond, where the defendant pays a fee to a private bail bond company and the company is then liable if the defendant fails to appear. The fee (typically 10 to 15 percent) paid to the commercial bail bond agent is the cost for posting the bail amount and assuming liability.

Setting the bail amount is in theory a judge's consideration of public safety risk (typically assessed in terms of prior criminal justice involvement), flight risk (reflected by ties to the community such as employment, school, family, owning property, etc.), and the recommendations by the prosecutor (and sometimes, by input from defense counsel).

In many instances, defense counsel is not present at the detention hearing. This is the case since roughly 80 percent of defendants are indigent and cannot retain counsel, and there is usually a time lag between booking and contact with a public defender or appointment of counsel. Often, the pretrial release hearing occurs during that time lag. One very important consequence is that the evidence shows that defendants who are represented at the detention hearing are more likely to be released on their recognizance and if released on bail, the bail amount is lower.[5]

PROBLEMS WITH BAIL SYSTEMS

The first criticism of bail is a very fundamental one of logic. The point of bail, presumably, is to deter flight from the jurisdiction (failure to appear) and reoffending. Maybe prosecutors and judges believe that when money is at stake, a defendant may think twice about fleeing the jurisdiction or forgetting a court date. And I suppose that same logic applies to reoffending—money is somehow a deterrent to recidivism while on pretrial release. First, if punishment (either the threat of punishment or actually being punished) does not deter crime and failure to appear, why would we expect money to deter? The evidence on this matter does not support the purported link between bail and pretrial misconduct. A study conducted in 2016 shows that contrary to the logic of the bail system, bail increases recidivism by 6 to 9 percent and has either no effect on failure to appear or actually increases it.[6]

> These results have implications for both our understanding of criminal defendants' economic circumstances and the institutional design of the American money bail system . . . Money bail imposes many costs on society—including those stemming from pretrial detention, convictions and recidivism—yet we find no evidence that money bail results in positive outcomes, such as an increase in defendants' rate of appearance at court.

A more recent 2020 analysis of the effects of bail on failure to appear and pretrial arrests reveals no relationship.[7]

> This [research] provides a unique opportunity to evaluate the main justification for the use of money bail: that it helps ensure appearance and prevent crime among released defendants. We find no evidence to support this.

Even if bail did deter reoffending or failure to appear, how on earth would judges and prosecutors know how much bail is necessary to deter a particular individual? Even if risk assessments are used to determine offender risk, which is a step in the right direction for improving court decision-making (something I discuss in depth below), that still does not answer the question of how much bail is enough to produce the desired outcome?

What seems to be the typical response from judges and prosecutors is to set a higher bail amount for individuals charged with more serious crimes, greater perceived dangerousness, or those determined to be high risk based on a risk-assessment instrument. This naively extends the flawed logic of bail as a deterrent simply by requiring higher bail for riskier and/or more dangerous offenders. Again, the idea that a greater amount of money will control the behavior of higher risk individuals is problematic, and the evidence indicates it does not work. If someone is dangerous and/or high risk, they should either be detained or carefully supervised.

Another characteristic of the bail system is that there is tremendous variation in bail settings across judges.[8] In many circumstances, judges have wide discretion in determining the bail amount as well as wide discretion in what information they consider and how they consider it in arriving at a bail amount.

Many jurisdictions around the country use what are called bail schedules that prescribe a set amount based on the severity of the crime(s) charged. A fundamental criticism of bail schedules it that they do not take into consideration a variety of important information that is related to offender risk. Nor do they consider an individual's ability to pay the amount indicated. That obviously contributes to the number of people detained pretrial for the simple reason that they cannot afford the bail or the commercial bond fee.

In addition to the Sixth Amendment issue regarding assistance of counsel during the detention hearing, there is also an Eighth Amendment issue regarding bail—"Excessive bail shall not be required." Unfortunately, the excessive bail clause is one of the least litigated protections in the Bill of Rights, thus there is a relative lack of understanding about what is excessive. In *Stack v. Boyle* (1951), the US Supreme Court held that bail should not be any greater than necessary to assure a defendant would appear to stand trial.[9] Since there was no evidence that the defendants were a flight risk in the case, the Court declared the bail excessive. The general understanding now is that a bail amount is not excessive if it is no greater than what is required to achieve a lawful goal of the court, whatever that means.

However, there are often failures to pay attention to the bail settings of judges. For example, a Pennsylvania law requires judges to consider a defendant's financial circumstances and ability to pay in the process of setting the bail amount. Ironically, there is essentially no supervision or oversight of the judicial decision-making process regarding setting bail amounts.[10]

A 2018 piece in the *Texas Tribune* described the bail process for offenders in Dallas County.[11] The headline is telling—"In Dallas County, Bail Is Set in Secret—And Often in Seconds."

> In most places around the country, bail hearings are open to the public . . . Not so in Dallas County, where people accused of crimes have their bail set behind closed doors . . . In most cases, the encounter between the judge and the accused lasts no more than 15 seconds. A judge ticks off each defendant's bail amount—often according to a predetermined bail schedule—asks if he or she is a U.S. citizen, then sends them off to jail. There's no discussion of the person's likelihood of returning to court or ability to pay the sum, or of the facts of the crime allegedly committed.

In St. Louis, there is a similar disregard for the accused's ability to pay, but much regard for speedy processing.[12]

> In 98% of the cases examined, a bond commissioner did not provide any information to the duty judge about a defendant's ability to pay and the judge set bail without any information on this constitutionally critical factor . . . court appearances lasted approximately 45–60 seconds.

First, a couple of observations. There is a presumption of innocence that in theory accompanies the defendant as he or she moves through the criminal justice process. As discussed above, the government's interest at this point is in public safety and flight risk. Pretrial detention is supposed to be used as a way to manage the risk of reoffending and flight from the jurisdiction for those the court believes must be incarcerated in order to mitigate that risk. However, there is clear evidence that substantial numbers of criminal suspects are detained pretrial not because they necessarily pose a significant risk, but because they cannot afford the bail amount set by the court. One could interpret detaining someone simply because they could not afford the bail or the bail bond agent's fee as punitive. In turn, many have argued that punishing someone before they have been proven guilty violates one of the pillars of American jurisprudence. Let's see what the evidence shows.

First, the vast majority of those in US jails on any given day are there for pretrial detention. The evidence indicates that out of one hundred individuals arrested who have a detention hearing, only a very small number (4 percent) are actually denied bail, presumably because the court determines the individual is too dangerous or too much of a flight risk to warrant release under any circumstances. One-quarter of the one hundred individuals arrested are released from detention on a nonfinancial basis (most typically their own recognizance or promise to appear). Thirty-eight percent are released by paying the bail set by the court (either directly or through a commercial bail bond agent).[13] Finally, one-third of the arrestees are detained pretrial because they cannot afford the bail amount set and/or they cannot afford the bond agent's fee. So, on any given day in the United States, there are 420,500 individuals in jail on pretrial detention not because bail release was denied, but simply because they cannot afford it.[14]

International comparisons show that the United States leads the other thirty-seven OEDC (The Organisation for Economic Co-operation and Development) countries in the use of pretrial detention. The US rate of pretrial detention varies between twice that to thirty-six times that of the other OEDC nations.[15]

The jail population in the United States has grown by nearly 300 percent over the past forty years. Most of that growth was due to the expansion of pretrial detention. Over the past twenty years, fully 95 percent of the growth in the jail population has been due to the expansion of pretrial detention, both in terms of number of individuals detained as well as the length of time detained.[16] The length of pretrial detention has increased over the past thirty years, ranging, for example, by more than 100 percent for rape, 45 percent for robbery, 40 percent for assault, and 35 percent for burglary.[17]

It is important to note that this was a period of substantially declining crime (27 percent decline in overall crime and a 40 percent decline in the crime rate between 2000 and 2018[18]). The evidence indicates that across the board, local jurisdictions are increasingly relying on pretrial detention. Statistical evidence also shows that jurisdictions are increasingly requiring financial conditions (bail) for pretrial release. Just more than one-half of defendants released in 1990 from pretrial detention were required to pay bail; in 2009, that had increased to 72 percent. That increase affected those accused of violent and nonviolent crimes alike. Moreover, the percent of those released from pretrial detention without bail required declined by 15 percentage points between 1990 and 2009.[19]

Bail amounts have increased as well. Across the board, the bail amount for felonies has increased by 120 percent over the past twenty-five years, from $25,400 in 1992 to more than $55,000 by 2006.[20] That average felony bail amount of $55,000 is higher than the annual pay of 80 percent of US wage earners. While bail amounts for property offenses did not increase, they did for violent crimes, drug crimes, and public-order offenses. So has the use of commercial bail bond agents. In 1990, about two-thirds of those released on bail did so with a commercial bond agent. By 2009, that had increased to 80 percent.[21]

A survey conducted by the Federal Reserve asked the general public how they would pay for a $400 emergency or unforeseen expense. Nearly 50 percent said that they would have to borrow it or sell something or that they simply could not cover it.[22] Compare that to the average bail amounts cited above. Even with a commercial bond, the typical felony defendant must come up with more than $5,000.[23] That helps put in perspective what millions of individuals face every year when it comes to pretrial release or detention after being arrested.

Not only have courts increasingly required bail, they have increasingly required bail amounts that are out of reach of many hundreds of thousands of arrestees. The Prison Policy Initiative has compiled data showing that most of those who are detained pretrial because they cannot afford the bail amount fall in the lower third of the income distribution. Men who were detained pretrial because they could not afford the bail amount had a median pre-incarceration income of $15,600, compared to that of their nonincarcerated counterparts, which was nearly $40,000, or 153 percent higher. By race/ethnicity, the median income of the nonincarcerated population compared to detained individuals who could not afford bail is 177 percent higher for Blacks, 58 percent higher for Hispanics, and 138 percent higher for Whites. For women, it is 162 percent higher for Blacks, 19 percent for Hispanics, and 100 percent higher for Whites. Moreover, the median incomes for detained Black males and detained White, Black, and Hispanic women fall below the federal poverty line.[24] The obvious conclusion is that disadvantage drives pretrial detention.

The decision to deny bail, release without bail, or release with bail is made by a judge or a magistrate, often considering the input from the prosecutor, and perhaps occasionally the input of defense counsel (if present). Judges have limited circumstances in which they can outright deny bail. That is reflected in data that indicate a very small proportion of arrestees are denied release. Judicial discretion is considerable when setting the conditions of release. The legally relevant evidence that a judge can consider includes the characteristics and severity of the charges, prior criminal history, and ties to the community. A bond interview, where pretrial-services personnel interview the arrested individual in jail about their financial circumstances, is used to assist the court in setting the bail amount. Research published in 2018 shows that in many instances, judges simply fail to consider ability to pay when setting a bail amount.[25]

What is surprising is that in many circumstances where judges have the defendants' financial information, bail still seems out of reach for many. In some instances, judges may set high bail as a way to achieve preventive detention since laws generally limit denial of release to exceptional situations. In other circumstances, financial information may not be required to be considered by the court in setting the bail amount. For example, in 2017, the Maryland Supreme Court established a rule that requires judges to consider ability to pay in setting the bail amount. In other states, the use of financial information is an unsettled issue.

A good bit of research consistently confirms the relationship between legally relevant considerations (charges, prior criminal involvement) and detention/release decisions. These are strong predictors of release versus detention as well as the bail amount.[26] However, there is clear evidence to support what Kamala Harris and Rand Paul assert in their recent *New York Times* op-ed.[27]

> Excessive bail disproportionately harms people from low-income communities and communities of color. The Supreme Court ruled in *Bearden v. Georgia* in 1983 that the Constitution prohibits "punishing a person for his poverty," but that's exactly what this system does. Nine out of 10 defendants who are detained cannot afford to post bail, which can exceed $20,000 even for minor crimes like stealing $105 in clothing. Meanwhile, black and Latino defendants are more likely to be detained before trial and less likely to be able to post bail compared with similarly situated white defendants. In fact, black and Latino men respectively pay 35 percent and 19 percent higher bail than white men.

Research reveals that extralegal factors, in particular race and ethnicity, influence the pretrial detention and release decision, as well as the bail amount.[28] For example, Black and Hispanic defendants are more likely to be detained pretrial, are less likely to be granted nonfinancial conditions of release, and more likely to be assessed higher bail amounts when bail is granted. These findings are controlling for other relevant predictors of these outcomes.[29] Another study found that being Black was associated with a 25 percent increased likelihood of pretrial detention as a result of courts setting higher bail amounts (35 percent higher for Blacks compared to Whites with similar characteristics, and 19 percent higher for Hispanics, compared to Whites), net of other factors. The authors conclude "estimates suggest discriminatory bail levels in at least one and possibly two, of these counties [out of five counties investigated], where estimates suggest judges set bail as if the value of blacks' lost freedom is less than two-thirds the value of whites' lost freedom."[30]

An investigation by the ACLU of race and ethnicity in the detention and bail-setting process in Miami-Dade County, Florida, shows similar disparities as other research. Non-Hispanic Blacks who have been arrested are 2.3 times more likely to be detained pretrial compared to their prevalence in the county population. Black defendants who are also Hispanic are 4.5 times more likely to be detained, again compared to their share of the population in Miami-Dade County.

Much research has focused on individual, case-level characteristics for explaining different pretrial outcomes regarding detention, release, and bail. More recent work has looked at the correlates of intercounty variation in detention and release decisions. Katherine Hood and Daniel Schneider document that declines in nonfinancial release and the doubling of bail amounts appear unrelated to changes in case composition or the characteristics of defendants. Rather, they show that trends over time and differences across counties in bail and pretrial release are the result of a variety of contextual factors, such as the political affiliation of the District Attorney, unemployment rates, income inequality, and the election of judges, among others.[31]

> Local politics shape pretrial decisions in predictable ways. Elected judges are associated with higher bail amounts than their appointed counterparts, and Democrats in the district attorney's office are linked to both higher rates of nonfinancial release and cheaper bail. This suggests that judges concerned about reelection make more conservative pretrial decisions, and on the other hand, Democrats reflect a partisan preference for less punitive pretrial regimes. Socioeconomic conditions are also important in predictable ways. Higher income inequality is linked to lower financial release and higher unemployment rates are linked to more expensive bail amounts.

Pretrial release and bail decisions are tied to individual, case-level characteristics as well as local contextual characteristics. In both cases, there is clear evidence that extralegal factors play a central role in pretrial outcomes. In turn, detention and release decisions have profound downstream effects, a topic I will turn to shortly.

The United States is one of only two countries in the world that relies on commercial bail bond agents for securing the pretrial release of accused felons and misdemeanants. The Philippines is the other. The for-profit bail bond industry in the United States posts $14 billion annually in bail to local courts. Adding together the typical bond fee (that is, the cost of borrowing the bail amount) with other related fees, the bail bond industry collects $2+ billion annually in revenue. The fee charged is nonrefundable, regardless of the outcome of the case, including dismissal of the charges or an acquittal.

The bail bond market is dominated by nine large insurance companies, which underwrite the majority of bonds that are issued in the United States. The insurers essentially have a financial firewall protecting them from losses by making the individual bond agents, those who set up the storefronts around local courthouses, responsible for any failure-to-appear bond forfeitures.

There are ethical issues regarding for-profit companies having financial stakes in the criminal justice system, as is the case with private prison corporations as well as bail bond companies. These concerns include bail bond companies profiting from the disadvantage of individuals who are unable to pay the bail amount in order to be released from jail. The reality is that they charge the poor for their freedom. Not the courts, not the jail, not the government, but for-profit, private-sector companies. It is important to underscore that trends in release and bail over the past thirty years or so (declining release-on-recognizance, increasing conditional release requiring bail, and increases in the bail amounts) clearly favor the bottom lines of these bail bond agents and their parent companies.

The bail bond industry occupies an unusual middle ground in that it is not really under the control of the courts, even though it plays a central role in the criminal justice system. Rather, what is described as piecemeal supervision is the responsibility of insurance regulators.

Despite many concerns, the for-profit bail bond industry lacks oversight and is not well regulated. A report issued in 2014 from the New Jersey State Commission of Investigation stated:[32]

> Operating in the shadows of poor government oversight, the system is dominated by an amalgam of private entrepreneurs who profit from the process but are subject to weak controls easily manipulated or ignored with little or no consequence.

It seems that what is described in New Jersey applies as well to much of the rest of the country.[33] New Orleans has a particularly egregious situation regarding commercial bail, a situation created by the Louisiana legislature. In New Orleans, 97 percent of felony defendants who are able to pay do so with a commercial bond. Seventy percent of misdemeanor defendants do so. The fee is 12 percent. However, 3 percent of the fee goes to local government—the court, the sheriff, the District Attorney, and the public defender. In addition, nearly 2 percent of the total bail amount paid by bond agents is reverted to the courts in New Orleans.[34] One could make an argument that there is an incentive to use bail more frequently and to require higher bail amounts.

Efforts at reform are hampered by the bail bond industry, which aggressively lobbies federal and state lawmakers. Between 2009 and 2017, the bail bond industry spent $6.4 million lobbying state legislators and $1.8 million in direct campaign contributions. Their lobbying and political campaign contributions target California, Florida, New York, and Texas, the four largest states in the country.[35] The industry also has worked with the American Legislative Exchange Council (ALEC) on multiple occasions to pass legislation to expand and protect its role. ALEC consists of legislators and corporations that write state legislative bills that promote its members' objectives.

A recent example of the bail bond industry's power is reflected in their success in at least temporarily halting the implementation of California Senate Bill 10. A California appellate court decision *In re Humphrey* compelled the state to pass bail reform to "correct a deformity in [California's] criminal justice system."[36] Senate Bill 10 would eliminate cash bail, replacing it with a system based on risk assessments and nonmonetary forms of pretrial release and preventative detention for those who are particularly high risk for flight and/or reoffending.

THE CONSEQUENCES OF PRETRIAL DETENTION

On the one hand, pretrial detention seems like a very effective way to manage the risk of reoffending and enhance public safety. It can be and is easily accomplished simply by setting bail amounts outside the financial reach of defendants. On the other hand, while pretrial detention seems like the safe choice and is quite consistent with our fifty-year mantra of tough on crime, there are a number of very negative consequences to jailing someone awaiting disposition of their case.

The research is extensive. There are profound short-term and longer-term consequences of pretrial detention. Failure to appear (FTA) is related to pretrial detention followed by release. But the key is length of detention. People detained in jail for two to three days and then released were slightly more likely to FTA compared to those detained one day. Those detained between two days and one week were 1.22 times more likely to fail to appear. That jumps to 1.41 for those detained fifteen to thirty days and then released.[37]

There is a strong and persistent relationship between pretrial detention and conviction. This holds for both felonies and misdemeanors.[38] For example, detained misdemeanants are 25 percent more likely to be convicted compared to similar defendants who were released pretrial.[39] For felons, the research indicates a 13 percentage point increase in the probability of criminal conviction.[40] Moreover, it is not just the fact of detention, but the length of time someone is incarcerated that is associated with increased probability of conviction. One study found that conviction for a felony increased from 22 percent for those who spent no time in jail to 72 percent for those who were incarcerated for more than two months.[41] The most common explanation of the relation between detention and conviction is a substantially higher rate of pleading guilty in a plea deal for those who are detained. Recent research shows that pretrial detention not only increases the likelihood of conviction, it also significantly speeds up the process. Specifically, individuals detained in jail plead guilty 2.8 times faster than defendants who are released.[42] In many misdemeanor situations, the government will offer time served in jail in exchange for a guilty plea. That can be quite an incentive for those facing loss of a job or housing.

Sentencing is also influenced by pretrial detention. At the federal level, pretrial detention is related to an increased probability of a prison sentence as well as a longer sentence.[43] In state prosecutions, being detained the entire pretrial period increases the probability of a jail sentence by 4.4 times and a prison sentence by 3.3 times compared to those released at some point prior to disposition. These incarceration sentences are longer as well—2.8 times longer for those detained the entire pretrial period and sentenced to jail and 2.4 times longer for those sentenced to prison. A 2018 study by Megan Stevenson estimates that sentence length is increased by 42 percent as a result of pretrial detention.[44] Another study looking at misdemeanor cases found those detained more than seven days were 43 percent more likely to be sentenced to jail and probation and for a longer period of time compared to those who were released.[45] A wide variety of other analyses confirm the detrimental effects on sentencing of pretrial detention, both for misdemeanors and felonies.

Pretrial detention is related to future offending, both during the pretrial period and longer term. Again, it is not just detention, but the length of time someone is incarcerated that is key. Data from St. Louis show a clear pattern of recidivism depending on the length of incarceration. Those held two to three days have a 17 percent higher reoffending rate. For those detained four to seven days, it is 35 percent higher, and it's 51 percent higher for offenders incarcerated between eight and fourteen days.[46]

The criminogenic impact of detention is also evident in terms of longer-term recidivism. Defendants detained two to three days were 17 percent more likely to reoffend within two years; those jailed for one to two weeks were more than 50 percent more likely to reoffend, compared to those released within twenty-four hours.[47] Another study shows a 32 percent higher likelihood of felony recidivism for individuals detained pretrial.[48]

The social and economic costs of pretrial detention are of considerable consequence.[49] It can lead to financial loss, housing instability, loss of government benefits, and family disruption, among other impacts.[50]

> Pretrial detention imposes direct economic costs on detainees. A detainee's inability to work causes the loss of income and, potentially, the loss of employment and property. If pretrial detainees lose employment, they often simultaneously encounter reduced wages if and when they find new employment, as serving time reduces hourly wages for men by approximately 11%, annual employment by nine weeks, and annual earnings by 40%. Furthermore, when property (either apartments or rented homes) is lost, as occurs in 23% of cases, extra funds are expended on a subsequent housing search.

There are other financial costs to pretrial defendants that are imposed by the criminal justice system. These costs are not limited to the pretrial system (for example, individuals on probation routinely pay a supervision fee as well as other costs associated with programs and services), but they do impose significant hardship on many, especially when we consider that the vast majority of criminal defendants are indigent and cannot retain their own counsel (I discuss additional characteristics of arrestees below). Here are some examples of pretrial fees that defendants are charged.

Perhaps the most pernicious are jail fees. In at least forty-one states, defendants who are being detained pretrial, usually because they cannot afford bail, are charged a daily jail fee, often called pay to stay. There is substantial variation across states as well as across counties in how much is charged. In Shelby County (Memphis), Tennessee, the fee is $38 per day; in North Carolina, it's $10 per day, and in twenty-three counties in Wisconsin, it's $20 per day. In Kentucky, it can be as much as $50 per day. In Oklahoma, pretrial jail inmates are required to pay the full cost of detention, including booking, receiving, discharge, food, clothing, housing, and medical care. Many other states charge this extensively as well.

This pay-to-stay fee in effect helps support local criminal court and jail systems around the country, and, despite what one might call the "bad smell," they have been held constitutional.[51] In some instances, the fees can be refunded if the defendant is acquitted or the case dismissed, but that is far from universal.

Private contractors routinely charge exorbitant fees for jail phone calls. For example, in New York State, jail inmates are charged $8.83 per phone call. In eighteen New York counties in 2017, inmates spent $4.8 million on phone calls. The counties received $1.7 million from the contractors in 2017 in what is most appropriately called kickbacks.[52]

In the vast majority of states (forty-three plus the District of Columbia), indigent defendants can be charged a fee for a public defender or assigned counsel. The irony is pretty glaring.

In Morgan County, Alabama, pretrial defendants are charged a variety of fees for supervision, including an administration fee, a monitoring fee, an offender database maintenance fee, court costs, and the costs of participating in any programs required by the director. Hamilton County, Indiana, and Sanpete County, Utah (among many, many other counties in the United States) require an initial supervision fee of $50 and $60, respectively. In Oklahoma, pretrial defendants are charged a $10 monthly supervision fee. Dallas County and Travis County in Texas charge personal bond fees ranging from $20 to $300. A final example is from Johnson City, Indiana, where the misdemeanor pretrial fees vary by level of misdemeanor: The fee for Class A is $454, for Class B, it is $334, and for Class C, the fee is $254.[53]

There are also variable charges for jail booking fees and medical care while in pretrial detention. Electronic monitoring, for higher risk defendants on pretrial release, is also something for which jurisdictions commonly charge.[54]

PRETRIAL SUPERVISION IS DRASTICALLY UNDERDEVELOPED

A 2015 survey of local jails conducted by the National Association of Counties found that the vast majority (about 70 percent) of individuals who are detained pretrial are low risk (among those counties that conduct risk assessments, which is about 40 percent of counties that responded to the survey).[55] Another study utilizing a very large sample of pretrial detainees found that large numbers of defendants are detained needlessly.[56]

> In other words, about half of those detained have a lower chance of being rearrested pretrial than many of the people released. Indeed, we would be able to release 25% more defendants while decreasing pretrial crime levels if we released defendants using our evidence-based model.

This once again underscores the dramatic overreliance on pretrial detention, which is, as I discussed earlier, mostly a consequence of individuals' inability to personally post bail or secure a commercial bail bond.

The courts have essentially two options regarding managing the risk of individuals who have been arrested and are awaiting processing—pretrial detention or release. Pretrial detention seems to be the safe choice politically (most judges are elected), as well as the choice that fits best with the broader agenda of tough on crime. And, it comes with little cost to the judge who sets bail amounts or the prosecutor who makes bail recommendations, but plenty of cost to local taxpayers, who must pay for the construction and operation of jails. The average daily cost of pretrial detention is $75 per inmate.[57] When aggregated, counties spend at total of $14 billion per year on pretrial detention.[58]

The other option is conditional release, such as bail and/or pretrial supervision. In this section, I focus on pretrial supervision.

Pretrial supervision is a concept much like probation, where individuals are diverted from incarceration to community-based, conditional supervision. The logic is to manage any risk of reoffending and failure to appear through the conditions of supervision, such as regular contact with a pretrial-services supervision officer, drug testing, and electronic monitoring, among others. Given what we know about the quite serious, negative consequences of pretrial detention, and the fact that such large numbers of pretrial defendants who are detained are nonviolent and low risk, pretrial supervision in lieu of detention seems like such an obvious policy choice. The benefits include substantially lower cost (the average cost for pretrial supervision is $7.17 per person per day, or one-tenth the cost of detention in jail[59]), as well as promoting public safety, both in the near term while individuals are under supervision, and the long term, by avoiding the criminogenic effects of pretrial detention.

The unfortunate reality is that pretrial supervision is quite limited. The available data indicate generally absent and/or underdeveloped pretrial-services offices, as well as a lack of use of pretrial supervision. A 2015 nationwide survey of local jails indicated that less than one-half of the jurisdictions that responded to the survey had any kind of pretrial supervision options.[60] That same survey revealed that only about one-third of counties reported releasing arrestees to any type of pretrial supervision.[61] Another relatively recent nationwide survey reported three hundred local jurisdictions that had a pretrial-services programs as of 2009, but noted that since then, six states had passed legislation establishing such programs.[62]

A 2016 survey conducted by the Supreme Court of Ohio demonstrates the relative absence of pretrial services in the seventh-largest state. Respondents indicated that slightly over half of the jurisdictions had a pretrial-services department. Of those that answered in the affirmative, pretrial services was not a separate entity, but housed in a probation department.

California has made a concerted effort to facilitate the implementation of pretrial services in order to alleviate jail crowding. Representatives from all of the state's fifty-eight counties responded to a survey. The vast majority (80 percent) of the counties indicated that they had some version of formal pretrial services, defined as providing information to judges for pretrial release decisions and/or monitoring the conditions of pretrial release. When asked about the four core pretrial services (screen defendants for release, administer risk assessments, provide information to the court in making release decisions, and supervise those on pretrial release), just a bit more than 60 percent of the county representatives indicated their county provides all four.[63]

On the other hand, a survey of Texas counties indicates that pretrial services are rarely available.[64] Respondents indicated that only 47 counties have any kind of pretrial services, out of a total of 254 counties in the state. The pretrial functions reported in the survey vary considerably, but the majority (60 percent of the respondents) stated that the primary service was pretrial supervision. A more recent survey (2017) reports that 40 percent of counties in Texas "have some capacity for pretrial supervision."[65]

What is evident from the survey results is that neither pretrial services nor pretrial supervision are well-established components of the American criminal justice system. Jail and bail are the defaults, with little in between. For those jurisdictions that do have some pretrial services and supervision, we have no evidence regarding capacity, funding, or quality of services. This is in spite of strong support for pretrial supervision by such high-profile organizations as the American Bar Association.

PRETRIAL REFORM: USE OF RISK ASSESSMENTS IS A STEP IN THE RIGHT DIRECTION

The bail reform movement has gained a good bit of traction in the past few years in promoting the use of validated risk-assessment instruments for pretrial decision-making. They are increasingly being used to assist in the detention versus release decision, as well as helping in determining the conditions of release. I applaud these efforts since the evidence indicates this is a good policy direction, but I want to be clear that this is just a step in the right direction in terms of true, comprehensive pretrial reform. At the end of this chapter, I will discuss what I consider to be the bigger picture of pretrial reform. But first, risk assessments.

The point of using risk assessments is to reduce the reliance on pretrial detention and to facilitate transitioning from a money-based system to a risk-based system of release. Among other things, that would reduce the "detention of the poor" system that currently exists in most pretrial systems in the United States, as well as reduce the pretrial incarceration of individuals who do not pose a significant risk of reoffending or flight.

Risk-assessment experts advise that assessments should not replace judicial decisions, rather that they be used as guidance for judges in making better, more informed decisions about release and detention, as well as the conditions of release. What that looks like varies considerably across jurisdictions and across courts.

Risk assessments for pretrial decision-making have become increasingly popular in recent years. Although there is no systematic, nationwide survey of the use of risk assessments, piecing together data from several sources indicates that they are in use in more than 175 counties and 10 states. About 35 to 40 percent of the US population lives in a jurisdiction that uses pretrial risk assessments.[66] A recent survey revealed that only 6 counties in Texas, the second-largest state in the country, use a validated risk assessment.[67] There are 254 counties in the state, so this amounts to 2 percent.

Typical risk-assessment instruments utilize offender characteristics and past behavior in trying to identify a general risk level. Typical items include: prior arrests, convictions, incarcerations, and probations; prior failure to appear in court; current age; age at first criminal justice involvement; substance use; employment stability; education; housing status; and ties to the community. These risk items are predictive of subsequent offending as well as failure to appear. The instruments do not make specific quantitative predictions. Rather, they classify individuals into categories of risk, usually low, medium, and high.

It is important to note that risk-assessment predictions are for groups of individuals, rather than a prediction for a particular individual. When someone is assigned a risk category, the inference is that this individual shares characteristics or traits with individuals who succeeded or failed with a particular frequency.

In addition, there is error in the predictions that risk assessments make, so the obvious question is: How accurate are they? The answer depends on which instrument we are talking about and how it is administered. The ballpark consensus is that the best risk-assessment instruments are correct (meaning, for example, that they correctly classify a low-risk person as low risk and a high-risk person as high risk) somewhere between 65 and 70 percent of the time.[68] Obviously as the quality of the instrument declines, so does accuracy.

There are two primary types of prediction errors to be concerned about. False positives predict someone will reoffend or flee, when in fact they do not. If the prediction leads to pretrial detention, then the error raises questions of unnecessary incarceration and all of the consequences of detention that I will discuss below. Moreover, erroneous pretrial detention violates the holdings of the US Supreme Court in *Salerno* that "liberty is the norm, and detention prior to trial or without trial is the carefully limited exception."[69] False negatives predict someone is low risk, when in fact they reoffend and/or flee. False negatives raise public-safety concerns, as pretrial detention is supposed to be used to protect the community from avoidable crime.

While risk factors predict negative outcomes, protective factors are predictive of decreased probability of reoffending and failure to appear. Many protective factors are simply the opposite of risk factors, but others are independent of risk factors. Examples of protective factors are: high IQ; negative attitudes about crime; religious involvement; self-control; pro-social peers; parents less engaged in antisocial behavior and supportive parents; living in a high-quality neighborhood and high-quality housing.

Protective factors are not typically included in instruments predicting reoffending and flight. Overprediction of risk as a consequence of this omission is one of the criticisms that have been leveled against risk assessments.[70]

Another criticism is that risk assessments perpetuate racial bias in criminal justice decision-making. A 2016 analysis of the COMPAS risk assessment by ProPublica found racial disparities in that the instrument disproportionally misclassified Black defendants as high risk in Broward County, Florida. Subsequent research conducted by the Center for Court Innovation found similar disproportionate classification errors for Black defendants.[71]

Since the goals of the use of risk assessments are to reduce reliance on money, increase reliance on risk, and reduce unnecessary use of pretrial detention, an important public policy question is how much has pretrial detention been affected by the use of risk assessments? The answer, unfortunately, is unclear. Some research shows an initial reduction of pretrial detention but a subsequent return to pre-assessment levels. Others show increases in pretrial detention.[72] Another study in Orange County, California, highlights that judicial buy-in is critical in that there are no significant increases in pretrial release after implementation of risk assessments.[73] On the other hand, emerging evidence shows increasing rates of pretrial release as a result of using assessments.[74]

It is important to keep in mind that risk assessments are not Mission Accomplished in terms of pretrial reform. They are, at best, decision-making tools. Their utility is based on the premise that more, accurate information is better when making decisions of such considerable consequence. However, they should not be used to replace judges and human deliberations. Rather, their value is in assisting court officials make decisions that, in turn, may result in desirable outcomes, such as reductions in the reliance on detention and bail and increases in pretrial supervision and providing of services. There is obviously no guarantee that the results of risk assessments will be used in ways that enhance the likelihood of accomplishing those goals.

I noted several problems with the use of risk assessments, such as the failure to include protective factors in the instruments, the potential for making incorrect predictions, and racial and ethnic bias. These are substantial concerns that should further reinforce the idea that risk assessments are not the silver bullet of pretrial reform.

There is one other concern that I believe is of paramount importance. Understanding and predicting human behavior is a complex enterprise. Consider human decision-making and our reliance on heuristics, cognitive shortcuts that significantly simplify the process. Judges are no different. The tendency is to engage in intuitive rather than analytical decision-making, especially in circumstances like a detention hearing where there typically are phenomenal time constraints.

For most of the history of American criminal justice, we have relied on rather crude processes for determining risk and dangerousness—rough guesses or gut feelings based on some review of legal and criminal justice information, such as seriousness of the offense, criminal history, and ties to the community. Things have improved with risk assessments, but we are still not there.

The Public Safety Assessment (PSA) is a commonly used, validated pretrial risk-assessment instrument. The PSA was developed by Arnold Ventures, a nonprofit committed to criminal justice reform. The PSA relies on administrative data to compute two risk scores, the risk of reoffending if released pretrial and the risk of failure to appear. The instrument consists of the following items:[75]

- The person's age at the time of arrest
- Whether the current offense is violent
- Whether the person had a pending charge at the time of the current offense
- Whether the person has a prior misdemeanor conviction
- Whether the person has a prior felony conviction
- Whether the person has prior convictions for violent crimes
- How many times the person failed to appear at a pretrial hearing in the last two years
- Whether the person failed to appear at a pretrial hearing more than two years ago
- Whether the person has previously been sentenced to incarceration

What is missing here, and what is missing from many pretrial risk assessments, is much consideration of criminogenic circumstances, such as mental illness, substance abuse, intellectual or cognitive deficits and impairments, employment problems, living/family situation, and housing, including homelessness, among others. Just as protective factors are typically not included in pretrial risk-assessment instruments, resulting in less accurate predictions,[76] so is the case with criminogenic factors. While risk assessments focus on economical statistical prediction, decision-making regarding pretrial status should include a consideration of the bigger picture of the circumstances of the individual.

There are two reasons for that. One is better decision-making that can result from considering assessed risk in conjunction with clinical circumstances as well as factors such as unemployment, family disruption, and housing instability. The second reason is that if we do not know these broader criminogenic conditions, then we do not know what needs to be treated or addressed in order to reduce the risk of reoffending and flight. Take for example a defendant with a significant mental health problem who is released on bail. If the court is not aware of his condition and simply treats this individual as any other offender (recall that 50 percent of individuals in the criminal justice system have a mental health problem), because of the mental illness, this individual may fail to comply with the conditions of release, resulting in revocation. Revocation is probably the worst thing that could happen both in terms of aggravating the mental illness and increasing the probability of recidivism. Tailoring the conditions of release (requiring case management to enhance compliance) and pretrial services (diversion to mental health treatment) to the needs of the individual can significantly increase success on pretrial release, reduce the likelihood of reoffending, and save money.

But we have to know what the issues are in order to make better decisions. I will discuss in more detail in the last chapter what I have been recommending in prior books that needs to be added to the pretrial process—panels of clinical experts (psychiatrists, psychologists, clinical social workers, primary care physicians, or nurse practitioners) who can assess, diagnose, and recommend interventions to prosecutors, judges, and defense counsel in order to address these criminogenic deficits, disorders, and impairments. To be clear, these criminogenic circumstances are the key to understanding our out-of-control recidivism rates in this country.

All of this goes back to the observation that what happens in the pretrial phase affects everything else. The decisions made early on have substantial downstream consequences. Problems left unaddressed up front are simply passed on and usually compounded.

PRETRIAL REFORM: THE EXPANSION OF PRETRIAL SUPERVISION

The lack of well-established pretrial supervision is a very unfortunate state of criminal justice since the evidence indicates that it can be a very

effective alternative to jail and bail, while avoiding the negative consequences of pretrial detention and money bail. Here is what we know.

The primary outcomes that pretrial supervision is typically tied to are
failure to appear (FTA) and misconduct while on supervision (such as
failure to meet with a supervision officer or failing a drug test, reoffending, and revocation from supervision). One of the earliest evaluations of
pretrial supervision targeted Miami, Milwaukee, and Portland, Oregon.
The experimental design approach revealed positive results, including
lower FTA rates and rearrests, compared to defendants released on recognizance, citation, or bail.[77]

A two-state study of the effects of pretrial supervision on failure to appear and new crimes committed before case disposition found: 1) significantly lower FTA for those receiving supervision compared to those who
did not; and 2) significantly lower levels of reoffending for those on supervision, especially for those on longer periods of supervision.[78] Another
study utilizing random assignment to supervision and nonsupervision
groups found significantly lower failure to appear and rearrests while
awaiting disposition.[79] An evaluation of supervised release in New York
City revealed very high success rates for those assigned to supervision.[80]
A review of six additional studies on the effectiveness of pretrial supervised release in a variety of different counties and states shows positive
outcomes in the majority of cases (lower FTA and reoffending).[81]

A 2016 meta-analysis of existing research on pretrial release reports
that court notification (reminding defendants of court dates via telephone
and/or email/text) is effective in reducing failure to appear, thus mitigating concerns about flight risk for individuals on supervision. The authors
also conclude that "neither bond type, drug-testing, nor supervision were
associated with reductions in arrest during pretrial release."[82]

Looking at pretrial services more broadly (which includes supervision,
targeted treatment, and other programs), research from multiple jurisdictions found either no increase in FTA and rearrest or increases in appearance rates and reductions in rearrests, compared to those on commercial
bond.[83]

Finally, an analysis of pretrial release modeled after the HOPE strategy
of supervising individuals on post-conviction probation shows positive
outcomes. The basics of the HOPE model include dedicated staff with
commitment to rehabilitation, programming, and swift, certain, and modest sanctioning for violations of conditions. The evaluation found substantially lower (40 percent less) rearrests while on supervision as well as
substantially lower terminal revocation from supervision.[84] The analysis
did not track FTAs.

The evaluation research on pretrial supervision is rather limited, in part
reflecting the relative absence of pretrial services and supervision. Juris-

dictions have relied heavily on pretrial detention and bail as the primary methods for managing public safety and court appearances.

It seems fair to conclude that at best pretrial supervision significantly reduces rearrests and FTAs, and at worst, there is no difference in outcomes between those on supervision and controls. The lower FTA and rearrest results clearly support efforts to develop and expand pretrial supervision and pretrial services. So do the no-difference results. That argument is based on the overwhelming evidence regarding the very serious problems with bail systems as well as the negative consequences of pretrial detention. Pretrial supervision can reduce FTAs and rearrests, or at least not increase them, and the criminogenic impacts of detention and bail can be avoided, as can much of the cost of detention.

Pretrial supervision is largely a foregone opportunity. In conjunction with expanded and funded pretrial services, supervision is an opportunity, much like probation, to engage with defendants, screen and assess, and begin the process of intervention in an effort to address the causes and correlates of criminality. The unfortunate reality of the American criminal justice system is no one takes responsibility for reducing recidivism, and much of what happens in the pretrial context (detention, money bail) has served to exacerbate reoffending.

Given where we are today, the expansion of pretrial supervision will require, among other things, significant investment in resources, getting smarter about determining the appropriate conditions of supervision, and better decisions about who should be detained and who should be on pretrial supervision. Add to the mix participation in pre-arrest and pretrial diversion and pretrial programs and services. I take that up next.

PRETRIAL REFORM:
EXPANSION OF DIVERSION AND PRETRIAL SERVICES

It is, in my mind, very hard to overstate the importance of pretrial diversion and providing services to those who have been arrested and are awaiting disposition of their cases. We know from volumes of research that most individuals enter the criminal justice system with a variety of criminogenic circumstances, often comorbid mental health and substance-use disorders as well as employment and housing instability. Detention simply serves to increase the likelihood of reoffending, and there are substantial costs. Research conducted in Illinois puts the cost of one recidivism event at more than $150,000.[85]

A 2015 survey revealed that pretrial release services are not a ubiquitous component of pretrial systems. Thirty-three states have some pretrial-services programs, but they vary considerably across states and counties in terms of how well developed they are, what services they provide, and how many individuals participate.[86] The same is the case for pretrial diversion. Like pretrial services, there is a patchwork of diversion programs across the country.[87]

Research conducted by the Substance Abuse and Mental Health Services Administration and analyzed by the Prison Policy Initiative profiled individuals who were arrested in 2017.[88] The findings are not particularly surprising, but they are compelling in terms of policy development. These are people at the front door of the criminal justice system, at the front end of the pretrial system. Approximately 4.9 million were arrested in 2017; 3.5 million (71 percent) of those were arrested once in that year, 930,000 (20 percent) were arrested twice, and 430,000 (9 percent) were arrested three or more times just in 2017. Those who were arrested once were three times as likely to be unemployed compared to individuals not arrested; those with two or more arrested were four times more likely to be unemployed. Those arrested once were twice as likely to not have a high school diploma, and individuals arrested two or more time were more than three times as likely not to have graduated from high school. One-fifth of the population not arrested had an income less than $10,000, compared to 36 percent arrested once and 49 percent arrested two or more times. Compared to individuals not arrested, persons with one or more arrests were two to two-and-a-half times more likely to have a mental illness, two to three times more likely to have serious psychological distress, and five to seven times more likely to have a substance-abuse disorder. These characteristics of arrestees are painfully obvious clues regarding what should be the focus of pretrial diversion and pretrial programs and services.

As things currently stand, the criminal justice system is, by default (and I would add, by irresponsible legislative and policy decisions), the set of agencies that has been given the responsibility for managing many of the consequences of the mental health crisis, the addiction crisis, and the affordable-housing crisis, among others. While we have had a drug problem in this country for many decades, and while the medical and behavioral health community declared in the 1950s that this is a public health problem, we have declared war on drug addiction and substance use and used the criminal justice system as the primary tool for managing it. It goes without saying, but I'll say it again, the war on drugs has been a miserable failure and has wasted countless lives and dollars in one of America's greatest policy disasters. The same conclusion holds for homelessness and mental health and how we use the police and jails to manage those crises.

Because pre-arrest diversion is relatively new and novel, evaluation research is limited. What we do know from well-established programs is there is a dramatic reduction in rearrest following participation and/or completion of the program. Participants in the Seattle Law Enforcement Assisted Diversion (LEAD) program are 60 percent less likely to be rearrested six months after entry into the program and 58 percent less likely to be rearrested two years after entry. The Leon County, Florida, pre-arrest diversion program has even better results—there is an 80 percent decline in rearrest for those who complete the program.[89,90]

The record is much stronger for the wide variety of pretrial diversion programs such as problem solving or diversion courts. There is an extensive network of such programs. For example, there are several thousand drug courts across the country. I, and many others, have reviewed the remarkable reductions in reoffending when programs are well designed, implemented, and operated. The problem is that while these diversion programs are common, their capacity is quite limited. They are still the exception to business as usual.

The point is that the evidence clearly points us in the direction of evidence-based pre-arrest and pretrial diversion and programs and services. We fortunately have many of the tools today to effectively manage risk and engage in effective behavioral change. What we lack is a fundamental shift in criminal justice policy that provides much enhanced funding and capacity for such programming.

PRETRIAL REFORM: RESTRICTING MONEY BAIL

There really is little to recommend bail. Whether one approaches it from a racial inequity perspective or the conclusion that bail does not effectively deter pretrial misconduct or the ethical concerns about the role of private business so involved in the pretrial system, the conclusion is that it should be eliminated or its use drastically reduced.

The proper expansion of pretrial supervision, diversion, and pretrial programs and services provides the court with evidence-based alternatives to bail. Perhaps a useful comparison is probation. Probation is conditional, supervised release to the community in lieu of incarceration. In the event of significant violation of conditions, a probationer can be revoked to prison (felony) or jail (misdemeanor). The vast majority of individuals under correctional control in the United States are on probation. If conditional release under supervision is acceptable for offenders convicted of a crime, why is it not the case for people accused of crimes?

Consider the following very common scenario and think about the convoluted logic. Assume Joe is arrested for a felony or misdemeanor, booked into jail, has a detention hearing where the bail is set beyond Joe's financial means and beyond his ability to come up with the bond fee, is kept in jail until he accepts a plea deal, and then is sentenced to time served or probation. In either case, he goes home. He somehow wasn't suitable (or wealthy enough) for pretrial release, but after a period of time in jail, and now with a criminal conviction, he is somehow suitable for release with or without supervision. An obvious irony is that his detention and criminal conviction place him at higher risk than when he was arrested. And we do this with tens of thousands of defendants every day, and hundreds of thousands every year!

There is a vocal bail reform movement in the United States, but there is not a uniform set of criteria that defines it. Rather, a number of states and local jurisdictions have engaged in a variety of steps to reduce reliance on cash bail and have demonstrated that jail populations can be reduced, public safety can be protected, and money can be saved without such negative consequences as increases in FTA.[91]

Washington, D.C., was an early adopter of bail reform. Bail has been eliminated there, and nearly all (94 percent) of defendants are released pretrial. The vast majority appear in court when required. New Jersey recently eliminated cash bail and reduced its local jail population by 20 percent without serious FTA problems (89 percent appear when required).

Larry Krasner, the progressive District Attorney of Philadelphia, implemented a policy to eliminate cash bail for twenty-five misdemeanors and felonies. An assessment of the policy indicates a decline in FTAs and no increase in reoffending. The chief prosecutor for Alexandria, Virginia, recently announced a new policy of prosecutors not requesting bail for misdemeanor cases. Other jurisdictions in Virginia are following suit.[92]

Harris County (Houston), Texas, has eliminated cash bail for misdemeanors. Forty percent of misdemeanants had been detained pretrial prior to the reforms. So has St. Louis, under the progressive District Attorney Wesley Bell. Bell announced that prosecutors will no longer request cash bail for nonviolent misdemeanors.

Illinois passed legislation in 2017 stipulating that the conditions of release for nonviolent misdemeanors and low-level felonies shall be nonmonetary. The effort also established the use of risk assessments and encouraged local jurisdictions to establish pretrial-services agencies.

New Mexico voters passed a constitutional amendment allowing the denial of release for high-risk defendants and the release of low-risk defendants who would have been detained because they could not afford bail.

The New York legislature passed a bill that eliminates cash bail with the exception of violent felonies. When cash bail is permitted, judges are required to consider the defendant's ability to pay in setting the bail amount.

Other states, such as California, Colorado, Delaware, Texas, Massachusetts, and Connecticut, are heading in the direction of reforming their bail systems. Moreover, many local jurisdictions are in the process of developing and implementing new pretrial release strategies that limit the use of money bail.

PRETRIAL REFORM: BETTER DECISION-MAKING

Reforming the front end of the pretrial system has many moving parts and requires fundamental changes and investment in resources that most jurisdictions have yet to do. The bottom line is that the negative consequences of pretrial detention can be eliminated for many pretrial defendants, pretrial supervision can be ramped up to manage risk, elimination of cash bail will reduce the unnecessary detention of hundreds of thousands of arrestees, and pretrial services can be adequately funded and provide diversion to treatment and appropriate assistance such as case management and court date reminders. However, all of this ultimately depends on the decisions that judges make and recommendations by prosecutors. The evidence is clear—the pretrial systems in this country grossly overdetain individuals, to the detriment of public safety, the individuals detained, and public resources.

Recent research indicates that large numbers of the detained pretrial population can be released without increasing crime.[93]

> This analysis suggests two important conclusions: First, judges often detain the wrong people. Judges often overhold older defendants, defendants with clean records, and defendants charged with fraud and public order offenses. Second, using our model, judges would be able to release 25% more defendants while decreasing both violent crime and total pretrial crime rates.

An econometric analysis of pretrial detention estimates that we could reduce pretrial detention by approximately 40 percent without subsequent increases in crime, including both violent and nonviolent crimes.[94]

What is it about the US criminal justice system that, at extraordinary cost, produces sky-high (85 percent) recidivism? The answer is simple. We do little to mitigate those circumstances, deficits, disorders, and impairments that study after study has demonstrated are fundamentally tied to recidivism. I offer that if we do not begin addressing this more seriously at the front end of the process, we simply hand it off to others downstream. And, depending on what was done up front, the individual may, in fact, be higher risk than when he or she entered the system, simply aggravating the situation.

I have made this point many times but it is foundational in understanding the dysfunctionality of American criminal justice. No one is responsible for reducing recidivism. No one is the designated recidivism czar. Think of it this way—who would you call to complain about the recidivism rate? I don't know either.

I will tie all of the pieces together in the last chapter but, for now, here is the point. First, we know from the discussion in chapter 2 that there is a natural tendency to overly rely on emotional, intuitive, shortcut processes for decision-making. That combined with severe constraints on time is a recipe for suboptimal decisions.

I'm not sure it can be overemphasized that the front end of the pretrial system is a tremendous opportunity to: 1) not do things, such as unnecessary pretrial detention, that increase the likelihood of short-term or long-term reoffending; 2) ramp up opportunities to improve the circumstances of those who enter the criminal justice system; and 3) drastically enhance decision-making by providing key individuals with more and better information.

Risk assessments are useful, but they are not the entire answer. We should consider the front end of the pretrial phase as high-stakes triage. Much like in a medical setting, multiple examinations and tests may be required to arrive at the proper diagnosis. Resources are limited and expensive, so we need to be able to invest wisely. We do that by having experts assess individuals and advise judges, prosecutors, and defense counsel regarding a path forward that protects the public from avoidable risk of harm, identifies the primary circumstances that bring a particular individual into the system, and devises a balanced plan that provides intervention, supervision, detention if necessary, and risk management.

Assuming the expansion of pretrial supervision, pretrial diversion, and pretrial programs and services, which obviously is a bold assumption and a massive undertaking, providing more and better expert information puts the key individuals in a position to make better decisions about such things as behavioral health, a topic in which lawyers are neither trained nor experienced. I would add that earlier is better. The evidence indicates that involvement with the criminal justice system is criminogenic, and the longer the involvement, the more criminogenic it becomes.

Cost-benefit analysis shows that continued use of cash bail and pretrial detention results in costs that exceed benefits. The analysis leads to the conclusion that alternatives to bail and detention, such as supervised release and diversion, provide many of the benefits (lower FTAs and reoffending) at considerable reductions in costs.[95]

Importantly, the public is on board with much of where the evidence takes us regarding recommendations about practices such as arrest, pretrial detention, and bail. The vast majority of the American public (between 80 and 90 percent) believes that nonviolent suspects should be cited and released and not arrested and booked into jail. They do, however, overwhelmingly believe that pretrial detention should be used for particularly violent offenders. There is a caveat to this opinion though, in that less serious violent offenders could be released with conditions such as pretrial supervision and absence of a serious criminal history.[96] Nevertheless, only 31 percent of pretrial detainees in the United States are violent offenders, so it is obvious that pretrial detention is much more broadly used than the public seems to support.[97]

Another survey revealed that three-quarters of respondents believe that the current bail system favors the wealthy. A majority (57 percent) call for a conditional end to the money bail system of incarcerating people simply because they cannot afford the amount. They do say there should be exceptions in extreme cases of risk. They add (72 percent) that there should be limits on how long someone can be detained pretrial because they cannot afford bail.

NOTES

1. OJJDP Statistical Briefing Book, "Estimated Number of Arrests by Offense and Race, 2018."

2. Trautman and Haggerty, "Statewide Policies Related to Pre-Arrest Diversion and Crisis Response."

3. Trautman and Haggerty, "Statewide Policies Related to Pre-Arrest Diversion and Crisis Response."

4. Texas Appleseed, "An Analysis of Texas Jail Bookings."

5. Liu, Nunn, and Shambaugh, "The Economics of Bail and Pretrial Detention."

6. Gupta, Hansman, and Frenchman, "The Heavy Costs of High Bail: Evidence from Judge Randomization," 22–23.

7. Ouss and Stevenson, "Bail, Jail and Pretrial Misconduct: The Influence of Prosecutors," 31.

8. Gupta, Hansman, and Frenchman, "The Heavy Costs of High Bail: Evidence from Judge Randomization."

9. Stack v. Boyle 342 U.S. 1 (1951).

10. Vaughn, "New Data Reveals the Racial Disparities in Pennsylvania's Money Bail Industry."

11. Mirza, "In Dallas County, Bail Is Set in Secret—And Often in Seconds," 1–2.

12. Patrick, "Judge Rules That St. Louis Jails Can't Hold Inmates Who Can't Pay," 5.

13. Prison Policy Initiative, "Detaining the Poor."

14. It is important to note that the 420,500 who are on pretrial detention because they could not afford bail is not a static group, meaning many of them are processed (most likely convicted and punished) and many new individuals are detained. The total number of individuals in a given year who have been detained pretrial because lack of resources is beyond my ability to calculate.

15. Dobbie and Yang, "Proposals for Improving the U.S. Pretrial System."

16. Pretrial Justice Institute, "Why We Need Pretrial Reform"; Liu, Nunn, and Shambaugh, "The Economics of Bail and Pretrial Detention."

17. Liu, Nunn, and Shambaugh, "The Economics of Bail and Pretrial Detention."

18. The Disaster Center, "United States Crime Rates 1960–2018."

19. Liu, Nunn, and Shambaugh, "The Economics of Bail and Pretrial Detention."

20. Justice Policy Institute, "The High Price of Bail."

21. Liu, Nunn, and Shambaugh, "The Economics of Bail and Pretrial Detention."

22. Gabler, "The Secret Shame of Middle-Class Americans."

23. Liu, Nunn, and Shambaugh, "The Economics of Bail and Pretrial Detention."

24. Prison Policy Initiative, "Detaining the Poor."

25. Stevenson, "Distortion of Justice: How the Inability to Pay Bail Affects Case Outcomes."

26. Hood and Schneider, "Bail and Pretrial Detention: Contours and Causes of Temporal and County Variation."

27. Kamala Harris and Rand Paul, "To Shrink Jails, Let's Reform Bail," *New York Times*, July 20, 2017.

28. See for example, Kutateladze et al., "Cumulative Disadvantage: Examining Racial and Ethnic Disparity in Prosecution and Sentencing"; Sutton, "Structural Bias in the Sentencing of Felony Defendants"; Wooldredge et al., "Is the Impact of Cumulative Disadvantage on Sentencing Greater for Black Defendants."

29. Hood and Schneider, "Bail and Pretrial Detention: Contours and Causes of Temporal and County Variation"; Demuth, "Racial and Ethnic Differences in Pretrial Release Decisions and Outcomes"; Schlesinger, "Racial and Ethnic Disparity in Pretrial Criminal Processing"; Color of Change, ACLU Campaign for Smart Justice, "Selling Off Our Freedom."

30. Bushway and Gelbach, "Testing for Racial Discrimination in Bail Setting."

31. Hood and Schneider, "Bail and Pretrial Detention: Contours and Causes of Temporal and County Variation," 143.

32. New Jersey Commission of Investigation, "Inside Out: Questionable and Abusive Practices in New Jersey's Bail Bond Industry."

33. Color of Change, ACLU Campaign for Smart Justice, "Selling Off Our Freedom."

34. Daniels, Weber, and Wool, "From Bondage to Bail Bonds: Putting a Price on Freedom in New Orleans."

35. O'Neill, "Bail Bond Businesses Buck for Bookings."

36. Barno, Martínez, and Williams, "Exploring Alternatives to Cash Bail," 364.

37. Digard and Swavola, "Justice Denied: The Harmful and Lasting Effects of Pretrial Detention."

38. Dobbie, Goldin, and Yang, "The Effects of Pretrial Detention on Conviction, Future Crime, and Employment"; Leslie and Pope, "The Unintended Impact of Pretrial Detention on Case Outcomes"; Heaton, Mayson, and Stevenson, "The Downstream Consequences of Misdemeanor Pretrial Detention."

39. Heaton, Mayson, and Stevenson, "The Downstream Consequences of Misdemeanor Pretrial Detention."

40. Leslie and Pope, "The Unintended Impact of Pretrial Detention on Case Outcomes."

41. Digard and Swavola, "Justice Denied: The Harmful and Lasting Effects of Pretrial Detention."

42. Petersen, "Do Detainees Plead Guilty Faster?"

43. Oleson et al., "The Sentencing Consequences of Federal Pretrial Supervision."

44. Stevenson, "Distortion of Justice: How the Inability to Pay Bail Affects Case Outcomes."

45. Digard and Swavola, "Justice Denied: The Harmful and Lasting Effects of Pretrial Detention."

46. Lowenkamp and VanNostrand, "Exploring the Effect of Supervision on Pretrial Outcomes."

47. Texas Appleseed, "Bail and Pretrial Release: Summary of Recent Research on What Works"; Heaton, Mayson, and Stevenson, "The Downstream Consequences of Misdemeanor Pretrial Detention"; Leslie and Pope, "The Unintended Impact of Pretrial Detention on Case Outcomes."

48. Heaton, Mayson, and Stevenson, "The Downstream Consequences of Misdemeanor Pretrial Detention."

49. Hood and Schneider, "Bail and Pretrial Detention."

50. Baughman, "Costs of Pretrial Detention," 5.

51. Hale, "Pretrial Detainees Are Being Billed for Their Stay in Jail"; Shapiro, "As Court Fees Rise, the Poor Are Paying the Price."

52. Fines and Fees Justice Center, "Paying for Jail: How County Jails Extract Wealth from New York Communities."

53. The Prosecutors Office, Johnson County Indiana, Frequently Asked Questions.

54. Zaluska, "Paying to Stay in Jail: Hidden Fees Turn Inmates into Debtors."

55. Ortiz, National Association of Counties, "County Jails at a Crossroads."

56. Baradaran and McIntyre, "Predicting Violence," 558.

57. Pretrial Justice Institute, "How to Fix Pretrial Justice."

58. Pretrial Justice Institute, "Why Are People in Jail Before Trial?"

59. Pretrial Justice Institute, "How to Fix Pretrial Justice."

60. Ortiz, National Association of Counties, "County Jails at a Crossroads."

61. Ortiz, National Association of Counties, "County Jails at a Crossroads."

62. Pretrial Justice Center, "Pretrial Services and Supervision."

63. Crime and Justice Institute, "Pretrial Progress: A Survey of Pretrial Practices and Services in California."

64. Texas Criminal Justice Coalition, "A Survey of Pretrial Service Providers in Texas."

65. Carmichael et al., "Liberty and Justice: Pretrial Practices in Texas," xvi.

66. Pretrial Risk, "Mapping Pretrial Injustice," retrieved from https://pretrial-risk.com/the-basics/; National Association of Criminal Defense Lawyers, "Making Sense of Pretrial Risk Assessments."

67. Carmichael et al., "Liberty and Justice: Pretrial Practices in Texas."

68. Yong, "A Popular Algorithm Is No Better at Predicting Crimes than Random People"; National Association of Criminal Defense Lawyers, "Making Sense of Pretrial Risk Assessments"; Lin et al., "The Limits of Human Predictions of Recidivism."

69. United States v Salerno, 481 U.S. 739 (1987).

70. Desmarais and Lowder, "Pretrial Risk Assessment Tools."

71. Picard et al., "Beyond the Algorithm; Pretrial Reform, Risk Assessment, and Racial Fairness."

72. Stevenson and Doleac, "The Roadblock to Reform"; Corey, "New Data Suggests Risk Assessment Tools Have Little Impact on Pretrial Incarceration"; Doyle, Bains, and Hopkins, "Bail Reform: A Guide for State and Local Policymakers."

73. Barno, Martinez, and Williams, "Exploring Alternatives to Cash Bail."

74. Desmarais and Lowder, "Pretrial Risk Assessment Tools."

75. Arnold Ventures, "Public Safety Assessment FAQs."

76. Desmarais and Lowder, "Pretrial Risk Assessment Tools."

77. Austin, Krisberg, and Litsky, "The Effectiveness of Supervised Pretrial Release."

78. Lowenkamp and VanNostrand, "Exploring the Impact of Supervision on Pretrial Outcomes."

79. VanNostrand, Rose, and Weibrecht, "State of the Science of Pretrial Release Recommendations and Supervision."

80. Redcross et al., "New York City's Pretrial Supervised Release Program."

81. Hatton and Smith, "Research on the Effectiveness of Pretrial Support and Supervision Services."

82. Bechtel et al., "A Meta-Analytic Review of Pretrial Research: Risk Assessment, Bond Type, and Interventions," 461.

83. Lam, "Pretrial Services: An Effective Alternative to Monetary Bail."

84. Davidson et al., "Managing Pretrial Misconduct: An Experimental Evaluation of HOPE Pretrial."

85. Illinois Sentencing Policy Advisory Council, "The High Cost of Recidivism."

86. Widgery, "Providing Pretrial Services."

87. Widgery, "Trends in Pretrial Release."

88. Jones and Sawyer, "Arrest, Release, Repeat: How Police and Jails Are Misused to Respond to Social Problems."

89. Trautman and Haggerty, "Statewide Policies Relating to Pre-Arrest Diversion and Crisis Response."

90. Kelly, *The Future of Crime and Punishment*; Kelly et al., *From Retribution to Public Safety.*

91. Doyle, Bains, and Hopkins, "Bail Reform: A Guide for State and Local Policymakers."

92. Pretrial Justice Institute, "What's Happening in Pretrial Justice."

93. Baradaran and McIntyre, "Predicting Violence."

94. Kleinberg et al., *Human Decisions and Machine Predictions.*

95. Dobbie and Yang, "Proposals for Improving the U.S. Pretrial System."

96. The Pew Charitable Trusts, "Americans Favor Expanded Pretrial Release, Limited Use of Jail."

97. Sawyer and Wagner, Prison Policy Initiative, "Mass Incarceration: The Whole Pie 2020."

4

Promising Prosecutors
Reform in the DA's Office

Prosecutors have played an important role in creating and perpetuating the dysfunction in the American criminal justice system. They can also play a substantial role in fixing it.

THE POWER OF THE PROSECUTOR

In 1940, the United States Attorney General Robert Jackson stated, "The prosecutor has more control over life, liberty and reputation than any other person in America."[1] Why is this the case? While police investigate and arrest, prosecutors decide whether and who to prosecute, what evidence to use, what offense(s) to charge, what to indict, how much evidence is enough, what to negotiate in a plea deal, what charges to enhance or dismiss, and what sentence to attach to a plea deal or what sentence to recommend to the court. In effect, the lawyers for the government serve as the key decision makers, determining what happens between the point when an individual is arrested and when the sentence is imposed. The entire pretrial phase is largely based on the decisions prosecutors make. To be clear, others, such as judges and defense counsel, play very important roles as well, but prosecutors are in the driver's seat. Because it is so important, I will repeat what Caleb Foote told us, which is that everything that is decided and done in the pretrial phase determines everything else.

The profound power of the prosecutor is the result of a number of circumstances. One is the long-term expansion of the criminal law. While there are examples of the elimination of some criminal laws, such as laws against sodomy and alcohol use, the trend over time has been to increase the reach of criminal liability by writing new laws reflecting behaviors that legislatures and Congress find need to be controlled or regulated by the threat of criminal penalty. This trend is referred to as overcriminalization and is a concern of a large number of organizations, including the American Bar Association, the Cato Institute, the Heritage Foundation, and the National Association of Criminal Defense Lawyers, to name just a few. As the late Harvard law professor Bill Stuntz wrote two decades ago in his very influential article "The Pathological Politics of Criminal Law":[2]

> As criminal law expands, both lawmaking and adjudication pass into the hands of police and prosecutors; law enforcers, not the law, determine who goes to prison and for how long.

The result, according to Stuntz, is that prosecutors become the de facto chief deciders of what crimes are prosecuted and, in turn, what criminal laws are enforced.

Longtime observers of prosecutors suggest that they may, in effect, legislate the criminal law through their charging decisions. As Stuntz argues, what laws are enforced determines what constitutes the criminal law. For example, while marijuana possession is still on the books in most states, many local law enforcement and local prosecutors are deciding not to enforce it and not prosecute it. The net effect is that laws against marijuana possession do not exist in those jurisdictions. Eric Luna makes a similar point in his piece "Prosecutor King."[3]

> Prosecutors provide the indispensable link between police investigation and courtroom adjudication, with the power to impact every decision along the way . . . Practice demonstrates a concentration of authority in a single office, where prosecutors not only execute the law in the conventional sense, but also effectively adjudicate matters by their decisions in individual cases. From another vantage point, prosecutors may even legislate criminal law, setting the penal code's effective scope over an entire caseload through collective decision making of varying levels of coordination.

Another critical trend in criminal law over the past fifty years that has enhanced the power of the prosecutor is the fundamental restructuring of sentencing laws, a series of changes that reshaped criminal sentencing at the federal level and in every state. Beginning in the 1970s, a coincidence of concerns about racial disparities in sentences (from the left) and the perception that judges are too lenient (from the right) led to the same remedy—getting judges out of the picture when it comes to sentencing, and, as a result, disparate and lenient sentences would be reduced or eliminated. This was accomplished by removing judicial discretion in sentencing through the implementation of determinate or fixed sentences, which replaced indeterminate sentences that provided wide ranges of punishment from which judges could select. Determinate sentences, including mandatory and mandatory minimum sentences, were primarily dependent on two criteria, the crime for which a defendant is being sentenced and the defendant's prior criminal history. The goal was to shift to a harm-based system where the punishment fits, or exceeds, the crime.

This change in criminal sentencing enhanced prosecutorial power because, in effect, it made prosecutors the sentencers through their charging and plea negotiation decisions. One of the two primary drivers of a determinate sentence is the conviction offense (the other is prior criminality).

The vast majority of all criminal convictions (more than 95 percent) do not occur in open court, do not see the light of day. They are accomplished through a plea deal that occurs over the phone, in courthouse hallways, in the prosecutor's office, or in jail interrogation rooms. These negotiations have few set rules and no written record. While the court will seek to determine if the plea deal was proper, this is often a pro forma inquiry.

Our extraordinary reliance on plea negotiation dramatically increases power and influence by making the prosecutor the jury as well as the prosecutor. In a plea deal setting, the prosecutor decides who is guilty and of what charge(s). What this reflects is the fact that prosecutors are not merely partisan advocates in litigation, but they also serve as the fact finder, determining who is innocent and guilty.

Also crucial for appreciating the power of the prosecutor is the relative underfunding of public defense. As I discuss in chapter 5, the vast majority of criminal defendants are indigent, too poor to retain their own defense attorney, and thus must rely on a government-paid lawyer in the circumstances where the law provides public defenders. The financial plight of public defense results in limited time to spend with clients and significant constraints in conducting investigations, interviewing witnesses, and a number of other pretrial activities. On the other hand, prosecutors have access to law enforcement for conducting investigations, to forensic labs for testing evidence, to expert witnesses, and to a variety of other resources that heighten the power of the prosecutor.

Another element in understanding prosecutorial power in the US court system is the adversarial approach to adjudicating criminal cases. While I discuss this in greater detail in chapter 6, I want to spend a little time in understanding the role of the adversarial system in accounting for prosecutorial power. The prosecutor in an adversarial system plays a very active role and has nearly all of the responsibility for initiating a case, gathering and assessing evidence, charging, presenting evidence to a grand jury, and ultimately proving the government's case. That, in and of itself, renders the prosecutor quite powerful. As another longtime observer of American prosecutors states:[4]

> Pursuant to the myth that they are mere litigants, prosecutors may tend to undertake their adjudicative role, not in the spirit of truth-seeking and balanced justice, but instead as a partisan in an adversarial contest.

Success in the adversarial system is defined as winning. Over the past fifty years, winning has meant criminal conviction and harsh punishment, which exemplify the tough-on-crime culture of many, if not most, prosecutors' offices. That punitive ideology, as Sklansky[5] observes, is a result of

> some combination of the adversary system of adjudication, a workplace culture that prizes victory above all else, the use of local elections to select lead prosecutors and the "politics of crime"—a political climate that has prioritized public safety and demonized criminal offenders.

So, for a variety of reasons, prosecutors occupy a very prominent and unique role in the American criminal justice system. Prosecutors serve as gatekeepers at the front door, sorting through those the police arrest and deciding who goes forward to criminal prosecution, conviction, and punishment. But the role of the prosecutor is broader than that because, in effect, they serve as law enforcer, adjudicator, and, in many important respects, sentencer. Many of these decisions are guided by an overarching, tough-on-crime ideology. In my 2018 book with Judge Pitman, *Confronting Underground Justice*, we interviewed public defenders and asked them, in their experience, if tough on crime defines the job of the prosecutor. It was a nearly unanimous acknowledgment that prosecutors are quite punitive. A few examples illustrate the point[6]—"they are prosecuting everyone," "not known for coddling," "giving tougher and tougher sentences," "they don't let the little things go," and "they are very unreasonable."

But the power of the prosecutor does not end there. Individuals who are diverted to probation or a problem-solving court like a drug court are subject to revocation if they violate the rules or conditions. The same holds for those on deferred prosecution or deferred adjudication. While the revocation decision is usually up to the judge, it is up to the prosecutor to determine if the transgressions are sufficient to warrant a motion to revoke. Importantly, the prosecutor is also involved in determining the conditions of probation, deferred adjudication, or diversion, or at least making recommendations to the judge.

Prosecutors also can and do influence decisions about release from incarceration for individuals who are eligible for parole. Parole is conditional early release from incarceration. In most instances, it is discretionary. Once the inmate becomes eligible for consideration for parole, the proper authority (a parole board, for example) will consider the case and make a decision. It is not uncommon for a prosecutor's office to offer the government's opinion about whether someone should be released.

All of these decisions involve discretion, that is, individual lawyers looking at evidence and the law and making a judgment. Prosecutors we interviewed for *Confronting Underground Justice* told us that their discretion is typically very broad, leaving a variety of decisions up to individual line prosecutors.[7] Most of the decisions that prosecutors make are subjective, as they should be. Reasonable people can disagree about things like the credibility of a witness, the results of a forensic examination of evidence, the state of mind of the defendant at the time of the crime, what someone deserves in terms of punishment, what is just and fair, and how to accomplish the goals of the criminal justice system, such as reducing crime and recidivism, to name a few.

However, the decisions that prosecutors make day-to-day are often without much accountability or oversight, especially in light of the tremendous caseload pressures that characterize most prosecutors' offices in the United States. Importantly, the decisions that prosecutors make are typically protected from liability. Prosecutors are generally immune from criminal and civil liability, even in situations where they engage in misconduct. In the case *Taylor v. Kavanagh*, decided in 1980 in the Southern District of New York and based on Supreme Court law, the court found:[8]

> The falsification of evidence and the coercion of witnesses . . . have been held to be prosecutorial activities for which absolute immunity applies. Similarly, because a prosecutor is acting as an advocate in a judicial proceeding, the solicitation and subordination of perjured testimony, the withholding of evidence, or the introduction of illegally seized evidence at trial does not create liability in damages.

Judges are generally very reluctant to intervene in controlling or regulating the decision-making of prosecutors. They usually have nothing to say about what prosecutors charge, nor do they often question the dismissal of charges. As Ronald Wright tells us, they view these as executive, not judicial matters.[9] While judges are generally required to approve of plea deals, they rarely interrupt the dizzying pace of case processing to question a plea. It is just not in their interest.

In theory, the jury trial serves as a check against the power of the prosecutor. The judge oversees the trial and determines when there are due process issues. The jury serves as the trier of fact, the evaluator of the evidence. The trial is where everything sees the light of day in open court, and, as the saying goes, sunshine is the best disinfectant. Moreover, jury trials can keep prosecutors accountable by requiring the government to prove its case using the reasonable doubt standard. But the reality is, as we already know, quite different as plea deals rule the courts.

Election of chief prosecutors historically has not served as an effective check either. Voters usually know very little about candidates, and incumbents have routinely been reelected until they move on to bigger and better things. We may, however, be beginning to see a shift in this with the election of progressive prosecutors. More on this shortly.

The role of the prosecutor, characterized and facilitated by broad discretion, expansion of the criminal code, changes to sentencing laws, the adversary approach to prosecution, the extraordinary reliance on plea negotiation, relatively little oversight and accountability, immunity from criminal and civil liability, the critical underfunding of public defense, as well as a nearly universal embrace of tough-on-crime solutions have placed prosecutors in a unique, powerful, and influential position. Prosecutors are essentially responsible for the processes and outcomes of the court system, historically perpetuating the tough-on-crime approach that defines how we do the business of American criminal justice.

THE ELECTION OF DISTRICT ATTORNEYS

With the exception of Alaska, Connecticut, Delaware, Rhode Island, and New Jersey, District Attorneys, the chief prosecutors in local jurisdictions, are elected. The United States is the only country in the world in which local District Attorneys are elected.

For most of the history of local prosecutor elections (District Attorneys or State's Attorneys), the strategy for messaging has been simple—fair, just, and tough. Of the three, tough is probably the only one for which any kind of metrics can be applied, often in terms of such measures as number of convictions, and a tough-on-crime DA can brag about the number sentenced to incarceration, or the number of death sentences imposed, among others. As long as no one digs any deeper, and historically they have not, these "body counts" sound pretty impressive. When the public is anxious about crime and safety, head in the direction of tough. Let fair and just serve as the bow on the package, and we are well on our way to reelection.

Often, however, incumbents are not challenged (recent data show that 85 percent run unopposed), thus voters are unlikely to learn much about the performance of the DA's office. Even when an incumbent had a challenger, DAs were reelected 70 percent of the time in elections between 1996 and 2006.[10]

The campaign narratives tend to focus on "personalities, not policies,"[11] or on a few high-profile cases, rather than the extent to which the DA is meeting community expectations and values and fulfilling promises. Prosecutor performance is most typically addressed by reference to case backlogs and slow processing of cases. New priorities are also a campaign staple, but analysis of messaging shows that such references are vague and/or unrealistic. Wright summarizes his analysis of campaign rhetoric in the following way: [12]

> The rhetoric of the election campaign puts too much weight on the wrong criteria and completely ignores some criteria that could help voters make meaningful judgments about the quality of prosecutor's work . . . These campaign talking points do not serve voters well because they offer too little of two commodities that voters need. First, voters need office-wide measures of competence . . . Second, voters need ideological markers or other clues about the values that guide the priorities of the prosecutor.

THE ELECTION OF PROGRESSIVE PROSECUTORS

Tough on crime was the safe choice for many individuals running in local, state, and federal elections. At the local level, tough-on-crime prosecutors were a perfect fix for an anxious public. That was then, this is now. The headlines began around 2015 and are from a wide variety of publications. But they share a common theme. Tough on crime is not as widely electable as it once was, at least for prosecutors. While tough is still very much alive and well, there are notable exceptions emerging in a number of prominent jurisdictions around the United States. Some selections from media headlines:

Overzealous Prosecutors Who Seek Excessive Sentences Face Removal from Office

Dallas County DA John Creuzot Calls New Reforms "A Step Forward in Ending Mass Incarceration."

District Attorneys Used to Brag about How Many Criminals They Threw Behind Bars. Now, an Increasing Number Boast of How Many They Kept Out of Prison

When Being Tough on Crime Is a Political Liability

Progressive Lawyer Wins San Francisco District Attorney Race, Continuing National Reform Trend

Hard-Line Prosecutors Face Rejection from Voters in Elections Across the U.S.

A New Strategy for Justice Reform: Vote Out the DA

A Wiser Generation of Prosecutors

Running for Elected Prosecutor Will Never Be the Same

The Progressive Prosecutors Blazing a New Path for the U.S. Justice
   System
Progressive DAs Are Shaking Up the Criminal Justice System
Prosecutor Elections Now a Front in the Justice Wars

The labels vary, usually something like progressive DAs or reform DAs
or reform-oriented DAs. Most tend to run on the Democratic ticket when
the elections are partisan, although there have been some notable Republican reform District Attorneys elected in recent years.

The locations tend to be larger metro areas such as Seattle, Denver, Dallas, Houston, Chicago, the Bronx, Brooklyn, Baltimore, San Antonio, San
Francisco, St. Louis, Boston, Orlando, Tampa, Jacksonville, and Philadelphia. There were also a number elected in smaller jurisdictions, such as
Nueces County, Texas, Caddo Parish, Louisiana, and a four-county district in rural Mississippi. Importantly, some reform candidates have been
successful in suburban areas, such as the suburbs of Fairfax, Loudoun,
and Prince William counties of northern Virginia.

Not every progressive candidate wins election. There have been some
notable defeats, such as Genevieve Jones-Wright in San Diego, Pamela
Price in Alameda County, California, Noah Phillips in Sacramento, and
Mark Hasse in Hennepin County, Minneapolis.

Progressive means different things to different people. There is
nibbling-around-the-edges progressive and there is fundamentally-
change-the-criminal-justice-system progressive, and everything in between. What progressive or reform or reform-oriented mean varies a
good bit by jurisdiction and by candidate. My terrific team of research
assistants conducted an analysis of the campaign materials of dozens of
progressive or reform prosecutor candidates who ran over the past four
to five years. This analysis uncovered a number of relatively universal
themes as well as issues that were more narrowly focused on a particular
candidate or on issues in a particular jurisdiction.

Much of what the first wave of progressive candidates campaigned on
(I am thinking of the first wave as those elected from 2014 to 2016) were
issues associated with law enforcement, such as use-of-force and racist
policies, the prosecution of low-level drug cases, and ending mass incarceration. That focus has expanded over time.

Common campaign themes include bigger-picture items such as ending mass incarceration, police use of force and police accountability, bail
reform (ending cash bail release), jail crowding, transparency of the District Attorney's office, racial bias in the criminal justice system, draconian
sentencing, reduction of fines and fees, expanding diversion programs,
and decriminalizing low-level drug possession. Some candidates took on

several of these issues in their campaigns, and a couple were single-issue candidates.

Some candidates focused on jurisdiction-specific issues, such as the shooting of a young Black male by police or a particularly corrupt DA. Other very specific concerns or issues that some candidates identified include expunging arrests, dealing with homeless youth, narrowing the use of three strikes laws, improving reentry programs, eliminating the death penalty, and improving juvenile justice.

Many of the progressive DA candidates received substantial campaign contributions from George Soros, either directly or through a political action committee (PAC). These include Larry Krasner in Philadelphia, Genevieve Jones-Wright in San Diego, Kim Ogg in Houston, Kim Foxx in Chicago, Aramis Ayala in Orlando, Rachael Rollins in Boston, James Steward in Caddo Parish, Louisiana, Chesa Boudin in San Francisco, and Andrew Warren in Tampa, Florida, among others. In some cases, campaign contributions from Soros were used as negatives in ads by conservative groups trying to discredit progressive candidates.

What is different in the recent elections of progressive District Attorneys is that the reform message has been particularly persuasive, as evidenced by the fact that, in many instances, incumbent District Attorneys were tossed out of office, something that historically has been uncommon. Whether in reaction to specific events like a police shooting, a particularly aggressive, tough-on-crime prosecutor, a corruption scandal, or promises for broader criminal justice reform, some communities appear to be voting in line with public opinion.

The Portland, Oregon, District Attorney election in May 2020 serves as a good example of the ongoing trend. Mike Schmidt decisively defeated Ethan Knight, the candidate endorsed by the outgoing incumbent (Schmidt garnered more than 76 percent of the votes). The election was ahead of the George Floyd death and the subsequent protests, but it clearly represented a sea change in the prosecutor's office.[13]

> Schmidt, 39, of Southeast Portland, campaigned on a platform of upending what he characterized as a business-as-usual approach to prosecution. He pledged to prioritize addiction and mental health treatment over prisons, ensure that cops who engage in brutality or misconduct are held accountable and review claims of wrongful convictions. He opposes the death penalty and mandatory minimum sentencing, and supports policies that aim to keep youth charged with crimes in juvenile court.

Alonzo Payne, endorsed by Bernie Sanders, defeated the incumbent prosecutor in the 12th Judicial District of Colorado by a substantial 62 percent to 38 percent margin. Payne is a reformer focused on reducing mass incarceration and ending the criminalization of poverty.

It is also important to note that progressive District Attorneys are getting reelected as well. Two of the three most prominent progressives, Kim Ogg and Kim Foxx, were both recently reelected (Larry Krasner of Philadelphia, the third of the three, is up for reelection in May of 2021). Several others will be up for reelection later in 2020 (primarily in August and then in the general election November 3) and in 2021.

The murder of George Floyd by Minneapolis police occurred on May 25, 2020, and was followed by nationwide protests on a scale unseen in this country in decades. It was estimated that at least 140 cities in the United States have had sizable protests centered around Floyd's murder and Black Lives Matter.[14] Protests continue in many cities as I write this in late July. Portland, Oregon, is an example that currently stands out, in part because the Trump administration has sent federal troops into the city without the request or consent of local government officials. These events have led to considerable debate about local law enforcement and criminal justice policy more broadly. What may make the key difference is the right candidate at the right time taking on the right issues.

As indicated above, many progressive DA candidates in recent years have identified local law enforcement as a target of reform. That focus has seemingly intensified in the past few weeks as DA candidates in major races are picking up the George Floyd and Black Lives Matter mantle. A recent *Politico* article reports:[15]

> In Los Angeles and a series of contests in Florida and New York, campaigns hope that demonstrators and their allies can supply critical votes in November, converting a generational outpouring of activism into district attorneys with the will and authority to prosecute police officers and advocate for broader policy changes . . . the prosecutorial movement has been growing for years fueled by Black Lives Matter . . . But activists . . . point to an unprecedented surge of anguish and activism now.

The seemingly unending examples of police use of excessive force and lethal force, made much more visible by cell phone video of the events, and, in particular, the massive protests that have occurred nationwide after the murder of George Floyd may signal a tsunami of sorts in local electoral politics. The momentum that the protests continue to generate may very well play out in local DA elections, especially those that have police accountability as a key campaign message. For example, Margaret Moore was elected as the Travis County (Austin), Texas, District Attorney in this longtime liberal capital city. Moore ran as a reformer and was elected in November 2016. She indicated that she would reduce the prosecution of marijuana possession cases and divert to treatment some individuals arrested for low-level drug possession. She also spoke in general terms about justice reform and racial disparities. However, the evidence shows that she failed to keep these promises.

Her opponent was Jose Garza, a former public defender and codirector of the Workers Defense Project. His campaign is a good example of a reform prosecutor outreforming his opponent. There was some overlap in their respective platforms, but Garza's went considerably further, including expanded diversion, treating substance abuse as a public health issue, eliminating cash bail, pursuing restorative justice, holding police accountable for misconduct, and never seeking the death penalty.

Garza received national funding from a variety of sources, including the Texas Justice and Public Safety Political Action Committee, as well as Real Justice. The Texas Justice and Public Safety PAC is partially funded by George Soros. Moreover, Garza had endorsements from Julian and Joaquin Castro, Bernie Sanders, and Elizabeth Warren.

The Moore-Garza primary runoff was July 14, 2020, well after the major waves of police protests were over. Austin had its share of large, vocal protests that occurred over a period of two weeks. As the July 14 election date neared, Garza's campaign increasingly emphasized police accountability and reimagining public safety. This messaging was coincidentally voiced by many local elected officials and opinion leaders throughout much of the community, and it certainly played a significant role in Garza's victory, winning a rather convincing 68 percent of the vote.

It is also important to point out that there was a police shooting on April 24, 2020, in Austin. Police were called to an apartment complex where someone claimed two people were doing drugs in a car in the complex parking lot. When they arrived, the police were able to corner Mike Ramos and his girlfriend in the parking lot, blocking them from leaving. A neighbor's cell phone video shows Ramos with his hands up and shouting he was unarmed. An officer fired a bean bag round (a less-lethal munition) that hit Ramos. At that point, he gets into his car and starts to pull out of the parking space. The police fire multiple rounds as Ramos drives toward the dead end of the parking lot. Ramos was killed. The Ramos shooting and what was perceived as a slow response from DA Moore's office to the shooting were certainly front and center in the local Austin protests.

The timing of the Travis County election gives us a glimpse of how the events of the spring and early summer of 2020 likely impact a local District Attorney election. How much of an impact is unknown, as is how long any effect will last.

Perhaps an acid test for the lingering of the effects of the Floyd murder and the protests is the election of the District Attorney in Los Angeles County, California. Jackie Lacey is the current Los Angeles DA, an African American female Democrat, first elected in 2012. She is seeking her third term in a runoff on November 3, 2020.

Lacey is a self-described "reasonable reformer," not a progressive but also not a hard-charging, tough-on-crime DA. She has implemented some reform measures in LA County, including a diversion program for individuals with mental illness who can get treatment and avoid jail. She also supports reform of the cash bail system, but not its elimination.

On the other hand, she supports the death penalty and opposes such reform legislation as Proposition 47, which reduced some nonviolent felonies to misdemeanors. Both of these positions have drawn considerable criticism. So has her prosecution of police shootings. The Los Angeles chapter of Black Lives Matter has held weekly protests outside of Lacey's office for the past two and one-half years, objecting to the fact that Lacey's office has only prosecuted one officer-involved shooting out of several hundred (Black Lives Matter claim 600 police shootings and Lacey's office says it is 340).

The point is that Lacey is seen as pro-police, and the opposition to her by Black Lives Matter Los Angeles has significantly intensified since the killing of George Floyd. The November election will serve as a natural experiment of sorts, since her opponent, George Gascon, has a strong track record as the previous progressive District Attorney in San Francisco.

Gascon is a former police officer who rose in the ranks to be deputy chief of the Los Angeles Police Department as well as chief of two big-city police departments. He supports holding police accountable for unlawful conduct, including prosecuting unlawful use of force. He prosecuted thirty such cases while DA in San Francisco. Also as DA in San Francisco, he led an investigation into racism and sexism in the San Francisco Police Department that resulted in more than eighty recommendations for reform, many of which were implemented.

Gascon was the first elected DA in the United States to oppose the use of cash bail. In 2016, he implemented the use of the Public Safety Assessment, a validated risk assessment that makes custody decisions based on assessed risk rather than financial means. Gascon also proposes to divert mentally ill offenders to treatment as well as those with substance-abuse problems, including the expansion of Law Enforcement Assisted Diversion (LEAD). Gascon is also a strong opponent to the war on drugs and the death penalty.

The wave of protests nationwide and the subsequent momentum that Black Lives Matter has may significantly impact local elections going forward, especially the election of reform-focused District Attorneys. I think it is without much debate that the most important District Attorney election this cycle is the Los Angeles race. We shall see.

At the same time, it is necessary to put this trend of the election of progressive prosecutors in perspective. There are approximately 2,500 elected District Attorneys in the United States. While there is not a running total that I have seen, it is clear that what we are looking at in the election of progressive or reform District Attorneys is a relatively small proportion of all elected District Attorneys. It is also important to point out that while small in numbers, many of the recently elected reform prosecutors tend to be high profile, vocal, in large jurisdictions, and receiving considerable media coverage.

The fact that reform-oriented District Attorneys are getting elected by campaigning about relatively bold criminal justice reforms as well as reforms that extend beyond the typical boundaries of the office (for example, reentry programs, abolishing the death penalty) highlights the fact that chief prosecutors are often seen as leaders of local criminal justice systems. Judges may assume such leadership positions. But there is only one DA in each county and they, unlike judges, typically have more freedom to dive into controversial topics. They, unlike judges, also have the ability to address many of the issues and concerns that they bring up at election time, such as police misconduct, prosecutor corruption, wrongful convictions, and prosecuting marijuana possession cases. Prosecutors have the power to investigate, charge, and prosecute, as well as decline to charge and prosecute, and that power can be a very decisive tool for reform.

I believe it is fair to conclude mid-year 2020 that the election of progressive prosecutors is neither a flash in the pan nor is it sweeping the nation. It is certainly driven by context and circumstances. Progressive prosecutors generally are elected in larger, more diverse, liberal metro areas (though not exclusively), and often are tied to some degree to a specific event(s) like police shootings or use of force. There is usually considerable discontent with the criminal justice system more broadly, such as mass incarceration and race and ethnic disparities in arrests, convictions, and incarceration. It seems to be the case that local voters recognize that District Attorneys are very powerful actors in local criminal justice systems, responsible for many of the system's dysfunctions, but also viewed as a solution, having the ability to implement meaningful reform.

PROGRESSIVE PROSECUTORS' REPORT CARDS

Simply declaring that a candidate is a progressive or reform prosecutor does not mean that reform is around the corner. First of all, there is no acid test that can be used to identify true reformers. As I mentioned above, what it means varies across jurisdictions and across candidates. How inclusive or broad it is also varies considerably. Some want to address very specific issues in their jurisdiction, and others want to change the entire criminal justice system. With those observations in mind, my research assistants collected considerable evidence regarding initial progress for DAs taking office between 2015 and 2019. This DA report card is simply designed to get a sense of progress made and challenges faced by some recently elected progressive/reform prosecutors.

Newly elected progressive prosecutors developed and implemented a variety of different initiatives. Common themes include: increasing opportunities for adult and juvenile pre-arrest and pretrial diversion, often for drug-possession cases and individuals with mental illness, and often wrapped around language about reducing mass incarceration; ceasing the prosecution of low-level marijuana-possession cases; making police accountable for misconduct; eliminating or reducing charging death penalty cases; bail reform (usually reflected in prosecutors' pretrial release decisions); conviction integrity/wrongful conviction units to review cases and assure proper conviction; and enhancing the transparency of the prosecutor's office.

The size and impact of these initiatives are highly variable. Some jurisdictions have a very long list of pre-arrest and pretrial diversion programs, others may have one or two. They also differ in terms of capacity and thus the number of eligible individuals who participate. In some jurisdictions, there is an outright refusal to charge under the death penalty statute. In others, there are review panels that assess cases and determine if the death penalty is appropriate. Efforts at bail reform range from policies not to object to release-on-recognizance requests from the defense, to the wholesale implementation of risk-assessment protocols and elimination of case bail entirely. Marijuana possession is the safe case for which to decline prosecution, but some jurisdictions have expanded that to low-level theft and other limited misdemeanors.

The specificity of reforms varies considerable as well. Some jurisdictions with progressive District Attorneys have more aspirational agendas while other hit the ground running. This is understandable since there are a variety of circumstances that facilitate or impede policy changes.

John Creuzot, the District Attorney of Dallas County, Texas, is an example of a reform DA who immediately implemented significant changes. Creuzot was elected in November of 2018 and took office in January 2019. In April of 2019, he published a document, a contract of sorts to the people of Dallas County, announcing what reforms he had implemented in the first ninety days in office.[16] These include:

- Decline prosecution of first-time misdemeanor marijuana possession and first-time third-degree and fourth-degree felony marijuana possession
- Decline prosecution of possession of trace amounts (less than .01 gram) of drugs

- No longer holding felony drug suspects in jail awaiting the results of laboratory testing
- To avoid criminalizing poverty, the DA's office will not prosecute theft of personal items under $750, unless there is evidence the theft was for economic gain
- Rather than prosecuting an individual for driving with their license suspended, the DA's office created a diversion program that results in charges being dismissed
- The DA's office will actively expunge arrests for individuals who successfully complete misdemeanor pretrial diversion programs
- Prosecutors have been instructed to limit probation sentence length with presumptive limits to recommended sentences—six months for misdemeanors and fourth-degree felonies, two years for second- and third-degree felonies, and five years for first-degree felonies; prosecutors are also instructed not to ask for incarceration for technical probation violations that do not threaten public safety
- The DA's office adopted bail guidelines to be used by line prosecutors when recommending bail amounts
  - A presumption of release without conditions for misdemeanors
  - A presumption of release for fourth-degree felonies with no prior convictions within the past five years
  - All other cases—the prosecutor's recommendation is based on an assessment of risk. While a tool will be used, it is not dispositive; rather it is a guide
  - Monetary conditions should never be requested by a prosecutor unless there has first been an ability to pay determination

The document then concludes regarding magistration, or the release/ detention hearing. Prosecutors are assigned to magistration so that they can screen cases and decline to prosecute those cases referenced above. There will also be defense lawyers at magistration.

Another example of a reform DA hitting the ground running is Rachael Rollins, the District Attorney for Suffolk County (Boston). She issued a rather extensive sixty-six-page memo ("The Rachael Rollins Policy Memo," March 2019) three months into her tenure as DA. This memo outlines reforms that are needed to accomplish her stated goals of filing fewer criminal charges, diverting more people into treatment and services, and sending fewer people to jail or prison. These include:[17]

- the presumption that all individuals should be released from pretrial detention without conditions; this can be overridden by clear evidence of flight risk or public safety risk

- declination to prosecute (decline or dismiss pre-arraignment without conditions) or divert fifteen offenses such as disorderly conduct, drug possession, larceny, destruction of property, driving with a suspended license, and trespassing; alternatives include referral to a public health professional or restitution for theft
- dismissal of marijuana cases without conditions
- instructing prosecutors to consider any collateral consequences, including immigration consequences, associated with charging and sentencing decisions
- creation of the Discharge Integrity Team responsible for assisting in the outside review of all fatal police-involved shootings
- recognition that the war on drugs has been an utter failure and that substance abuse and mental illness are public health, not criminal justice matters; commitment to expand diversion to community-based substance abuse and mental health treatment
- plea negotiations shall be driven by several overarching principles:
  - incarceration is a last resort
  - diversion shall be offered whenever possible
  - substance abuse, mental illness, poverty, and the behaviors that often result from them should never be a justification for incarceration

Another strategy that is becoming increasingly common is the creation of progressive prosecutor interest groups or associations that leverage their increasing numbers to lobby for criminal justice reform at the state legislative level. For example, elected progressive prosecutors in Virginia have formed an alliance to counteract the traditional tough-on-crime lobbying activities of the Virginia Association of Commonwealth's Attorneys (VACA). The Virginia Progressive Prosecutors for Justice (VPPJ) consists of eleven reform-focused District Attorneys in the state.[18]

"[VACA] is down in Richmond every single day of session, and opposes reform after reform," Parisa Dehghani-Tafti told me during her campaign in Arlington County. She cited VACA's opposition to decriminalizing marijuana. In neighboring Fairfax, Steve Descano told me he wished to build a counterpoint to VACA with which to head to Richmond and say, "Hey legislators, you've heard this regressive view of the world. Let me tell you a progressive view of what justice looks like." Both won, ousting incumbents, and now joined the new coalition.

The VPPJ's inaugural statement to the Virginia legislature noted that they represent more than 40 percent of the population of Virginia and included proposals to increase police accountability for use-of-force misconduct and other unlawful behavior, eliminate mandatory minimum sentences, expand deferred dispositions in all cases where the commonwealth's attorney and defense attorney agree, expand the ability to expunge arrests, and eliminate the mandatory six-month driver's license suspension on all drug convictions.

INTERVIEWING PROGRESSIVE PROSECUTORS

Part of the research for this book involved directly interviewing elected progressive or reform-focused District Attorneys. Telephone interviews were conducted with eighteen self-identified reform-oriented, progressive District Attorneys, most of whom were elected into office between 2016 and 2019. Those interviewed were selected based on news reports regarding their election and reform platform. There was an effort to inject diversity regarding a number of dimensions. They are from seven different states and represent large and medium metro areas as well as small, more rural counties. The majority of interview respondents are from large metro areas. Four are female and five are minorities, either African American or Hispanic. Several of the reform DAs came from a criminal defense background. The rest were former line prosecutors. Two had been DAs who then implemented reforms over a longer period of time, rather than being elected as a progressive and starting the reform process when entering office. Three ran and were elected as Republicans. The rest were elected as Democrats.

The interviews typically took forty-five to sixty minutes to complete. Notes were taken during the interviews. The respondents were assured confidentiality, although several stated they were fine with my using their names and attributing quotes to them. Despite that, I have maintained confidentiality herein. While I do quote certain statements from respondents, I do not attach any names or other identifying information to those quotes.

The questions covered a range of issues including their election campaigns (how they positioned themselves, their opponents, funding, problems encountered), their thinking about reform, their perceptions about the power and influence of prosecutors for affecting reform, their role regarding reducing recidivism, and barriers they have encountered since in office, among others.

Election of Progressive Prosecutors

Most of the reform prosecutors I interviewed indicated that their election platforms were well received, representing a range of reform initiatives and positioning of candidates. In many of the elections, there was a pretty stark contrast between the reformer candidate and the business-as-usual, tough-on-crime incumbent. Most of the elections were landslide victories. In several cases, the election campaigns were reportedly quite negative.

In some cases, there was a particular event that a campaign targeted, such as use of force by police or an officer-involved shooting. Others focused on fairness, justice and equality, transparency, or corruption in the prior administration. Smart on crime was a common election theme, implicating such things as prosecution of minor drug crimes and retail theft.

Three of the DAs I interviewed had been in office for some time and became converts to reform, initiating changes over longer periods of time.

Overall, the election campaigns offered a more balanced approach, by prosecuting and punishing serious and violent offenders and declining to prosecute low-level drug offenses and / or diverting drug offenders to treatment.

The majority of the DAs I interviewed benefitted from outside money, most commonly from George Soros or one of his political action committees. That money was reportedly very helpful in electing these progressive DAs.

Reform Initiatives

Most of what the progressive prosecutors who were interviewed are proposing or implementing are fairly standard reform initiatives. They include increased diversion for lower-level offenders and offenders with mental health and substance-abuse problems, bail reform such as increasing the number released without conditions, not prosecuting low-level drug and retail theft cases, changing the culture of the prosecutor's office, holding police accountable, and expanding pretrial services.

I was impressed that in addition to the nuts and bolts of pretrial reform in these jurisdictions, progressive DAs expressed a variety of compelling big-picture ideas about criminal justice. It is important to note that what follows are responses to general, open-ended questions about what is wrong with the criminal justice system and where it should go from here.

Several discussed changing what success looks like.

> When the case is closed and the sentence is issued, people think we won. But most reoffend, which means we lost. We failed to achieve our purpose.
> Recidivism is the name of the game. That [reducing recidivism] is what we should be doing.
> Recidivism means the system failed.
> Conviction is not always the right outcome. We need to think differently about what we're trying to achieve.

We need to stop this endless cycle of repeatedly convicting and punishing people. That doesn't work.
Just because we can convict doesn't mean we should.
We should not continue to criminalize poverty.
We should be minimizing the collateral consequences.
We really have to think differently about drug abuse and mental health.

Others spoke of how the criminal justice system has the wrong operational philosophy.

The criminal justice system is too shortsighted. There is way too much focus on retribution and punishment without thinking about the consequences.
I think the biggest problem is that the justice system is shortsighted.
Lack of empathy is a huge problem in the criminal justice system.
The criminal justice system is rooted in hate and retribution. We need to be positive, not angry.

Many noted that DAs or State's Attorneys play very important roles in their communities with regard to reform.

Prosecutors have the power to make the right thing happen.
Discretion is a prosecutor's superpower. We should use it to make a difference, for change.
Prosecutors should lead change in their community.
The DA is in a unique position to make reform happen.
It's up to the prosecutor to lead reform.

Changing the Culture

Many newly elected reform DAs either selectively fired prosecutors that were not in step with the philosophy or initiatives of the new DA or experienced significant exodus of prosecutors who saw the handwriting on the wall and decided this was not for them. For example, Larry Krasner of Philadelphia had a 30 percent turnover in staff, Stephanie Morales of Portsmouth, Virginia, lost nearly 50 percent of her staff, and Aramis Ayala of the Ninth Judicial Circuit Court of Florida lost 20 percent of her office when she took over.

Nearly all of the progressive DAs I interviewed indicated that they fired some line prosecutors and/or prosecutors in administrative positions upon taking office. The goal was to change the culture of the office, to transition from traditional tough-on-crime to a smart-on-crime environment.

Getting Outside Help

A common characteristic of these progressive prosecutors is their reliance on outside expertise for formulating reform initiatives. These resources include universities, nonprofits such as Fair and Just Prosecution, the Vera Institute, the Institute for Innovation in Prosecution, and the Pretrial Justice Institute, as well as collaborating with other reform prosecutors. There is a general consensus that there are important resources available outside of the prosecutor's office.

> A couple expressed the idea that lawyers have limited expertise.
> You don't want a lawyer to build your next skyscraper.
> I'm not a researcher, so I need the right people advising us.
> Another indicated that he relies on the "veteran" reform prosecutors.
> I'm learning from the pioneers, people like Larry Krasner, Dan Satterberg, and George Gascon.

Reducing Recidivism

In our 2018 book *Confronting Underground Justice*, Judge Pitman and I reported on the results of interviews we conducted with line prosecutors. One of the questions was "What is your role in terms of reducing recidivism?" The vast majority stated that they did not think that reducing recidivism was in their job description. Most did not see it as their responsibility. Several added that they believe it is up to the offender.

> I'm not sure we play a role.
> We don't look at recidivism, we just look at the case before us.
> Reducing recidivism is a great thing, but I don't see that as my job.
> I'm jaded, but I just don't think people change . . . People just don't give a crap anymore. They don't care about going back to jail.
> I don't know . . . I think it's up to the defendant.
> We are here to punish people for conduct. Whether or not someone chooses to reoffend after they have been punished is up to them . . . They reoffend because it is their choice.

I think people make choices. I can't do much about that.

The line prosecutors who said they do play a role were asked "How do you reduce recidivism?" The most common answer was by imposing punishment. The more serious the offender—in terms of severity of crime and/or criminal history—the greater the punishment.

> We play a huge role because if someone is going to be a repeat offender, then we will increase the punishment.

I think the best way to prevent recidivism is a long prison sentence.
I think it's a big role. I think we need to look at the risk of recidivism and if the risk is high then we need to be more severe on the punishment.
Our general philosophy is that if we hold them accountable, then they won't want to do it again.

I asked this same question about recidivism reduction to reform-minded or progressive District Attorneys. Across the board, without hesitation, every one stated that reducing recidivism is one of the most important things they do.

Absolutely. That's my job. That's why I'm here.
That's our job.
That should be our laser focus.
That is why I became a prosecutor. Reducing recidivism is my #1 goal.
That is the whole point.
Prosecutors have a lot of power to do this.

When asked the follow up of how they believe recidivism is reduced, the vast majority replied with expanding diversion programs, attacking the underlying causes of crime, harm reduction, and limiting the footprint of the criminal justice system on offenders.

I think we can do that [reduce reoffending] by reducing the negative footprint of the criminal justice system.
We need to minimize the collateral effects [of the criminal justice system].
We need to attack the underlying causes [of crime].
Diversion, diversion, diversion.

In the course of the interviews, I told the progressive DAs what line prosecutors had said about reducing recidivism (not my job, or if it is, use punishment). Most were incredulous, and a couple were angry.

That's the problem.
Prosecutors with tunnel vision.
I'm in the process of getting rid of prosecutors that think that way.

There could be a couple of things going on to account for these differences between progressive DAs and line prosecutors in thinking about recidivism. One is that progressive DAs are more likely to think about innovative ways to accomplish broader criminal justice goals, such as reducing crime and recidivism, compared to line prosecutors who are probably more concerned with the day-to-day pressure to dispose of cases and manage caseloads.

The results of our interviews with progressive prosecutors are very consistent with interviews conducted in 2020 with twenty-two mainly chief prosecutors (District and State's Attorneys). These interviews were sponsored by the National District Attorneys Association (NDAA).[19] While our interviews were with progressive prosecutors in mainly larger jurisdictions, the NDAA interviews were with some self-identified progressives, but also a good number of mainstream chief prosecutors, many of who are from smaller jurisdictions.

What is particularly interesting is that thinking differently today about crime and punishment is not limited to progressive prosecutors or large jurisdictions. The consensus among these twenty-two prosecutors is that it is time to think more broadly about the roles and responsibilities of prosecutors, to cure the myopia of only responding to crime with punishment, by considering longer-term, collateral consequences, the circumstances of individuals, and effective ways to address recidivism. It seems the goal is to achieve more of a balance between punishment on the one hand (for serious and violent offenders) and behavior change and diversion on the other (for less serious crimes and offenders with significant disorders, impairments, and deficits). Here are some verbatim quotes that illustrate some central themes from the NDAA interviews.

Lyndsey Olson, a City Attorney in St. Paul, Minneapolis:

> We framed victory around conviction rates and weren't looking at how to work on recidivism at the front end. The traditional mindset ensured that the cycle of recidivism would continue.[20]

David Angel, an Assistant District Attorney in Santa Clara County, California:

> I think the challenge for prosecutors and the interest they represent is that rehabilitation is often viewed as an afterthought, to be dealt with by prison or probation . . . we need to start thinking about it in a broader way.

Leon Cannizzaro, District Attorney, New Orleans, Louisiana:

> Diversion is the process of not only diverting individuals from the traditional prosecution track but also diverting them from the negative paths they are currently walking. Our goal is for individuals to leave us better than when they came in. Prosecution tends to focus on things that are objective, like

facts and legal analysis. But our work in diversion is about individuals and is therefore quite fluid and subjective.

John Chisholm, District Attorney, Milwaukee County, Wisconsin:

We believe that the purposes of the system include being preventive and remedial. We wanted to move away from thinking about the criminal justice system as simply reactive and punitive. That new mindset allows us to consider the root causes of crime.

John Hummel, District Attorney, Bend, Oregon:

My role as a prosecutor is to be a community leader for public safety. One way to keep a community safe is to prosecute people who commit crimes, and my office does not hesitate to do this. Another way for a prosecutor to keep a community safe is to work with the community to develop programs to prevent crime in the first place. In Deschutes County we focus on crime prevention. Failing to work upstream to prevent crime would be a dereliction of duty.

Mark Vargo, State's Attorney, Pennington County (Rapid City), South Dakota:

In thinking about my new role as State's Attorney in Pennington County, I took a hard look at the misdemeanors coming through. It dawned on me that, instead of deciding that I am the mechanical hand of God who imposes the penalty for what someone did, a better practice is to attempt to see whether we can effectuate change so we never see that person again.

Andrew Warren, State Attorney, 13th Judicial District (Tampa), Florida:

For the past generation, prosecutors have traditionally viewed the system as a way to implement a punishment rather than implement a long-term problem-solving approach. The question has been: How do we win this case? Prosecutors weren't thinking about long-term or collateral consequences. That approach is myopic because it only considers one of the goals of the criminal justice system, which is accountability. For me, there are additional goals: reducing recidivism, rehabilitating offenders, and supporting victims. We've focused too much on punishment alone without really thinking about what happens when people get out of the system and reducing the number of people there in the first place.

PUSHBACK AND CHALLENGES

Getting elected and having good ideas are necessary but not sufficient for reform-oriented District Attorneys to implement significant change.

Leadership is critical, and many elected DAs are ready to carry that mantle. However, there are many players involved in criminal justice in local jurisdictions, and their assistance, cooperation, approval, buy-in, and funding are fundamentally linked to successful reform efforts. Local law enforcement, judges, pretrial services, line prosecutors, and city councils and county commissioners who have budget authority are key to successful reform.

Probably the most vocal opposition to progressive DAs is law enforcement. Police associations are typically very powerful organizations, and many have not hesitated to register their opposition. For example:

> The president of the Chicago Police Union—"[Kim Foxx] could care less about what police think. She's anti-police and pro-criminal."[21]
>
> [San Francisco District Attorney] Boudin ran on the promise to address racial bias in the criminal justice system, overhaul a cash bail rule that he says discriminates against the poor and hold police accountable in misconduct cases. Local police groups spent $650,000 for ads and mailers during the election that lambasted Boudin as a "dangerous choice" for the city.[22]
>
> "San Francisco's newly elected district attorney literally has a criminals-first agenda," wrote Paul Kelly, president of the United Coalition of Public Safety, a consortium of thirteen Western law enforcement associations.[23]
>
> "Police officers sense their lives are in danger if they feel the prosecutor doesn't have their back," Pasco [executive director of the National Fraternal Order of Police] says. "You arrest people who are breaking the law, but sometimes they're then not even held. That has a chilling effect on the enthusiasm of officers."
>
> Ultimately, Pasco says, the result of progressive prosecutorial policies is "chaos and anarchy," and he predicts the end result will be a pendulum swing back to tough-on-crime policies.[24]

Law enforcement officials from across Cook County (Chicago), Illinois, declared in 2019 that they had no confidence in Kim Foxx's ability as the chief prosecutor in the county. A group of forty police chiefs and other police officials from Cook County called for Foxx to resign.

Rachel Rollins, the DA of Suffolk County (Boston), Massachusetts, has drawn the anger of the Massachusetts Secretary of Public Safety Thomas Turco. Turco stated the "unconventional practices of Boston's Suffolk County District Attorney Rachel Rollins could put children at risk, make the opioid crisis worse, and help gang members and ex-cons while also undermining drunken driving and pot laws."[25]

John Creuzot, a longtime District Judge in Dallas County, Texas, and now the progressive District Attorney, has been on the radar of police associations that call him a socialist and because of his policy regarding low-level shoplifting, which they said will "allow the common criminal to feast on the business retail community."[26]

Joe Gonzales, the District Attorney of San Antonio, Texas, declared his office will not prosecute criminal trespass for individuals who are homeless. The police union called this "a total abdication of a DA's responsibility."[27]

Several of the progressive DAs I interviewed noted that judges were barriers to moving forward on certain reforms. For example, reducing the number of defendants on pretrial detention and releasing more individuals without bail require the cooperation of judges. Prosecutors can make recommendations regarding detention and bail, but the decision is ultimately up to judges. The same holds for sentencing. Prosecutors can recommend sentences, but it is the judge who imposes the sentence.

The origin of judicial opposition varies, but it is likely a result of a number of factors, including differing political ideologies, turf wars, the distribution of power, and theories about how to do the business of the criminal justice system. It is not hard to envision a tough-on-crime judge coming face-to-face with a progressive prosecutor and challenging the actions that DA has taken. It is also not difficult to conceive of a judge who believes a DA is violating ethical standards or the informal rules of the courthouse. Moreover, judges may not take kindly to a DA who is perceived to be usurping power or trying to interfere with judicial decision-making.

State officials have also attempted to intervene in local DA's actions and decision-making. An analysis by the *New York Times* found[28]

> Governors, state attorneys general and state legislators have tried to hobble prosecutors by limiting their cases, blocking retrials, stripping them of authority, pressuring the media to criticize them or pushing for extraordinary and paralyzing levels of oversight.

In 2019, the Republican governor of Maryland Larry Hogan instructed the Attorney General of the state to take over the prosecution of violent crimes in Baltimore. His reasoning was that the Baltimore District Attorney Marilyn Mosby, a reform-oriented DA, was too soft on crime—"far too often in Baltimore City, violent offenders get a slap on the wrist and are released back onto the streets to commit yet another violent offense."[29]

In 2017, Aramis Ayala, a reform State Attorney for the Ninth Judicial Circuit Court in Florida, implemented a policy of not seeking the death penalty. The Republican governor Rick Scott quickly responded by reassigning twenty-nine capital cases from her office.

Kimberly Gardner, the first Black female DA in St Louis, has faced a barrage of opposition from a variety of sources, including the governor and Attorney General of Missouri, as well as police unions and the St. Louis Police Officers Association. Despite the criticism, legal challenges, and unrelenting scrutiny that the *New York Times* called "virtually unheard of for an elected prosecutor,"[30] Gardner was reelected to office in the August 4, 2020, primary, with 60 percent of the vote.

Pushback from line prosecutors is a very common issue for DAs who want to implement significant reform initiatives. As I mentioned above, weeding out line prosecutors and administrators who oppose such changes is a very common practice when progressives take office. Nearly all of those I interviewed relayed their ongoing struggle with changing the culture of their office.

Implementing reform, including making significant changes to policy and procedure, is difficult in and of itself. Changing the culture of an organization is often much more challenging, especially when ways of thinking and doing business have been well entrenched for decades and seem to work well in the organizational framework that reformers inherit.

Changing the culture is also difficult because it is not something that prosecutors may know much about. Prosecutors are lawyers, and implementing certain changes, such as declining to prosecute certain cases, investigating and when warranted prosecuting excessive use of force by police, and reducing the reliance on bail, may seem fairly straightforward from the perspective of a lawyer (although as I argue in the final chapter, these are matters that require expertise that typical prosecutors' offices do not have). Changing thinking about crime and punishment and the goals and objectives of the office is another matter. It is typically a long-term process that requires considerable attention and expertise. I will return to this in the final chapter.

Inadequate funding is one of the most commonly cited challenges that reform prosecutors face when implementing policies. While several of the reform prosecutors I interviewed stated that they were receiving support from local government including funding, others cited inadequate funding as a major barrier to advancing reform initiatives. Most commonly mentioned were the lack of funding for diversion programs, problem-solving courts, pretrial services, and supervision.

Many of the twenty-two prosecutors interviewed for the NDAA research mentioned lack of funding as a significant risk to their efforts, noting that while supportive, local and state government are not as forthcoming with funding as is necessary. Most stated that they rely heavily on external grants to help fund diversion programs and treatment capacity. I believe that a fair takeaway from these interviews is that few reform prosecutors have the funding necessary to meet the goals of their efforts. In fact, it is reasonable to suggest that the goals of many of these reform efforts are toned down by the realities of funding. The implication is that the impact of reform efforts on jail and prison populations, as well as recidivism rates, is mitigated by lack of funding, as well as other constraints.

Despite a number of very significant challenges and rather consistent resistance from very strong organizations like police associations and unions, as well as some district attorney associations and the United States Department of Justice, the election of reform-oriented prosecutors has gained substantial momentum, and many are well on the way to implementing significant changes in jurisdictions across the United States. The NDAA interviews demonstrate that there are different ways to get to the same place—meaningful reform is not just the purview of progressives elected in large metro areas. Rather, reinventing the role of the prosecutor has spread more broadly than perhaps previously assumed, especially among more traditional prosecutors and those in smaller jurisdictions.

Is prosecutorial reform the future of criminal justice in this country? Will local jurisdictions continue to elect progressive DAs or support more traditional prosecutors interested in doing the business of criminal justice in a different way? I don't know, but I do know that there are some important circumstances that suggest the ongoing election of progressive and reform-oriented prosecutors and local support for prosecutor reform.

Two-thirds of the one hundred largest cities in the United States are led by Democratic mayors. Hillary Clinton won eighty-eight of the one hundred largest counties in the 2016 presidential election. These election results reflect the geography of electoral politics, which is that larger metropolitan areas tend to be more Democratic and more liberal, thus they are more likely to elect progressive prosecutors and support prosecutor reform. Moreover, several of the largest one hundred cities that are led by Republican mayors have progressive or reform-oriented District Attorneys.

I pointed out earlier that the interviews that were sponsored by the NDAA suggest that reform-oriented prosecutors are showing up in smaller jurisdictions as well as the higher-profile metro areas such as Philadelphia, Dallas, Houston, San Antonio, San Francisco, Denver, Seattle, and Tampa. There is increasing evidence that DAs in smaller jurisdictions are getting elected and starting to implement reforms. Recent elections, including primaries during the summer of 2020, have resulted in the election of reform prosecutors in a variety of smaller jurisdictions. Daniel Nichanian, the founding editor of *The Appeal: Political*

Report, has followed the election of prosecutors. Nichanian notes nearly a year ago:[31]

> The movement to elect prosecutors intent on fighting mass incarceration has been largely associated with big cities like Chicago and Philadelphia until now. But it broke new ground on Tuesday when a group of decarceral candidates won in suburban and rural counties across the nation.

Five progressive candidates defeated incumbents in Virginia counties, including Arlington County, Albemarle County, Fairfax County, Loudoun County, and Prince William County. Delaware County, a Philadelphia suburb, elected Jack Stollsteimer, who campaigned with a ten-point Smart on Crime platform.

Rural Mississippi has had Scott Colom as the DA since 2015. His efforts at reforming prosecution in his rural district were rewarded with reelection. He will be joined by Shameca Collins and Jody Owens, who were also elected in rural counties on progressive platforms.

Even in defeat, progressives are having impacts on prosecutor elections. Tiffany Caban lost to Melinda Katz in the Queens, New York, DA race, but Caban's campaign pushed Katz further to the left in terms of bail reform and conviction integrity.

More recently (August 5, 2020), Nichanian observed:[32]

> The circle of progressives elected to prosecutors' offices of cutting incarceration will gain three new members come 2021, due to elections and related events over the past week . . . Initially associated with the nation's biggest cities, successful efforts to overhaul the criminal legal system through the ballot box have spread to suburban and rural jurisdictions.

Progressive candidates won election over longtime prosecutors with tough-on-crime records in Pima County (Tucson), Arizona, Washtenaw County (Ann Arbor), Michigan, and the 12th Judicial District in Colorado (the San Luis Valley).

Karen McDonald, formerly a felony court judge, resigned the bench because she realized that the only person who can really effect change in a local jurisdiction is the prosecutor. She ran for District Attorney in the suburban county of Oakland, Michigan, and defeated the hard-line incumbent by a two to one margin.

In Maricopa County (Phoenix), Arizona, home of the tough as they get Sheriff Joe Arpaio, progressive candidate Julie Gunnigle won the Democratic primary. She will face her Republican opponent, also a woman, in the November general election.

Despite strong opposition from police organizations and former prosecutors, Mark Dupree, an African American, was reelected as the District

Attorney in Wyandotte County (Kansas City), Kansas. His opponent was a former prosecutor who had significant backing from local officials.

Portland, Oregon, just elected one of the most progressive DAs in the country. Mike Schmidt won with 75 percent of the vote, despite a long-standing punitive culture in Oregon and a DA association that has repeatedly fought reform.

Another consequence of the prosecutor reform movement is that more and more incumbent DAs with more conservative records are being challenged. Some of them do not win, but the campaigns raise important issues and may shift the thinking of more traditional candidates who do win.

A wild card in all of this is the murder of George Floyd, the nationwide protests that followed that incident, and the substantial role that Black Lives Matter is currently playing in the national and local political landscapes. If this momentum is sustained for the longer term, there could be interesting local election results in November of 2020 and beyond.

Finally, there is a risk factor that should not be ignored. The venue for much criminal justice reform is local jurisdictions, initially large metro areas with progressive prosecutors, and now expanding more broadly. The issue is the extent to which governors, state legislatures, and state Attorneys General may preempt local efforts at reform. Preemption refers to the assumption that state law trumps local law. We have seen battles between city and state government over sanctuary cities, bathroom use by LGBT individuals, homelessness, the use of plastic bags, and, more recently, responses to COVID-19, to name just a few. I identified a few instances above where state government intervened regarding decisions and policies by the DA in Baltimore, the Ninth Judicial Circuit Court in Florida, and in St. Louis. I also cited the *New York Times* analysis of state intrusion in the business of the prosecutor. As more progressive DAs are elected in conservative states, we may see more intrusion into local criminal justice policy, which may hamper reform efforts.

I will return to the matter of prosecutors and comprehensive criminal justice reform in chapter 7.

NOTES

1. Jackson, "The Federal Prosecutor."
2. Stuntz, "The Pathological Politics of Criminal Law," 509.
3. Luna, "Prosecutor King," 57.
4. Luna, "Prosecutor King," 78.
5. Sklansky, "The Problems with Prosecutors," 458; see also Stuntz, *The Collapse of American Criminal Justice*; Tonry, "Prosecutors and Politics in Comparative Per-

spective"; Pfaff, *Locked In: The True Causes of Mass Incarceration and How to Achieve Real Reform.*

6. Kelly and Pitman, *Confronting Underground Justice,* 192.

7. Kelly and Pitman, *Confronting Underground Justice.*

8. Block, "Let's Put an End to Prosecutorial Immunity," 2–3.

9. Wright, "How Prosecutor Elections Fail Us."

10. Wright, "How Prosecutor Elections Fail Us."

11. Sklansky, "The Changing Political Landscape for Elected Prosecutors."

12. Wright, "How Prosecutor Elections Fail Us," 605.

13. Crombie, "Portland Gets First Outsider District Attorney in Mike Schmidt, Part of a National Wave of Progressive Prosecutors," 2.

14. Taylor, "George Floyd Protests: A Timeline."

15. White, "Floyd Death Propels Police Reformers in Key Prosecutor Races," 1.

16. John Creuzot, Criminal District Attorney, Dallas County, April 10, 2019.

17. Nichanian, "Rachael Rollins Announces New Prosecutorial Policies in Boston," *The Appeal,* March 28, 2019.

18. Nichanian, "Eleven Prosecutors Form a Progressive Alliance in Virginia," 2.

19. Lagratta, "To Prosecute: Interviews About Early Decision-Making."

20. Lagratta, "To Prosecute: Interviews About Early Decision-Making," 150.

21. Bogira, *The Hustle of Kim Foxx,* 44.

22. della Cava, "New, More Progressive Prosecutors are Angering Police, Who Warn Approach Will Lead to Chaos," 3.

23. della Cava, "New, More Progressive Prosecutors are Angering Police, Who Warn Approach Will Lead to Chaos," 4.

24. della Cava, "New, More Progressive Prosecutors are Angering Police, Who Warn Approach Will Lead to Chaos," 8.

25. Crime and Justice News, *The Crime Report,* "MA Official Says DA's Practices Threaten Public Safety."

26. Vera Institute of Justice, "Reform-Minded Prosecutors—Especially Black Women—Face Pushback," 4.

27. Vera Institute of Justice, "Reform-Minded Prosecutors—Especially Black Women—Face Pushback," 4.

28. Robinson, "The People Who Undermine Progressive Prosecutors," 2.

29. Vera Institute of Justice, "Reform-Minded Prosecutors—Especially Black Women—Face Pushback," 1.

30. Vera Institute of Justice, "Reform-Minded Prosecutors—Especially Black Women—Face Pushback," 3.

31. Nichanian, "Voters Beyond Big Cities Rejected Mass Incarceration in Tuesday's Elections," 1–2.

32. Nichanian, "Progressives Score New Wins in Prosecutor Elections, Adding to the Movement's Breadth," 2.

5

Indigent Defense

The Sixth Amendment provides a variety of protections and rights regarding criminal adjudication, including the right to have a lawyer assist in one's defense.

> In all criminal prosecutions, the accused shall enjoy the right . . . to have the Assistance of Counsel for his defense.

As is evident from reading the passage above, the Sixth Amendment is silent regarding the mechanics and logistics of assistance of counsel. There is nothing about when this right begins, how counsel should assist defendants, and, importantly for this chapter, what to do in circumstances when a defendant is too poor to retain their own counsel.

The retention of counsel for poor or indigent defendants was initially addressed in the 1963 landmark case *Gideon v. Wainwright*. Gideon was an indigent defendant in Florida who represented himself in a felony prosecution. Under the law in Florida at the time, the only requirement for providing counsel for indigent defendants was in capital cases. Gideon was convicted and sentenced to prison. He petitioned the US Supreme Court, and fortuitously it was the Warren Court that agreed to hear the case, a court that was responsible for a number of important decisions regarding criminal defendants' rights. These decisions include *Mapp v. Ohio* (which established the exclusionary rule in cases of Fourth Amendment violation of the right against unreasonable search and seizure), *Escobedo v. Illinois* (which clarified right to counsel during custodial interrogation),

Miranda v. Arizona, and *Brady v. Maryland* (requiring prosecutors to provide exculpatory evidence to the defense), among others.

The Warren Court took the *Gideon* case as the opportunity to apply across the states the requirement of providing counsel to indigent defendants in any felony prosecution. The following is an excerpt from the *Gideon* decision (Gideon v. Wainwright, 372 U.S. 335 (1963).

> reason and reflection require us to recognize that, in our adversary system of criminal justice, any person hauled into court, who is too poor to hire a lawyer, cannot be assured a fair trial unless counsel is provided for him. This seems to us to be an obvious truth. Governments, both state and federal, quite properly spend vast sums of money to establish machinery to try defendants accused of crime. Lawyers to prosecute are everywhere deemed essential to protect the public's interest in an orderly society. Similarly, there are few defendants charged with crime, few indeed, who fail to hire the best lawyers they can get to prepare and present their defenses. That government hires lawyers to prosecute and defendants who have the money hire lawyers to defend are the strongest indications of the widespread belief that lawyers in criminal courts are necessities, not luxuries. The right of one charged with crime to counsel may not be deemed fundamental and essential to fair trials in some countries, but it is in ours. From the very beginning, our state and national constitutions and laws have laid great emphasis on procedural and substantive safeguards designed to assure fair trials before impartial tribunals in which every defendant stands equal before the law. This noble ideal cannot be realized if the poor man charged with crime has to face his accusers without a lawyer to assist him.

Subsequent Supreme Court cases established similar rights in misdemeanor prosecutions where a defendant is subject to incarceration upon conviction (for example, *Argersinger v. Hamlin* 407 U.S. 25 (1972)).

Gideon and *Argersinger* established the fact of indigent defense but did not clarify when a defendant shall have the assistance of counsel. Over time, the Court has addressed many of these issues. *Escobedo v. Illinois* and *Miranda v. Arizona* both dealt with the right to representation during post-arrest interrogation. The court also extended the right to counsel for lineups (*United States v. Wade*), preliminary hearings (*Coleman v. Alabama*), and arraignments (*Hamilton v. Alabama*).[1]

Imbedded in the reasoning behind *Gideon* and *Argersinger* is the risk of incarceration. That is, the Court argued that when a defendant is in jeopardy of losing his or her liberty, they should have assistance of counsel and if indigent, counsel shall be provided by the government. We now encounter a very profound irony in the law of indigent defense.

As problematic as indigent defense systems are in the United States, something I will discuss in detail shortly, there is a gaping hole in when indigent defendants have access to counsel in criminal proceedings.

Many probably believe that the right to counsel applies to the very early proceedings, typically called an initial appearance, magistration, or a detention hearing. However, in the majority of states, there is no provision in codes of criminal procedure for indigent defense at this very early, important stage of criminal processing. In fact, in at least thirty-two states, indigent defense counsel is not present at the initial appearance, according to analysis of state codes of criminal procedure.[2]

Importantly, the US Supreme Court has failed to address this glaring omission in the law of indigent defense.[3]

> The U.S. Supreme Court has done little to protect the constitutional rights of indigent criminal defendants when they initially appear before a judicial officer that has the power to restrict their liberty, despite the fact that the setting of bail implicates an indigent defendant's right to counsel under the Sixth Amendment and the right to due process and equal protection under the Fourteenth Amendment. The Court has never found the setting of bail to be a critical stage of the proceedings that would require the presence of counsel or discussed what procedural safeguards should be in place to protect the rights of indigent defendants. These failures may contribute to rising rates of pretrial incarceration, a trend that the Court should take steps to reverse by finding a right to counsel at an indigent defendant's initial appearance where a judicial officer has the power to place restrictions on their liberty.

The troubling irony here is that the Supreme Court has held that an indigent defendant shall have a public defense attorney appointed for any "critical stage" of processing. A critical stage is defined as[4]

> proceedings between an individual and agents of the State (whether "formal or informal, in court or out") that amount to "trial-like confrontations," at which counsel would help the accused "in coping with legal problems or . . . meeting his adversary."

The initial appearance may sound harmless enough, but it can and does involve very serious decisions. The most important is the decision to detain someone pretrial or release him or her pending disposition of the case. This is important because pretrial detention has considerable downstream consequences. These include loss of a job, loss of housing, medical and psychological/psychiatric complications, family disruption, and difficulty assisting with one's defense, among others. There is also clear evidence that pretrial detention increases the probability of conviction (pretrial detention is a major motivator for agreeing to a plea deal), results in harsher punishment, and increases the likelihood of recidivism.

The fact that the detention decision is made in a hearing where the government is represented by the prosecutor but, in the majority of states, the defendant is not represented and is essentially on his own raises a number of legitimate questions. These consist of constitutional concerns, including the Sixth Amendment right to counsel and the Fourteenth Amendment due process clause and equal protection clause.

The due process clause of the Fourteenth Amendment (in the context of the initial appearance) protects against being punished prior to being convicted of a crime. The point of detention is not to punish but to protect the public and assure that the defendant does not flee the jurisdiction. The problem is that there is considerable evidence that pretrial detention is inappropriately used for defendants who are not a public safety risk or flight risk. Thus, to the extent that pretrial detention is excessive relative to the harm it is intended to deter (a test for distinguishing punitive from regulatory), the more legitimate it is to claim that it is punitive.

The Supreme Court has been clear that the right to counsel "attaches" at a defendant's first appearance before a judge or magistrate. However, the right to counsel and access to counsel are two different things. The equal protection concern pertains to the access to counsel for those with resources compared to those without. As John Gross puts it:[5]

> In *Gideon v. Wainwright*, the Supreme Court noted that "there are few defendants charged with crime, few indeed, who fail to hire the best lawyers they can get to prepare and present their defenses." The fact that the wealthy have an absolute right to have counsel present at their initial appearance and the poor do not raises equal protection concerns. In addition, the continued reliance on financial securities when making pretrial release decisions means that the wealthy go free while the poor remain in jail.

While *Gideon* was a major step forward in terms of providing substance and meaning to the Sixth Amendment right to counsel, it left many questions unanswered. For example, what are the necessary qualifications that defense attorneys must possess in order to provide "procedural and substantive safeguards designed to assure fair trials"? Moreover, what constitutes an adequate defense in terms of time devoted to a case and quality of representation? Then there are logistical questions such as what level of government—state or county—is responsible for assuring counsel is provided and, ultimately, who pays for it?

These issues have been left up to the states and counties across the country to address. As a result, the United States does not have anything close to a uniform system for providing indigent defense. In some states, the primary responsibility falls on state government. In others, it falls entirely on counties. In others still, it is a combination of state and county responsibility. What we have ended up with is a patchwork of approaches to fulfilling the promise of *Gideon*.

Not only has the US Supreme Court recognized the value of protecting fundamental rights of criminal defendants, especially indigent defendants, so has the public. There is generally strong agreement among the public regarding the right to have counsel provided to indigent defendants. A recent public opinion poll[6] found that two-thirds of surveyed adults believe government should use tax dollars to provide counsel to indigent defendants. Nearly two-thirds believe that government should increase spending of tax dollars for indigent defense.

Interestingly, public opinion is pretty realistic regarding access to indigent defense and the quality of representation. About 50 percent of those surveyed believe public defenders do not provide adequate representation nor take much of an interest in their indigent clients. Eighty percent do not believe that public defenders have enough time for their cases. Nearly three-quarters believe that states are doing only a fair or poor job of providing criminal defense for those too poor to retain counsel.[7]

Federal indigent defense is governed by the 1964 Criminal Justice Act, which mandated local adoption of defense systems consisting of the appointment of local, private attorneys as well as an alternative system of a Federal Public Defender Service (a government agency) or a Community Defender Organization (a private, nonprofit agency). Because the federal judicial system is uniform throughout the United States, the federal public defender system is also considerably more uniform than the state and local systems. Moreover, federal indigent defense caseloads are lower than most state/county caseloads, and federal public defenders are generally paid more, have more experience, and have access to more resources for investigation and so on.

We now turn to an in-depth assessment of the state of indigent defense in the United States today. This discussion will focus on state and local indigent defense systems.

THE STATE OF INDIGENT DEFENSE

There are three primary ways in which defense counsel is provided to indigent defendants. The public defender model typically relies on full-time or part-time salaried lawyers who do only indigent criminal defense work. These public defender offices are either public or semipublic agencies. The appointed counsel model relies on local private criminal defense attorneys who are assigned by the court for an hourly rate or other agreed-upon amount. Finally, the contract attorney approach relies on private lawyers who are under contract to provide criminal defense, often in cases where the public defender may have a conflict of interest.

The most glaring and persistent problem with indigent defense is lack of funding and excessive caseloads and workloads. There is nothing new about too many cases and too few lawyers. Observers and critics have been pointing out the problems for decades. Ten years ago, two major national reports vividly highlighted the critical caseload and workload problem. The Constitution Project's "Justice Denied: America's Continuing Neglect of Our Constitutional Right to Counsel" described it as follows.[8]

> Frequently, public defenders are asked to represent far too many clients. Sometimes the defenders have well over 100 clients at a time, with many clients charged with serious offenses, and their cases moving quickly through the court system. As a consequence, defense lawyers are constantly forced to violate their oaths as attorneys because their caseloads make it impossible for them to practice law as they are required to do according to the profession's rules. They cannot interview their clients properly, effectively seek their pretrial release, file appropriate motions, conduct necessary fact investigations, negotiate responsibly with the prosecutor, adequately prepare for hearings, and perform countless other tasks that normally would be undertaken by a lawyer with sufficient time and resources. Yes, the clients have lawyers, but lawyers with crushing caseloads who, through no fault of their own, provide second-rate legal services, simply because it is not humanly possible for them to do otherwise.

The second 2009 report, by the National Association of Criminal Defense Lawyers and titled "Minor Crimes, Massive Waste: The Terrible Toll of America's Broken Misdemeanor Courts," took aim at the misdemeanor system.[9]

> Almost 40 years later, the misdemeanor criminal justice system is rife with the same problems that existed prior to the *Argersinger* decision. Legal representation for indigent defendants is absent in many cases. Even when an attorney is provided to defend a misdemeanor case, crushing workloads make it impossible for many defenders to effectively represent clients. Too often, counsel is unable to spend sufficient time on each of their cases. This forces even the most competent and dedicated attorneys to run afoul of their professional duties. Frequently, judges and prosecutors are complicit in these breaches, pushing defenders to take action with inadequate time, despite knowing that the defense attorney lacks appropriate information about the case and the client.

The Justice Policy Institute reports that national standards for indigent defense caseloads are as follows: 150 felony or 400 misdemeanor or 200 juvenile or 200 mental health cases or 25 appeals per year. Based on these caseload guidelines, only 21 percent of state-based and 27 percent of county-based public defender officers are able to meet these standards.[10] There is a considerable amount of documenting caseloads across the country, and they all pretty much tell the same extraordinary stories. For example, average caseloads for a public defender in Kentucky is 460 per year. In Florida, the average felony caseload is 500 per year. In Miami-Dade County, Florida, the indigent defense caseload recently increased from 370 to 500 per year.[11] In Fresno, California, the average is around 600.[12]

Among other things, the report discussed above by the National Association of Criminal Defense Lawyers noted that public defenders in Miami, Atlanta, and Chicago handled in excess of 2,000 misdemeanor cases per year.

In Washington state, public defenders are able to devote about an hour to each felony case. In New Orleans, it is an average of seven minutes.[13]

Then there is Melinda Cameron, an assigned criminal defense lawyer in Detroit. Over the past five years, she has had 3,802 cases, 1,800 of which were felonies. Eli Hager, who wrote the piece for the Marshall Project, observes:[14]

> With such a caseload, it would be impossible for Cameron to put in the hours of research, witness questioning, and strategizing with her clients that legal experts agree are needed in such serious cases. Since 2014, for example, she has only visited one client in jail, according to court receipts. Cameron emphasized in an interview that she doesn't take shortcuts, and does what's best for her clients. And in a specialty—indigent defense—that is among law's least lucrative, she's also trying to make a living . . . "The money is not there," she said, "unless you do some volume."

Encouraging high-volume defense representation is largely a function of the pay structure. Detroit pays indigent defense lawyers by court event:[15]

> $40 for an arraignment, $110 for a plea-deal hearing, $90 for a half-day of trial, and so on, no matter how long or involved each hearing is. This encourages attorneys to stay at the Murphy Hall of Justice accumulating quick court appearances rather than doing unpaid but crucial out-of-court work such as reviewing crime-scene footage, visiting their clients' families, and discussing their options with them even if they're in jail.

Detroit is certainly not alone regarding public defense lawyers who specialize in volume business. Take, for example, Ray Espersen, who was a court-appointed public defense attorney in Travis County (Austin), Texas. In one year, Espersen had been appointed to and paid for 331 felonies, 275 misdemeanors, and 46 felonies in neighboring Williamson County. Then there is James Barr, an appointed defender in Harris County (Houston), Texas, who was paid for more than 430 felonies in one year, or Artie Aguilar, who had a contract to handle all of the indigent felony cases in a four-county area, resulting in 322 cases.[16] The Texas Indigent Defense Commission conducted research to determine appropriate caseloads. Their results indicated that in Texas, a defense lawyer could effectively handle 128 felonies or 226 misdemeanors.[17]

A feature story in the *New York Times* on February 3, 2019, detailed the caseload of Louisiana public defender Jack Talaska. The story describes Talaska's caseload on a particular day, thus the title of the article, "One Lawyer. One Day, 194 Felony Cases."[18] The article puts this in context.[19]

> Bottom line: Mr. Talaska would have needed almost 10,000 hours or five work years, to handle the 194 felony cases he had on that April day alone, not to mention the dozens more he would be assigned that year.

Another story about public defenders in Louisiana, this one focusing on the 16th Judicial District, shows just how bad it can get.[20] There is one full-time public defender, Rhonda Covington. Her office receives about $35,000 from the state to handle 900 cases across the two parishes that comprise the 16th Judicial District. She has a part-time secretary, two part-time paralegals, and two contract lawyers who work two days per week. Covington is required to represent defendants who en masse, fifty at a time, together plead guilty to and are sentenced for serious felonies in these group plea hearings that take perhaps two to three hours. The prosecutor's office in the 16th Judicial District has a caseload similar to the public defender's office, but with a $1 million higher budget.

Walter Stokley is a public defender in Kansas City, Missouri, a state with a particularly poor indigent defense system. Responding to a report that public defenders spend about 21 percent of the time that is actually needed for an adequate defense, Stokley stated: "You're not getting an attorney. You're getting a sliver of an attorney."[21]

Research conducted by the National Association for Public Defense on a handful of state public defender systems found that defense lawyers in Colorado, Missouri, and Rhode Island had two to three times the workload required for an adequate defense. In Louisiana, it was five times the workload, and in Texas the researchers discovered that public defense lawyers spent about two hours assessing evidence and investigating witness accounts. This amounts to about one-quarter of what is required in felony cases.

Stephen Hanlon, general counsel for the National Association of Public Defense, stated:[22]

> When obstetricians have five times as much work as they can handle competently, terrible things happen. When public defenders have five times as much work as they can competently handle, terrible things happen too.

According to a report by the National Association of Criminal Defense Lawyers, at least twenty states today have flat-fee pay structures for public defense representation. For example, the fee for a misdemeanor case in Florida is $400, $250 in Connecticut, $300 in North Dakota, $180 in New Mexico, and in Virginia, it is $158.[23]

In Travis County, Texas, appointed defense attorneys are paid $600 per felony case, regardless of what is involved. On average across the state of Texas, court-appointed attorneys were paid $247 per misdemeanor and $598 per felony. In New Mexico, the fee paid to a public defender for a felony case is limited to a maximum of $700. In Missouri, a public defender is paid a flat fee of $500 for each noncapital felony. Oregon has a more complicated flat-fee structure. For example, a public defense attorney is paid between $565 and $626 for a domestic violence case and between $221 and $255 for a probation revocation hearing.

In Potter County, Texas, where Amarillo is located, defense attorneys representing indigent defendants are paid a flat fee. One attorney, noting that appointed lawyers are paid only $500 for a misdemeanor, stated, "How often are you going to meet with your client?"[24]

Harris County (Houston), Texas, serves as the illustration of another serious problem associated with public defense. In Houston, indigent defense is provided either through a public defender office or through an appointed counsel system. Very recent research on the appointed counsel system in Harris County[25] reveals that judges, who are responsible for appointing private attorneys, are twice as likely to appoint lawyers who contribute to the judge's election campaign, compared to lawyers who did not contribute. If that still isn't problematic enough, these appointed attorneys are paid flat fees for their services, encouraging them to seek large numbers of cases in order to maximize their income. And if that isn't problematic enough, the research reveals that these campaign-contributing attorneys may compromise the defense of their clients.[26]

> We find that defense attorneys who donate to a judge are, if anything, less successful than non-donor attorneys in attaining charge reductions, dismissals, and acquittals, or avoiding prison sentences. We contend that donor attorneys might underperform simply because they take on so many cases from their donee judges, and hence spend less time on each matter.

Mississippi leaves it up to cities and counties to fund public defense. Only eight of the state's eighty-two counties have public defender systems. The rest rely on appointed counsel. In all felony cases, payment is capped at $1,000, motivating the moving of cases and relying on high volume to make money.[27]

Returning to Eli Hager's piece "One Lawyer. Five Years. 3,802 Cases" for the Marshall Projects' investigation of indigent defense in Detroit, we meet Christine Grand, a stark contrast to Melinda Cameron, who I discussed earlier.[28]

> Grand makes a point of spending hours with her clients in jail, going over court documents and other records in a case. "That's the evidence against them. They have an absolute right to see that," she said. "[That's] why I became a lawyer and what the ethics rules require."
>
> For a serious felony, this often entails sitting in the jail visiting room with her client, watching dozens of hours of video footage from the crime scene and from the police interrogation room on her laptop. It also means making copies—often hundreds of pages—of police reports, witness statements, cell phone records and other evidence, and waiting in security lines, sometimes for hours, to get into the jail. For all of that work—not to mention paying for the copies and for parking—Grand earns a flat fee of $50 for a jail visit. It doesn't matter whether she spends 20 minutes or 20 hours. "A lot of cases, I make less than $5 an hour," she said, "but I stopped calculating it because it's so depressing."

At the root of the dysfunction of indigent defense is the profound lack of resources, including, but not limited to payment to the attorneys who do this work. Over the past twenty-five years, there has been an aggregate 2 percent increase in spending in real dollars for indigent defense. Over this same time period, there has been a 40 percent increase in the number of felony cases.[29]

The American Bar Association, in its 2004 assessment of the state of indigent defense in the United States, described the funding for public defense as "shamefully inadequate."[30] The ABA reached similar conclusions in 1983 when it marked the twentieth anniversary of the landmark *Gideon v. Wainwright* decision. More recently, the Bureau of Justice Statistics conducted a survey of county-based public defenders and reported that only about 25 percent of them had sufficient resources to manage their caseloads.[31] The situation was further aggravated by the recession that began in 2007, as states and counties cut or failed to increase funding for indigent defense.

One way to gauge the relative underfunding of public defense is in comparison to funding for prosecution. Since 80 percent of criminal defendants are indigent, public defenders and prosecutors' offices have roughly the same caseload. Nevertheless, the funding/resource disparity is striking, especially when we appreciate that prosecutors can rely on other agencies such as law enforcement for such things as investigation and forensic analysis.

The Orleans Parish Public Defenders Office handles 85 percent of all people charged with crimes in New Orleans but has a budget that is one-third that of the prosecutor. The 2016 budget for prosecution in New York City's five boroughs was $331 million. The budget for public defense that same year was $250 million. The budget in 2016 for the Washtenaw County, Michigan, prosecutors' office was $5.9 million. The budget for the public defender office was $2.9 million.[32]

Another way to assess the indigent defense funding problem is by looking at individual salary disparities. The National Association for Law Placement reports median salary differences between local prosecutors and public defenders (not including assigned counsel or contract defense attorneys) of between $3,500 and $6,000 per year, depending on experience.[33] In the Fourth Judicial District in Florida, beginning public defenders earn about $10,000 less per year than beginning prosecutors. Junior-level prosecutors in Denver earn $15,000 more per year than junior-level public defenders.[34] Staten Island legal aid lawyers make $11,200 less per year than their counterparts with the same experience in the District Attorney's office. The disparity is $4,700 in Manhattan.[35] In Multnomah County (Portland), Oregon, the highest paid, most experienced indigent defense attorney makes only $2,888 more than the lowest-paid prosecutor in that jurisdiction.[36] In Loudoun, Virginia, an entry-level public defender makes $59,523, compared to $65,135 that an entry-level prosecutor makes. The disparity grows with experience—a public defender with fourteen years of experience makes $93,703, compared to $126,103 for the prosecutor with similar experience.[37]

Statewide in Virginia, the disparity is dramatic. The *Virginia Mercury* reported in September 2019:[38]

> With salaries starting at $53,000, public defenders make almost 40 percent less on average than their counterparts in the prosecutor's office, according to the defender's office, which used Freedom of Information Act requests to obtain and compare salary data. Among their findings: 27 of their 29 attorneys make less than the highest paid administrative assistant in the prosecutor's office.

One consequence of inadequate funding for indigent defense is high caseloads. Another is turnover. In 2019, 25 percent of the public defenders statewide in Virginia quit due to low pay and high caseloads.[39] In that same year in Miami-Dade County, Florida, 25 percent of the public defenders quit, again, reportedly over low pay and high caseloads.[40] There is a similar story in Kansas. In 2018, twenty-two of the state's ninety-three public defenders quit. The cause? High caseloads, low pay, and poor benefits.[41]

Not only are there serious concerns with funding of public defense, several states provide no meaningful oversight of their indigent defense systems, such as assessing and monitoring adequate defense. The ACLU testified more than ten years ago that inadequate funding and oversight of indigent defense has created a constitutional crisis in Michigan.[42]

> The poor are frequently provided with counsel in name only. The failure of states to adequately fund and administer public defender services infects the entire criminal justice system.

> Michigan has one of the worst indigent defense systems in the country . . . The state delegates to 83 counties the responsibility for funding and administrating trial-level public defense services. But Michigan provides no fiscal or administrative oversight and does nothing to ensure that the counties' funding, policies, programs and guidelines enable their public defenders to provide constitutionally adequate legal representation.

David Carroll, the executive director of the Sixth Amendment Center, which conducts research on the right to counsel, says the indigent defense system in Detroit is:[43]

> as bad as anything I have seen in my career—including in the deepest parts of the Deep South, where funding for indigent defense is nonexistent and relationships between judges and attorneys are notoriously cozy.

There is no state oversight of indigent defense in Mississippi. In that state, felony defendants are not provided counsel until after indictment and arraignment. According to a report by the Sixth Amendment Center, it can be a few months and up to a year before a defendant has counsel.

Unfortunately, the lack of sufficient state oversight of indigent defense systems appears to be as common as underfunding. Lack of supervision and oversight are tied to inadequate representation.

Several organizations, such as the ACLU and the Southern Poverty Law Center, have filed lawsuits against states' public defender systems. I look at three such lawsuits to provide examples of the types of issues that are being litigated.

In 2017, the Southern Poverty Law Center filed a class action lawsuit against Louisiana for providing inadequate defense for indigent defendants. The plaintiffs allege that chronic deficient funding for public defense resulted in violations of due process, equal protection, and adequate representation.

The American Civil Liberties Union filed a class action lawsuit in 2017 against the state of Missouri and the state public defender system. The issues revolved around funding and adequacy of representation.[44]

For more than two decades, Defendants have failed to provide the resources required to adequately represent poor people accused of crimes in Missouri, leading to an actual and constructive denial of counsel for, and ineffective representation of, indigent defendants across the state.

The lawsuit claims that public defenders have three times the number of manageable cases. As a result, lawyers are unable to devote sufficient, if any, time to conducting interviews, investigating, and assessing evidence, activities that are critical in an adequate criminal defense. The ACLU claims that on average, public defenders in Missouri are able to spend about 20 percent of the recommended amount of time.

Another class action suit filed by the ACLU takes on public defense in Nevada. Among the pleadings is the following:[45]

A state does not satisfy its obligation under *Gideon* simply by appointing someone with a law license to represent indigent defendants. The state must instead appoint attorneys under circumstances—financial, administrative, logistical, political—that permit those attorneys to do their jobs. The appointed lawyer must be in a position to provide *meaningful* assistance—otherwise the state effects a "denial of Sixth Amendment rights that makes the adversary process itself presumptively unreliable."

Among other things, the lawsuit cited inadequate resources, flat-fee contracts, and lack of appropriate qualifications, training, and supervision of public defenders. The claims for relief include violation of the Sixth Amendment right to counsel and violation of the Fourteenth Amendment due process protection.

National Public Radio, in conjunction with the Brennan Center for Justice and the National Center for State Courts, conducted a state-by-state survey of court-imposed fees assessed against indigent defendants. A total of forty-three states charge indigent defendants fees to cover some portion of public defense. This often involves an application fee for a public defender that ranges between $10 and $400, according to the survey. Courts can also charge a defendant some portion or the total cost of a public defender. Failure to pay can result in prosecution and incarceration. The irony is these defendants are indigent, and that is why they have public defenders.

As Lars Troutman observes in his piece "The Bill of Rights 'Shouldn't Come with a Bill'":[46]

The Hobson's Choice between a defendant's money and her rights often revolves around whether to claim the Sixth Amendment right to an attorney—and to require the government to fulfill its obligation to provide a court-appointed one if necessary. Indeed, the cruel irony of charging a defendant for public counsel immediately after determining she is too poor to hire her own lawyer has done little to cool the ardor with which states assess public counsel fees.

THE CONSEQUENCES

There are several very significant consequences resulting from the problems with indigent defense that I discussed above. A common denominator to many of the issues is inadequate funding, leading to, among other things, extraordinarily high and unmanageable caseloads and lack of resources for investigation and experts. The primary effects include concerns about adequacy and quality of representation, due process shortcuts and/or violations, and the fairness of justice.

The most grievous result of this is wrongful conviction. The Innocence Project researched exonerations in recent years and found that about 20 to 25 percent of the exonerees had filed ineffectiveness of counsel claims.[47] Moreover, many of these original convictions were in part based on the analysis of forensic evidence, something for which public defenders often fail to have resources.

The American Bar Association's National Right to Counsel Committee's report "Justice Denied: America's Continuing Neglect of Our Constitutional Right to Counsel"[48] documented the consequences of an uneven playing field in the US court system. In particular, when under-resourced public defense lawyers go against better-funded prosecutors, the risk of serious errors occurring is heightened.

> The committee report also addresses why the right to counsel matters. The most compelling answer is that, in our adversary system of justice, fairness is served if both sides are represented by lawyers who are evenly matched in areas such as available time to devote to the case, training, experience, and resources. When the defense does not measure up to the prosecution, there is a heightened risk of the adversary system of justice making egregious mistakes . . . Whatever the reasons, for innocent persons to lose their liberty is a travesty. Equally troubling, it means that guilty persons roam free, victimizing others, while the state pays to incarcerate those who have not transgressed against society. Well-trained lawyers and adequately funded systems of defense are essential to prevent this.

Resource constraints promote public defense lawyers' phenomenal reliance on plea negotiation. Whether it is caseload pressure or low, fixed fees for indigent representation, the result is the same—clear incentives to move cases, as many and as quickly as possible. Hand in hand with plea negotiation are a variety of due process matters. Acceptance of a plea deal requires the defendant to waive fundamental constitutional rights, such as the Sixth Amendment right to "a speedy and public trial by an impartial jury" and to be "confronted with the witnesses against him" as well as the Fifth Amendment right against coerced confession (a very realistic element of the plea negotiation process), the right to appeal the conviction, often the right to appeal the sentence, as well as due process protections more broadly.

The current state of indigent defense is truly unconscionable, but it is not new. Public defenders, academics, and other interested individuals have been pleading for more funding for indigent defense for decades, and the due process and inequity concerns raised over the prosecution of poor defendants has been the subject of commentary for decades as well.

Unfortunately, the only realistic option at the moment is business as usual, meaning processing as many cases as possible to spread around to as many indigent defendants as feasible some benefit from criminal defense representation. Let me be clear that is not my recommendation, just the reality. What this means is continued reliance on plea negotiation at the extraordinary levels we currently see.

Let's now turn to what does make sense for indigent defense going forward.

THE REMEDIES

There is clear consensus among informed observers of a very serious need to fundamentally reform indigent defense. The advocates vary from the ACLU (national and state ACLUs), the Brennan Center for Justice, the CATO Institute, the Vera Institute of Justice, Mark Holden (the senior vice president at Koch Industries), the National Association of Criminal Defense Lawyers, Right On Crime (the conservative criminal justice reform organization), the Sixth Amendment Center, the American Bar Association, and many, many more, including hundreds of academics and researchers. The concerns are essentially the same—grossly inadequate funding, extraordinarily high caseloads and workloads, lack of sufficient oversight, and few resources for investigation and expert assistance. The universal remedy is more money.

I could not agree more. Critical underfunding is the source of much of the failure of indigent defense to meet the promise of *Gideon* and the Sixth Amendment. Making indigent defense functional through adequate funding is foundational. That will lead to manageable caseloads and workloads, increased access to defense counsel, strengthening of due process protections, and enhancement of the quality of defense.

However, I do not think that should be the entirety of indigent defense reform. Funding per se does not address the broader dysfunctions of the court system and the criminal justice system. My idea of reform is more fundamental than fulfilling the constitutional vision of indigent defense. That should be an obvious first step—providing an adequate defense to those too poor to retain counsel. Beyond that, the logic seems to fundamentally reinvent it.

Comprehensive reform of indigent defense serves as one very important piece of many, including prosecutors, defense counsel, judges, and pretrial officials, among others. All of these elements of the court system are implicated in our fundamentally flawed criminal justice system and all should be subject to significant renovation.

In our recent book *Confronting Underground Justice,* Robert Pitman and I interviewed prosecutors, judges, and indigent defense counsel. One of the things we learned is that essentially any attempt to identify and address underlying criminogenic circumstances associated with criminal justice involvement, things such as mental health problems, substance-abuse disorders, cognitive and intellectual impairment, among others, was primarily up to defense counsel!

While there is variation across and within jurisdictions, the stark reality we discovered in the interviews with both prosecutors and public defense counsel is that screening and assessment for underlying causes and correlates of criminality was not systematically done and when it is done, it is usually at the initiative of the defense. In other words, most of the burden for trying to reduce recidivism, by diverting someone away from purely criminal prosecution and punishment to some kind of treatment, is the responsibility of defense counsel.

Here is the dilemma. Public defense lawyers often do not have the time and resources to adequately defend indigent clients, often with just basic services. How are they supposed to take on the added burden of triage? The answer is that they usually don't. This helps us understand why there is so little effort in the US criminal justice system to identify and transform the circumstances, situations, deficits, and disorders of criminal defendants in order to reduce the likelihood of reoffending. No one realistically has the time or motivation to focus on these considerations when the day-to-day priority of the courts and the key individuals in the courts is to move cases. So, where do we go from here?

Presuming adequate funding and collateral resources (which, granted, is hard to envision at the moment), an important element in reforming indigent defense already exists in quite limited form. It is called holistic defense, problem-solving defense, community-oriented defense, holistic advocacy, and a variety of other things. While there are various approaches to holistic defense, they tend to share in common the overarching theme of attempting to identify and mitigate criminogenic circumstances. Typical are poverty, trauma, mental illness, substance-use disorders, employment problems, educational deficits, housing instability, and cognitive dysfunction, as well as the coincidence of comorbidity of multiple circumstances. Holistic defense also can take care of collateral legal issues such as immigration and civil and family matters.

In order to address the client's legal issues as well as the variety of other circumstances, holistic defense relies on interdisciplinary teams of individuals trained to address the variety of nonlegal issues. These include not only criminal defense lawyers, but social workers, staff with clinical expertise, case managers, and civil, immigration, and family law attorneys, among others. Cross-discipline communication and collaboration is critical in order to coordinate interventions/treatment as well as legal proceedings.

Holistic defense was created as an alternative to doing the business of indigent defense.[49]

> A primary goal of holistic defense is to improve public safety by decreasing crime. This goal can be accomplished by helping citizens to avoid system involvement in the first place, as well as by reducing recidivism and future justice involvement among clients. Mitigating collateral consequences and addressing social service needs are two primary methods through which holistic defenders attempt to prevent recidivism.

The logic is simple and evidence-based. In order to reduce the extraordinarily high recidivism rates we see as a result of current punishment-focused criminal justice policy, we need to identify and address the reasons individuals engage in crime and end up in the criminal justice system. Not only in theory can holistic defense provide advocacy and counsel in legal proceedings, it can also link offenders with local community-based resources to assist with mitigating these criminogenic circumstances. In turn, holistic defense has the potential to save substantial sums of public money by reducing reoffending and reentry into the justice system. One of the early advocates for holistic defense adds that it can also enhance justice.[50]

> Government bears the cost of higher crime, as well as chronic family violence, alcoholism and substance abuse, homelessness, and mental illness. So, any significant moves to address those problems in communities where people cannot seek help easily can significantly reduce costs. The goals of justice, too, are served in the process for those who believe justice is better served by those who provide services, solve problems, and strengthen communities than by those who blindly arrest, prosecute and incarcerate.

In theory, holistic defense makes sense. Advocating not only in the courtroom but also problem-solving the variety of circumstances that indigent defendants typically face seem well designed to reduce the risk of subsequent criminal involvement. The obvious question is what do we know about the effectiveness of holistic defense? Does it work and if so, in what ways?

Research evaluating holistic defense is sparse. It is simply not something that has garnered much attention in the research community. One notable exception is the National Institute of Justice, an agency within the United States Department of Justice, which sponsored a couple of recent evaluations. Here is what we know.

One study by James Anderson, Maya Buenaventura, and Paul Heaton assessed holistic defense outcomes for the Bronx Defenders (a provider of holistic defense) compared to the New York Legal Aid Society (a provider of traditional indigent defense). Anderson and colleagues report that while holistic defense did not impact subsequent criminal justice involvement one year after arraignment, it did reduce the likelihood of incarceration by 16 percent and reduced the sentence length for those who were sentenced to incarceration by 24 percent.[51] The reduction in incarceration was particularly pronounced for drug offenders and those convicted of larceny, where holistic defense reduced incarceration by 63 percent and 72 percent, respectively. Overall, holistic defense resulted in 1.1 million fewer incarceration days and saved New York taxpayers $160 million.

The other study investigated the outcomes of holistic defense in several jurisdictions. Two key findings emerged from this research. Defendants who received holistic defense services reported greater client satisfaction and a greater sense of procedural justice. Moreover, those who were convicted and sentenced to incarceration received a sentence approximately four months shorter than comparison groups.[52]

The research that has been conducted so far has failed to document any effect of holistic defense on subsequent reoffending or criminal justice involvement. This is despite an approach that is designed and intended to "provide services, solve problems, and strengthen communities" rather than "blindly arrest, prosecute and incarcerate."[53]

So, what does this mean regarding holistic defense and indigent defense reform? While the research does not allow a definitive conclusion regarding recidivism, I am not persuaded that it is time to reject it as a valuable approach. There are several reasons for that conclusion.

First, the concept of holistic defense emerged from evidence-based principles that punishment does little to reduce reoffending, but addressing criminogenic circumstances does. It certainly passes the "face validity" test, and there is overwhelming evidence that diversion programs such as drug courts are quite successful at reducing drug relapse and recidivism.

We have seen from decades of evaluation research on criminal justice diversion programs that there can be a substantial gap between design and implementation. For example, not all drug courts are created equal. Some adhere to the evidence-based recommendations quite closely. Others end up with versions that depart in significant ways from the blueprints derived from careful, comprehensive research. The reasons for such departures include funding limitations, lack of expertise, politics, cultural barriers, and less-than-optimal decision-making.

So, the point is that holistic defense efforts may suffer a variety of real-world limitations that force compromises. The most obvious one is funding since wholly inadequate funding is characteristic of indigent defense. There could also be any number of constraints that thwart the proper execution and operation of holistic defense, such as lack of available capacity for mental health or substance-abuse treatment or lack of affordable housing. One thing I have learned from firsthand experience developing and evaluating such diversion programs as problem-solving courts is that any number of circumstances can intervene and frustrate proper execution.

The basic holistic defense model is certainly worth pursuing, with the premise that certain components are absolutely essential, including having the proper clinical expertise for assessing defendants and identifying those criminogenic circumstances that need to be addressed. Both criminal and civil lawyers can certainly provide the necessary legal expertise, but given the often complex, comorbid situations that indigent defendants often have requires professional experts—psychiatrists, psychologists, clinical social workers—who can make appropriate assessments/diagnoses on the clinical side of things. Others can provide assessments and interventions for such things as housing, educational deficits, and employment problems.[54] I will discuss this concept of professional experts assisting decision-making in greater detail in chapter 7.

Prioritizing a client's needs and developing an intervention or treatment plan is essential. For example, the research is clear that attempting to provide substance-abuse treatment for someone who is homeless is far from optimal and will be seriously compromised. Housing is often a critical first step. Thus, it is necessary that someone or a team gets the big picture of needs and develops a logical sequence of interventions.

Another very important consideration is the availability of local resources for addressing these circumstances. Treatment capacity, affordable housing, employment training, and other related assets all require available capacity in a timely manner. It would certainly be counterproductive to determine that a client needs mental health treatment but there is a six-month waiting list to get in to see a psychiatrist. That is an unfortunate reality in many communities in the United States today.

The context and culture within which holistic defense efforts occur is fundamental. In our decidedly adversarial system, the two opposing parties typically have different interests and goals. While there is variation across and within jurisdictions, it is generally fair to say that in many circumstances, prosecutors pursue criminal convictions and punishment and defense counsel typically pursue mitigation of punishment and preservation of due process protections.

How well holistic defense works may very well depend on prosecutors and judges and how they view their roles and responsibilities. While holistic defense is largely the responsibility of defense counsel, its success may very well hinge on the willingness of prosecutors and judges to consider alternatives to business as usual. An expressed agreement by the prosecutor may not be required, but cooperation by the government can facilitate the successful implementation of a holistic defense approach.

Let me illustrate this point by referencing the Harris County (Houston, Texas) Public Defender's Office approach to holistic defense. The Harris County Public Defender defines it in the following way:[55]

> Holistic defense combines aggressive legal advocacy with a broader recognition that for most poor people arrested and charged with a crime, the criminal case is not the only issue with which they struggle. The key insight of holistic defense is that to be truly effective advocates for our clients, we as defenders must broaden the scope of our work to include both the collateral consequences of criminal justice involvement as well as the underlying issues, both legal and non-legal, that have played a part in driving our clients into the criminal justice system in the first place.

In order to accomplish this broader vision of identifying and addressing client needs, public defenders must present to the prosecutor and judge "the charged offense within the context of the client's entire life."[56] In order to be successful and produce the desired effect, the prosecutor and judge need to be willing to consider the client's circumstances and cooperate with defense counsel in order to determine an appropriate resolution to a case.

The point is that holistic defense should not be just the purview of the defense. Rather, accomplishing the goals of holistic defense should reflect the collaboration of all parties in the court system. If the culture of a particular court is tough on crime and conviction and punishment driven, it is difficult to see how a holistic defense approach would be successful. Moreover, if the culture of a court is purely adversarial, where the government's interests and the defense's interests are in direct conflict, it is difficult to see how that could lead to a collaborative resolution.

At the same time, not every case should be a holistic defense case. There are many crimes for which punishment is simply the right thing to do, in the interest of justice, accountability, or retribution. The point is that the use of holistic defense obviously must be selective, just as the process of prosecutors identifying cases as appropriate for diversion is selective.

Holistic defense, or something similar, is a very important step in the direction of meaningful and comprehensive criminal justice reform. It is not the entire picture, but a necessary element in a comprehensive effort to expand the menu of options well beyond the business-as-usual approach of plea and punish. That requires not only innovative defense counsel willing to embrace holistic defense; it also requires prosecutors and judges who share a vision of rethinking the American courtroom, pursuing evidence-based recidivism reduction strategies and increasing the capacity or ability of defendants to become productive members of the community.

NOTES

1. Escobedo v. Illinois, 378 U.S. 478 (1964); Miranda v. Arizona, 384 U.S. 436 (1966); United States v. Wade, 388 U.S. 218 (1967); Coleman v. Alabama, 399 U.S. 1 (1970); Hamilton v. Alabama, 368 U.S. 52 (1961).

2. Gross, "The Right to Counsel but Not the Presence of Counsel: A Survey of State Criminal Procedures for Pre-Trial Release."

3. Gross, "The Right to Counsel but Not the Presence of Counsel: A Survey of State Criminal Procedures for Pre-Trial Release," 831.

4. Gross, "The Right to Counsel but Not the Presence of Counsel: A Survey of State Criminal Procedures for Pre-Trial Release," 865.

5. Gross, "The Right to Counsel but Not the Presence of Counsel: A Survey of State Criminal Procedures for Pre-Trial Release," 881.

6. Justice Programs Office, "Americans' Views on Public Defenders and the Right to Counsel."

7. Justice Programs Office, "Americans' Views on Public Defenders and the Right to Counsel."

8. Constitution Project, "Justice Denied: America's Continuing Neglect of Our Constitutional Right to Counsel, Report of the National Right to Counsel Committee," 7.

9. National Association of Criminal Defense Lawyers, "Minor Crimes, Massive Waste: The Terrible Toll of America's Broken Misdemeanor Courts,"14.

10. Schoneman, "Overworked and Underpaid: America's Public Defender Crisis."

11. Hastings, Associated Press, "Public Defender Offices Are in Crisis."

12. Schoneman, "Overworked and Underpaid: America's Public Defender Crisis."

13. Schoneman, "Overworked and Underpaid: America's Public Defender Crisis."

14. Hager, "One Lawyer. Five Years. 3,802 Cases."

15. Hager, "One Lawyer. Five Years. 3,802 Cases."

16. Satija, "How Judicial Conflicts of Interest Are Denying Poor Texans Their Right to an Effective Attorney."

17. Satija, "How Judicial Conflicts of Interest Are Denying Poor Texans Their Right to an Effective Attorney."

18. Oppel and Patel, "One Lawyer. One Day, 194 Felony Cases."

19. Oppel and Patel, "One Lawyer. One Day, 194 Felony Cases," 14.

20. Hager, "When There's Only One Public Defender in Town."

21. Crime and Justice News, "MO Defender Crisis: 'You're Getting Sliver of an Attorney.'"

22. Oppel and Patel, "One Lawyer. One Day, 194 Felony Cases."

23. Gross, "Gideon at 50: A Three-Part Examination of Indigent Defense in America."

24. Collins, "Potter County Criminal Defense System Is Lambasted in a New Report."

25. Sukhatme and Jenkins, "Pay to Play? Campaign Finance and the Incentive Gap in the Sixth Amendment's Right to Counsel."

26. Sukhatme and Jenkins, "Pay to Play? Campaign Finance and the Incentive Gap in the Sixth Amendment's Right to Counsel," 1.

27. Bayram, "Left Behind: Public Defenders Underpaid, Have Little Oversight."

28. Hager, "One Lawyer. Five Years. 3,802 Cases."

29. Pfaff, "A Mockery of Justice for the Poor."

30. Hanson, "Gideon's Broken Promise: American's Continuing Quest for Equal Justice."

31. Laird, "Starved of Money for Too Long, Public Defenders Are Suing—And Starting to Win," *ABA Journal*, January 1, 2017.

32. Jaffe, "'It's Not You, It's Your Caseload': Using *Cronic* to Solve Indigent Defense Underfunding."

33. National Association for Law Placement, "New Findings on Salaries for Public Interest Attorneys."

34. Brennan Center for Justice, "A Fair Fight: Achieving Indigent Defense Resource Parity."

35. Filter Staff, "Public Defenders are Hugely Overworked—But Also Underpaid Compared with Prosecutors."

36. Shepherd, "Public Defenders Make Far Less Than Prosecutors," *Willamette Week*, October 24, 2018.

37. Loudoun Now, "Loudoun Lawyers Urge Better Pay for Public Defenders."

38. Oliver, "Most Public Defenders in Richmond Make Less Than a Secretary in the Prosecutor's Office. They Want a Raise," *Virginia Mercury*, September 30, 2019.

39. Ujiyediin, "One in Four Kansas Public Defenders Quit Last Year, Leaving Agency 'in Crisis.'"

40. Crime and Justice News, "Miami Prosecutors, Defenders Quit Over Low Pay."

41. Ujiyediin, "One in Four Kansas Public Defenders Quit Last Year."

42. ACLU, "Inadequately Funded Public Defender Services Threaten Criminal Justice System."

43. Hager, "One Lawyer. Five Years. 3,802 Cases."

44. Ford, "A 'Constitutional Crisis' in Missouri."

45. Diane Davis, Ryan Cunningham, and Jason Enox v. State of Nevada; Brian Sandoval, Governor, The First Judicial District Court of the State of Nevada in and for Carson City, Class Action Complaint for Injunctive and Declaratory Relief, 2.

46. Trautman, "The Bill of Rights 'Shouldn't Come with a Bill,'" *The Crime Report*, March 7, 2019.

47. West, "Court Findings of Ineffectiveness of Counsel Claims in Post-Conviction Appeals."

48. Lefstein, National Right to Counsel Committee, American Bar Association, "A Broken Indigent Defense System: Observations and Recommendations of a New National Report."

49. Lee, Ostrom, and Kleiman, "The Measure of Good Lawyering: Evaluating Holistic Defense in Practice," 1230–31.

50. Steinberg, "Beyond Lawyering: How Holistic Representation Makes for Good Policy, Better Lawyers, and More Satisfied Clients," 633.

51. Anderson, Buenaventura, and Heaton, "The Effects of Holistic Defense on Criminal Justice Outcomes"; Anderson, Buenaventura, and Heaton, "Holistic Representation: An Innovative Approach to Defending Poor Clients Can Reduce Incarceration and Save Taxpayer Dollars—Without Harm to Public Safety."

52. Ostrom and Bowman, "Examining the Effectiveness of Indigent Defense Team Services."

53. Steinberg, "Beyond Lawyering: How Holistic Representation Makes for Good Policy, Better Lawyers, and More Satisfied Clients," 633.

54. My colleagues and I have discussed the expertise issue in two recent books—*From Retribution to Public Safety: Disruptive Innovation of American Criminal Justice* (with Robert Pitman and William Streusand) and *Confronting Underground Justice: Reinventing Plea Bargaining for Effective Criminal Justice Reform* (with Robert Pitman).

55. Harris County Public Defender's Office website, Holistic Defense. Retrieved from http://harriscountypublicdefender.org/holistic-defense-2/.

56. Harris County Public Defender's Office website, Holistic Defense. Retrieved from http://harriscountypublicdefender.org/holistic-defense-2/.

6

Rethinking the
Adversarial Approach

The foundation of American criminal jurisprudence is the adversarial system. It is characterized as a theoretical battle of equals, where partisan advocates—the state (represented by the prosecutor) and the defendant (represented most commonly by a public defender or appointed defense counsel)—engage in a struggle that is supposed to result in the discovery of the truth, preservation of the defendant's procedural rights, and justice. While partisan, adversarial proceedings define the American court process, there are advocates and dissenters alike.

As Supreme Court Justice Potter Stewart wrote in *Herring v. New York*, "the very premise of our adversary system of criminal justice is that partisan advocacy on both sides of a case will best promote the ultimate objective that the guilty be convicted and the innocent go free."[1] Or as Justice Handler of the New Jersey Supreme Court put it, "Because we do not know which side truth has taken, we let the sides fight it out . . . In this contest, the truth will out."[2] That is the theory of how our criminal justice system goes about the business of litigating criminal cases. In the real world, things are quite different.

The adversarial system has its critics, and some have been heavyweights in American jurisprudence, including Roscoe Pound, Jerome Frank, and Marvin Frankel, all academics and the latter two federal judges. Pound argued in 1906 before the American Bar Association that adversarial proceedings are based on a "sporting theory of justice" when in reality it was not sporting.[3] In his 1949 book *Courts on Trial*, Jerome Frank saw the adversarial process as a "battle of wits and wiles" and called for the elimination of the "martial spirit" of litigation.[4]

More recently, but still forty years ago, Marvin Frankel in his book *Partisan Justice* laid out his criticisms of the adversarial system.[5]

> Excessive reliance on the adversary process has come to permeate our legal institutions. The fundamental conception of rules of warfare as the route to peace characterizes our approach to both civil and criminal disputes. Our reliance upon adversary premises and techniques has led to an array of disorders and dissatisfactions—from glutted courts to the travesties of plea bargaining to the rituals and endless tinkerings attending the Miranda warnings, and the injustices that result because effective access to justice depends too heavily on the wealth necessary to pay for effective lawyering . . . We have fashioned a regime of individual competitive struggle, freeing the contestants to war against each other, decreeing in large measure that the state or its judicial representative should serve as passive umpire to keep the conflict within broad limits.

Alfred Meyer in the early 1990s describes adversarial proceedings as competitive, contentious, and aggressive, designed to result in zero-sum outcomes where one party wins at the expense of the other.[6] Professor Menkel-Meadow charges that the adversarial system falls short of being the ideal method for discovering the truth—"oppositional presentations of facts in dispute are not the best way for us to learn the truth; polarized debate distorts the truth, leaves out important information, simplifies complexity and obfuscates rather than clarifies."[7]

THE ADVERSARY SYSTEM, DUE PROCESS, FAIRNESS, AND JUSTICE

A hallmark of our adversarial system is procedural fairness or justice, assuring that the proceedings conform to due process requirements set forth in the Constitution and amended by the US Supreme Court. Monroe Freeman, a strong advocate, seems to believe that the promises of the Bill of Rights are fulfilled by our adversarial approach. Freedman concludes: "These rights [presumption of innocence, rights to counsel and confrontation of witnesses, the privilege against self-incrimination] are essential components of the adversary system as it has evolved in American constitutional law."[8] Let's take a closer look at this assertion.

The pressures and constraints on the typical public defender or appointed counsel and the pressures and conflicting interests of prosecutors make ensuring due process often a rather unrealistic goal for indigent defendants who are unable to retain their own lawyers.[9] In their recent book *Rebooting Justice*, Benjamin Barton and Stephanos Bibas describe the day-to-day challenges faced by public defense counsel.[10]

In theory, American criminal justice depends on a contest of equals. In this boxing ring, the defense lawyer is the champion in the defendant's corner. Our adversarial system counts on the defense lawyer to challenge the prosecutor's case vigorously, to test whether a defendant is guilty and what punishment he deserves . . . He must negotiate over a possible plea bargain, stand ready to try a case if needed, and advocate at sentencing . . . All of these steps take time—weeks or days, not just hours. The reality falls far short of this ideal.

While not representative of appointed counsel or public defenders nationwide, a Brennan Center for Justice study illustrates the situation many criminal defendants face. The Brennan Center research found that a court-appointed lawyer on average spends less than six minutes per case in hearings where a defendant pleads guilty and is sentenced.[11]

A prominent critic of the adversarial system questions the ability to achieve fairness given the often extreme inequities in resources.[12]

In litigation, the unequal resources of the parties will often determine the hierarchy of opposition . . . the adversary system clearly contemplates adversaries of equal skill and economic support; the result should not depend on the resources or skill . . . We all know, however, that the "haves" come out ahead.

In 2015, Sen. Charles Grassley (R-IA) stated that governments routinely fail to comply with the provisions of the Sixth Amendment right to counsel for indigent defendants, and innocent defendants plead guilty to crimes and suffer a variety of collateral consequences as a result. Subsequently, Senator Grassley called the first US Senate Judiciary Committee hearings on this matter in May 2015. The Sixth Amendment Center provided testimony at the Judiciary Committee's hearings.[13]

Despite the necessity of competent counsel to fair and equal justice, state and local governments regularly fail their Sixth Amendment duties. Though indigent people accused of felonies have attorneys appointed to their cases more regularly than not, those public attorneys are far too often appointed so late in the court process, or are so financially conflicted, or experience such undue judicial interference, or do not have the legal training/experience to match the complexities of the charges filed, or juggle far too many cases at any one given time (and usually all of the above) that defendants have, in effect, no legal counsel advocating on their behalf.

It is unfortunate that there is relatively little case law that speaks to the quality or competence of representation.

When we consider misdemeanors, the circumstances are particularly troubling since they constitute the vast majority (estimated at 80 percent) of all criminal cases.[14] In many misdemeanor cases, defendants go through the process, from arrest through plea negotiation, conviction and sentencing, not only with overworked public counsel who realistically have little time and resources to devote to defending clients, but often without the assistance and advise of any defense counsel at all.

Under current law, the government is required to provide defense counsel for indigent defendants charged in misdemeanor cases only when the defendant is subject to incarceration upon conviction. This effectively excludes public defense for low-level misdemeanors such as fine-only crimes where statute prohibits jail time as punishment. Even though they are classified as less serious offenses, these fine-only misdemeanors carry significant penalties as well as downstream consequences such as restrictions on employment and housing.

In cases of more serious misdemeanors, which involve potential jail time upon conviction, indigent defense is even more problematic. We lack comprehensive data on how often indigent misdemeanor defendants do not receive assistance of counsel. One study conducted in all twenty circuits in Florida found statewide that less than one-half (45 percent) had a public defender present (13 percent had privately retained counsel). It was worse in the larger metro areas of Miami-Dade County (39 percent had counsel), Jacksonville (32 percent), and Broward–Ft. Lauderdale (24 percent).[15] Alexandra Natapoff has studied the misdemeanor system for years and concludes, "The routine failure to honor the constitutional right to counsel thus explains much of the broader lawlessness and dysfunction of the misdemeanor process. It also means that many misdemeanor defendants must effectively face the court on their own."[16] Testimony before the US Senate Judiciary Committee in 2015 affirms that conclusion—"But the problems of our nation's misdemeanor courts are starker [compared to felony courts]. Many misdemeanor courts simply fail to provide any lawyers at all, despite the constitutional imperative to do so."[17]

A research project conducted by the Constitution Project in collaboration with the National Right to Counsel Committee involved observations in misdemeanor courts in a number of different states. The purpose was to discover common practices regarding access to public defense. In many cases, prosecutors engaged in plea negotiation directly with defendants without counsel, even though they had a right to a lawyer and had not actually given up that right. In some courts, judges required defendants to talk with prosecutors before they would appoint counsel for indigent defendants.[18]

Our adversarial approach for the processing of criminal cases is premised on fairness and due process. The goal is to find the truth and do it in a way that preserves defendants' constitutional and procedural rights. The result is a fair, just outcome.

Consider Professor Freeman again. He claims, as do many other advocates of the adversary system, that "these rights are also included in the broad and fundamental concept that no person may be deprived of life, liberty or property without due process of law—a concept which itself has been substantially equated with the adversary system."[19]

It seems that Freedman and others who hold the adversarial system in high regard are not aware that: 1) 80 percent of criminal defendants are indigent and if they get a lawyer, he or she is a public defender or appointed counsel; 2) there is a very serious, chronic crisis in the public defense systems in this country that substantially impedes the ability to provide proper representation; 3) 97 percent of criminal convictions are based on a negotiated plea, precluding the right to trial, the right to confront and examine witnesses, and proving guilt beyond a reasonable doubt; and 4) there are a number of ways that prosecutors can persuade, convince, and compel a defendant to agree to a plea deal, including charge stacking, the trial penalty, and pretrial detention, among many others.[20]

As even the casual observer must conclude, the day-to-day reality of what happens in America's criminal courts is a far cry from what the architects probably envisioned. It is certainly not a level playing field for the vast majority of felony and misdemeanor defendants. If we ignore outcomes for a moment and just focus on process, one would conclude it probably is relatively expedient and efficient, but the same observer would be hard-pressed to call it fair and just.[21] Simply contrast the power and resources of the prosecutor against the deficient funding and lack of resources of public defense, and the adversarial process is anything but a fair fight.

If one is not compelled by the lack of fairness and due process in our adversarial system, or the problematic justice it routinely delivers, consider the relationship between our adversarial approach and the dysfunctions of the criminal justice system. The point is simple—I contend that the failures of the American criminal justice system, exemplified by extraordinarily high recidivism, are, to a significant degree, a direct result of our adversarial process. Let me explain.

THE ADVERSARIAL PROCESS EXPEDITES CASE DISPOSITION

The overburdened criminal courts have been written about many, many times. Excessive caseloads for prosecutors, excessive caseloads and lack of funding for collateral activities for public defense lawyers, and the excessive dockets that judges must manage require systems that permit or facilitate the quick, efficient processing of cases. Plea negotiation is one example of a mechanism that fast-tracks cases to conviction and sentencing.[22] So is the adversarial system.

The adversarial approach to the disposition of criminal cases tends to promote relatively simple, binary reasoning and decision-making, such as conviction versus acquittal and freedom versus incarceration.[23] This type of decision-making facilitates the efficient operation of the criminal court system by focusing the activities of the prosecution and defense on just a couple of questions—guilty of what and how much punishment.

The adversarial model clearly defines the roles and interests of the key players—the prosecutor is the partisan who is responsible for the interests of the government, the defense lawyer is the partisan responsible for the defendant's interests, and the judge is responsible for the interests of due process and keeping cases moving. Clearly defined roles and interests, and generally binary, guilty–not guilty decision-making, help keep things simple and in turn, moving pretty quickly. That is especially true when combined with plea negotiation. Whether it's charge bargaining (dismissing charges or downgrading charges) or sentence bargaining (either a sentence embedded in the plea deal or a promise to recommend an agreed-upon sentence), the issues are rather straightforward. I suggest that the adversarial process and plea negotiation go hand in hand in allowing the criminal courts to expediently proceed with the business of disposing of cases. However, there are bigger-picture consequences of the adversarial system and expedited case processing that go to the heart of the dysfunction of the American criminal justice system.

THE ADVERSARIAL PROCESS SUBSTANTIALLY CONTRIBUTES TO THE DYSFUNCTION OF THE CRIMINAL COURTS AND THE CRIMINAL JUSTICE SYSTEM

Eric Fish is a federal public defender with a PhD and JD from Yale University. He has written a very influential article titled "Against Adversary Prosecution."[24] Fish argues that the adversarial system logically focuses prosecutors' attention on winning, which means obtaining criminal convictions.[25]

> Prosecutors as well as the general public see the criminal justice system as an adversarial contest between two sides. The government wins this contest if the defendant is convicted and punished. The government loses if the defendant is acquitted or the conviction is later vacated.

This view of prosecutors as pursuing convictions is common in the literature on American prosecutors.[26] It is also a perspective that was supported by the interviews Robert Pitman and I conducted with public defenders for our recent book *Confronting Underground Justice*.[27]

Fish goes on to explain why prosecutors typically are conviction-driven. The incentives include electoral politics, where tough-on-crime District Attorneys have to fulfill their campaign promises by prioritizing criminal convictions and tough sentences, and the generally competitive culture of prosecutors' offices. I would add to this the idea that crime and punishment is the currency of the American prosecutor. Their job is to enforce the law and what they know about that, what they are taught, is charging, convicting, and punishing, all in a competitive, partisan setting.

This rather narrow role of the typical prosecutor is clearly portrayed by the responses I referenced in chapter 4 to interviews conducted with prosecutors in our book *Confronting Underground Justice*. We asked prosecutors what they believe their role is in terms of reducing recidivism. By far, the most common answer was "none" or "it's not my job." Several prosecutors we interviewed believe that it is out of their hands and is all up to the offender. A few prosecutors said that they do play a role in reducing recidivism and the tool they have for doing that is punishment. We also asked what it would take to reduce recidivism (other than punishment), and the vast majority responded "I have no idea" or something similar.

While there is variation in how prosecutors think about and go about the business of prosecution, they typically see their roles pretty clearly and narrowly defined in terms of law enforcement, criminal charging, indictment, conviction, and punishment. This is what they are socialized to do and this is what is reinforced in the day-to-day administration of most prosecutors' offices. This rather narrow law enforcement role for prosecutors is supported by the interviews referenced above. Typical answers to the question "How do you think of your job as a prosecutor, what are your primary responsibilities?" include:

"I enforce the criminal laws . . . if someone is accused of a crime we convict if there's enough evidence. If we believe they're innocent, then we dismiss the case."

"I enforce the law."

"My job is to impose consequences on people for their criminal choices."

"My job is to prosecute the cases that are presented by a police department and get indicted by a grand jury."

"We look at what they [defendants] do and figure if they should go to jail or not."

"I determine who is guilty and then impose the right punishment."

Not only does the adversarial process declare partisan victory as the ultimate outcome, it also defines what victory looks like—conviction and punishment for the prosecutor, and acquittal, charge reduction, charge dismissal, and/or reduction in sentence for the defense. Unfortunately, there appears to be relatively little in the day-to-day administration of the adversarial process that promotes looking beyond partisan victory and how success is defined in the context of the adjudication of criminal cases.

PROBLEMS CREATED BY THE ADVERSARIAL PROCESS

Where does all of this leave us? There are several points to make here. First, there are very serious due process, fairness, and justice concerns with the adversarial process and the collateral circumstances discussed above, issues such as critical underfunding of public defense. As Eric Fish tells us, "the powerful cultural and professional forces that push prosecutors to seek convictions and harsh punishments, causes adversarialism to dominate American prosecution. Often values like due process get pushed aside in the zeal for a conviction."[28] In essence, the adversarial role of the prosecutor takes priority over the prosecutor's other role of seeking justice and preserving the rights of defendants. Do we really think the promises of the Bill of Rights are being fulfilled?

Second, I suggest that the emphasis on quick processing of criminal cases, combined with the fact that the key decision makers in the criminal courts—prosecutors, public defenders/appointed counsel, and judges— all share the common interest in moving cases quickly, requires the courts to rely heavily on plea negotiation and the adversarial framework of decision-making. That, in turn, reinforces the norms of prosecution, conviction, and punishment.

Third, the adversarial process promotes tough-on-crime policies by reinforcing the driving forces of conviction and harsh punishment. The simplicity of adversarial plea negotiation reduces everything to how much harm was done in the commission of the instant offense and prior crimes, and how much harm should the government impose on the defendant. We know from many, many sources that harsh punishment does not change behavior and thus does not effectively reduce crime and recidivism.

CONSEQUENCES AND FAILURES

However, there is more to a reconsideration of the adversarial system. Conflict does not beget collaboration. Competition is not conducive for problem solving. Winning, defined as conviction and punishment, comes at the expense of collaboration, problem solving, and recidivism-focused alternatives to case resolution. In other words, the pressures on the courts and the priorities of the officials working in the courts as reinforced by the adversarial process keep us entrenched in moving cases and doling out tough punishment, with neither the time nor the inclination to think differently about criminality, criminal offenders, and reducing recidivism. That thinking tends to dominate all aspects of the disposition of criminal cases, including the very common process of plea negotiation.[29]

> Even if some form of the adversary system was defensible in particular settings for purposes of adjudication, the adversary model employed in the courtroom has bled inappropriately into and infected other aspects of lawyering including negotiations . . . we need to examine why this one mode of dispute resolution [the adversarial system] still so thoroughly dominates our thinking about legal problem solving.

The adversarial process values victory, and that is defined in terms of criminal conviction and criminal sentencing, not as much in terms of diversion and rehabilitation. The focus is generally on crime and punishment and much less on psychiatry, psychology, public health, neuroscience, addiction medicine, or all of the other resources and expertise for addressing educational, vocational, housing, poverty, and other deficits, disadvantages, and criminogenic circumstances that are so characteristic of many criminal offenders.

It is my belief that the adversarial system for adjudicating criminal cases is largely a failure, and a failure on several fronts. First, it does not function to promote due process and justice. Second, it facilitates quick, assembly-line justice. Combined with plea negotiation, we have the two necessary elements that allow the criminal courts to remain open. It seems that we have been satisfied if courts can conduct business. But I see it a bit like the sausage analogy regarding the legislative process. Don't look too closely.

A related failure, and in my mind the most important, is that the adversarial process imposes blinders on the court (meaning prosecutors, defense counsel, and judges) that discourage considering alternatives to traditional conviction and punishment. Yes, there certainly are exceptions to this. We have a variety of diversion programs, such as drug courts and deferred adjudication, but let's be clear, these opportunities for alternative disposition are by far the exception. For example, the three thousand or so drug courts in the United States today have the capacity to meet about 10 percent of the need or demand.[30]

By directing attention to crime and punishment, the adversarial system keeps the engine of the criminal justice system laser-focused on conviction and punishment. What gets lost is thinking differently about crime and punishment. What gets lost is problem solving beyond the very

limited tools of punishment. What gets lost is collaboration and cooperation. What gets lost is consideration of the circumstances that bring individual offenders to the justice system.

Therein lies the dysfunctionality of the adversarial system. It simply
fails to fulfill the mission of our criminal justice system, which is public
safety.

Now, how do we fix this? I will briefly outline what I believe needs to
change and then will expand on it in the next chapter, where I put the
various pieces of criminal court reform together. Very simply, I believe
there is good reason to eliminate the adversarial process for large numbers (probably the majority) of criminal cases. In its place, we need to
develop a system that is focused on individuals and their circumstances,
understanding what brings a particular individual into the justice system.
That requires problem solving and collaboration. It also requires appreciating that many criminal offenders enter the criminal justice system with
rather complex circumstances and comorbidities. That in turn requires
expertise that we do not currently have in the court system.

The questions we should be asking in most cases, rather than what will
Johnny plea to and how much punishment does he deserve, is what will
it take to significantly reduce the likelihood Johnny will reoffend? The
criminal courts in this country are generally not in a position to answer
that question accurately. What I propose is rethinking the structure, function, goals, objectives, and culture of the criminal courts so that question
is the most consequential we can ask.

NOTES

1. Herring v. New York, 422 U.S. 853, 862 (1975).
2. Quoted in Meyer, "To Adjudicate or Mediate," 369.
3. Quoted in Meyer, "To Adjudicate or Mediate," 365.
4. Quoted in Meyer, "To Adjudicate or Mediate," 366.
5. Frankel, *Partisan Justice*, 86, 11; Quoted in Meyer, "To Adjudicate or Mediate," 366.
6. Meyer, "To Adjudicate or Mediate."
7. Menkel-Meadow, "The Trouble with the Adversary System in a Postmodern, Multicultural World," 6.
8. Freedman, "Our Constitutionalized Adversary System," 62.
9. Lynch, "Our Administrative System of Criminal Justice."
10. Barton and Bibas, *Rebooting Justice: More Technology, Fewer Lawyers, and the
Future of Law*, 20–21.
11. Cohen, "How Americans Lost the Right to Counsel."
12. Menkel-Meadow, "The Trouble with the Adversary System in a Postmodern, Multicultural World," 22–23.

13. Sixth Amendment Center, "Actual Denial of Counsel in Misdemeanor Courts," Testimony to the United States Judiciary Committee, May 20, 2015.

14. Alexandra Natapoff interview with Terry Gross, "*Punishment without Crime* Highlights the Injustice of America's Misdemeanor System," January 2, 2019, National Public Radio.

15. Equal Justice Initiative, "Thousands in Florida Face Misdemeanor Charges without a Lawyer."

16. Natapoff, *Punishment without Crime*, 79–80.

17. Carrol, Sixth Amendment Center, "Why Our Misdemeanor Courts Are Filled with Uncounselled Defendants."

18. Hanlon, Harvey, and Lefstein, "Denial of the Right to Counsel in Misdemeanor Cases: Court Watching in Nashville Tennessee"; The Constitution Project, "Justice Denied: America's Continuing Neglect of Our Constitutional Right to Counsel."

19. Freedman, "Our Constitutional Adversary System," 57.

20. See Kelly and Pitman, *Confronting Underground Justice*.

21. See Wilets and Imoukhuede, "A Critique of the Uniquely Adversarial Nature of the U.S. Legal, Economic and Political System and Its Implications for Reinforcing Existing Power Hierarchies."

22. See Kelly and Pitman, *Confronting Underground Justice*.

23. Menkel-Meadow, "The Trouble with the Adversary System in a Postmodern, Multicultural World."

24. Fish, "Against Adversary Prosecution."

25. Fish, "Against Adversary Prosecution," 1419–21.

26. Fish, "Against Adversary Prosecution," 1419.

27. Kelly and Pitman, *Confronting Underground Justice*.

28. Fish, "Against Adversary Prosecution," 1422.

29. Menkel-Meadow, "The Trouble with the Adversary System in a Postmodern, Multicultural World," 7, 25.

30. Kelly, *The Future of Crime and Punishment*; Kelly, Pitman, and Streusand, *From Retribution to Public Safety*.

7

Putting the Pieces Together
Fundamental Pretrial and Court Reform

There is certainly no shortage of serious problems with the American criminal justice system. Police use of force, profiling, and racial bias are front and center in the moment (September 2020). Mass incarceration and racial and ethnic disparities throughout the justice system continue to be the focus of many justice reform advocates and organizations.

The fact that this book is not directly about policing or mass incarceration does not mean they are somehow less important than what I focus on here. The very front end (policing) and the back end (corrections, reentry) are in critical need of substantial evidence-based reform. At the same time, it seems to me that what happens between the point of arrest and sentencing is profoundly consequential and accounts for a substantial amount of the dysfunction of American criminal justice.

It is now time to turn to solutions. What I hope to do in this chapter is lay out what I believe are key components of effective reform of the court system. As I asserted early on, it seems to me that much of what is wrong has to do with decision-making. That will be the guiding principle here.

It may be obvious by now that I have some clear, evidence-informed priorities when it comes to comprehensive criminal justice reform. The goals, among others, are to reduce recidivism and victimization, reduce inequality and racial disparities, release individuals from custody or supervision in better condition than when they went in, and increase cost effectiveness.

How we achieve these goals is a monumental enterprise. In 2016, the US criminal justice system employed more than 2.1 million people and spent $240 billion.[1] The scale is sobering. By way of comparison, Walmart is currently the largest corporation in the United States, with 2.2 million employees and 4,756 stores. Its net worth is estimated at $515 billion.

Much attention is currently focused on prosecutors, premised on the observation that prosecutors are the most powerful actors in the US criminal justice system, and fueled by the recent election of significant numbers of progressive or reform-minded chief prosecutors. The logic is compelling.[2]

> Because prosecutors stand at the gateway to the criminal justice system, mediating between the police and the courts, and because they are vested with such wide discretion, they are able to redirect the energies of the criminal justice system, to recalibrate its severity, and to change its tactics. They can make these changes rapidly, in individual cases or at the wholesale level. Prosecutors can tailor charges, plea offers and sentencing recommendations to particular defendants. They can go further and offer to defer criminal prosecution altogether . . . by aggregating many such decisions, or by adopting explicit policies to guide their discretion, prosecutors can steer the entire criminal justice system in new directions.

This thinking is also enshrined in judicial decisions. For example, in *Cheney v. United States District Court for the District of Columbia*, the federal court held that there is an expectation that prosecutors use their discretion for goals other than punishment: "the rigors of the penal system are mitigated by the responsible exercise of prosecutorial discretion."[3]

I agree that prosecutors play a central role in this, but I believe that it does not stop with prosecutors, nor do I think we should expect prosecutors to go it alone. What I hope to convey in this concluding chapter is a broader, more ambitious agenda for fundamentally changing how we administer criminal justice, what outcomes it produces, and how it can lower costs.

Before we begin, let me reiterate one important clarification. American criminal justice consists of several layers of government—a self-contained federal system (which I do not discuss here), fifty states, and more than 3,100 local jurisdictions. While all participate in the administration of criminal justice in a variety of ways, most of criminal justice is local. More than 52 percent of total direct criminal justice expenditures are incurred by local government, compared to 18 percent by the federal government and 31 percent by state government. Much of that is law enforcement, but local jurisdictions also spend more on the court and pretrial systems than state governments.[4] Moreover, local jurisdictions employ considerably more (nearly 60 percent) of all individuals employed in the criminal justice system.[5]

State legislatures play a critical role in a variety of activities, such as creating the criminal code that delineates all state crimes, defining proper criminal procedure, setting sentencing procedures and laws, and funding and operating prisons and parole. While all of these statutes, regulations, and policy decisions shape the nature of criminal justice in each state, I am effectively sidestepping an extensive discussion of what needs to change at the state level in order to achieve effective justice reform. Certainly, sentencing laws need to change as they are historically a primary vehicle for imprisoning more and more people, especially people of color, for longer periods of time. Parole laws and policies need to change as well since restrictions on early release have increased time served in prison and revocation of parole is a common way of reincarcerating those who have been released, often for what are called technical violations. How we operate prisons is in drastic need of fundamental change. It is no coincidence that Norway's recidivism rate is 20 percent when one takes a look at how they approach incarceration (in Norway, essentially everything that is done when someone is incarcerated is designed to prepare that person for release to a productive, crime-free life without harsh punishment).

The point is there is much to be done at the legislative level to facilitate fundamental change. However, at the end of the day, I believe it is critical to put more of our effort at the local level, especially the pretrial/court systems, where the most consequential decisions are made.

PROSECUTORS: RECENT RECOMMENDATIONS FOR REFORM

There is no shortage of advice (I certainly plead guilty!) for how prosecutors and prosecution should change. Three very recent articles cover a good bit of the reform terrain: "A Vision for the Modern Prosecutor" (produced by the Executive Session of the Institute for Innovation in Prosecution at John Jay College, which includes a number of progressive prosecutors as signatories), "21 Principles for the 21st Century Prosecutor" (by Fair and Just Prosecution, the Brennan Center for Justice, and the Justice Collaborative), and "Prosecutors, Democracy and Justice: Holding Prosecutors Accountable" (by Jeremy Travis, Carter Stewart, and Allison Goldberg).

The recommendations made in these three articles include a variety of changes. One ("A Vision for the Modern Prosecutor") emphasizes rethinking conceptions of justice (away from case processing and the going rate of punishment and toward a consideration of a variety of outcomes that are just), modes of operation (taking a proactive role in effecting change), the culture of the office (by thinking less in terms of us versus them and more collaboratively to understand and address the complex situations of offenders), and performance, including expanding measures of success such as public safety. The authors of "Prosecutors, Democracy, and Justice" recommend broader, more aggressive changes. Their own words are compelling.[6]

> The tangible impact on peoples' daily lives drives a dissatisfaction with incremental reform and a call for deep, tangible change. Today's criminal justice reform movement is more than a series of policy suggestions, or a catalogue of demands, or a simple criticism of the status quo. The movement is powered by a set of big ideas, grounded in a deep critique of our history and elevated by an expectation for a fundamentally different approach to justice.

They then concentrate on reinventing the role of the reform prosecutor, especially the leadership role, including being a leader in the profession, among criminal justice stakeholders and in the public sphere. Next, Travis, Stewart, and Goldberg illustrate how the use of prosecutorial discretion is affecting changes to charging decisions, bail and pretrial detention recommendations, plea negotiation, sentencing recommendations, and, finally, post-sentence reviews (also known as conviction integrity). Finally, they emphasize that the District Attorney is a CEO, responsible for establishing policies to accomplish reform, driving culture change within the office, and developing metrics for measuring progress. A particularly important role they note is that of the leader of criminal justice reform. There are many examples of reform prosecutors who have taken that mantle and been quite vocal on the local, state, and national stages promoting fundamental reform. These include Dan Satterberg (Seattle), Kim Foxx (Chicago), Kim Ogg (Houston), John Creuzot (Dallas), Mark Gonzalez (Corpus Christi, Texas), John Chisholm (Milwaukee), Beth McCann (Denver), and Scott Colom (16th District, Mississippi), among others.

The third article, "21 Principles for the 21st Century Prosecutor," recommends a series of both general and specific reforms that are aimed at reducing incarceration and increasing fairness. Those targeting incarceration include increasing diversion, expanding pretrial release, treating mental illness and substance-use disorders, exercising restraint in charging decisions, negotiating plea deals fairly (something Judge Pitman and I discuss extensively in *Confronting Underground Justice*), appreciating the important differences of juveniles compared to adults and acting accordingly, minimizing the prosecution of misdemeanors, especially those associated with poverty, mental illness, and homelessness, and promoting restorative justice. Enhancing fairness involves changing the office culture, reducing racial disparities, effectively reviewing convictions and sentences, holding police accountable for misconduct, broadening discovery rules (providing the state's evidence to the defendant), expunging and sealing criminal records, and using forensic evidence fairly, among others.

Collectively, these three sets of reform recommendations cover quite a bit of ground. There is a great deal of overlap with my thinking about the roles, responsibilities, and expectations of prosecutors and broadening the scope of their work so that success is defined as reducing recidivism and enhancing public safety. Crime prevention is a foreign concept to many traditional prosecutors, but it is absolutely key to proactive justice reform. Minimizing the criminogenic impact of the criminal justice system while preserving public safety should be a guiding principle moving forward. Diversion is essential, but it is only one piece of a much bigger effort. Leadership is fundamental for successful reform. Because of their position in the justice system, their relative power, and their visibility, prosecutors are in a position to take the lead in setting policy, collaborating with other policy makers and justice officials, bridging divides in local criminal justice, serving as opinion leaders, and garnering public support for fundamental change. Navigating local politics will also require the DA's attention.

SHORTCOMINGS OF RECENT REFORM RECOMMENDATIONS

While the reforms that have been set forward by a variety of experts and organizations are, in my mind, very much on target, I believe they miss a few very essential points. One is that the nature of the decisions they make requires expertise that is in short supply in the typical court system. Prosecutors are lawyers. They are trained as lawyers and they generally think like lawyers. They know the law and criminal procedure. Some recently elected progressive DAs come from prosecution backgrounds and some come from criminal defense backgrounds. Nevertheless, they are lawyers. That is what they know.

But the criminal justice reforms that are proposed and are being implemented, especially those targeted in the prosecutor's office, take us far outside the realm of the law. Criminal justice reform involves critical decisions regarding such things as mental health, addiction and substance-use disorders, trauma, neurodevelopmental and neurocognitive impairments, the impacts of poverty, and a variety of other disorders, deficits, and impairments that are implicated in criminal offending. While those decisions generally fall within the prosecutor's purview, they are admittedly outside their areas of expertise.[7] The same holds for judges and defense attorneys. As we move away from the quick-and-simple convict-and-sentence mentality, the issues at hand and the decision-making become much more complex.

The point is that prosecutors cannot develop, implement, manage, and evaluate reform alone. The tasks that lie before them are extraordinary, requiring not quite a 180-degree change, but close to it. The goal is to balance public safety with behavioral change, putting some offenders in prison (for public safety, justice, retributive, and/or accountability reasons), managing risk and diverting many to programming designed to address the reasons for their criminality, and dismissing charges against others.

There are a variety of circumstances—such as offenders with complex disorders, impairments, and deficits; lack of appropriate clinical and other professional expertise, time, and resource pressures; and a bias toward shortcut, nonanalytical, emotion-based decisions—that conspire to perpetuate problematic decision-making by key individuals in the court system. The perceived need to focus on expedient case processing, rather than careful, analytical, evidence-informed problem solving is a key example of that. It is unfortunate that in many jurisdictions we have the perfect combination of offenders with serious behavioral health disorders and impairments and a pretrial system that does little to mitigate those circumstances and a good bit to aggravate them.

Moreover, prosecutors, and many judges as well, rarely see the consequences or outcomes of the decisions they make. They may not be aware of the short- and longer-term results of pretrial detention, plea deals, convictions, sentencing recommendations and sentences, and collateral consequences of all of these decisions on recidivism, for example. As one expert on prosecutorial decision-making puts it, many prosecutors "fly blind." Flying blind refers to the tendency for many prosecutors to be rather unaware of the bigger-picture operation of the criminal justice system, such as crime rates, court processing, and local concerns about crime.[8] This lack of feedback, metrics, and analysis may keep prosecutors from being aware of system dysfunctionalities and alternatives to business as usual.

IMPROVING DECISION-MAKING

Assuming the ultimate goal is to promote public safety, reduce recidivism, and enhance fairness, equity, and justice, an important step in that direction may be providing decision makers with relevant expertise. In *From Retribution to Public Safety*, a book I wrote with Hon. Robert Pitman, a US District Judge, and Dr. William Streusand, a psychiatrist, we made a case for moving away from anger-based, retributive, punishment-focused thinking about crime to a behavioral change model based on detailed analysis of the complex circumstances that are associated with criminality. One of our recommendations is to create panels of clinical and behavioral experts who screen and assess offenders early on in the pretrial phase and advise prosecutors, judges, and defense counsel about an informed path forward for managing and reducing risk of reoffending. The point is to make recommendations to prosecutors regarding alternatives to prosecution, supervision, diversion to treatment, and release/detention decisions, among others. Our logic is that giving court officers a clinically or professionally informed assessment—similar to what many jurisdictions do regarding the psychiatric assessment of defendants for competency—will allow them to consider clinical recommendations and make better decisions about longer-term outcomes.

The goal is to promote analytical problem solving over case processing and intuitive, shortcut decision-making, to identify key reasons for an individual's criminality and develop intervention plans to mitigate those circumstances. This requires, among other things, an environment of cooperation and collaboration. It also requires an ambitious scaling up.

Much of what I am proposing is aspirational. There are dozens of progressive or reform-oriented DAs in office across the country, and what they are doing is largely aligned with evidence-based practices. However, what they have accomplished to date is limited. Frustration with some of the efforts is understandable. Many candidates promised to end mass incarceration, and they have come up short. In some cases, they have not delivered on even their more limited campaign promises.[9]

I do not mean this as a criticism. Rather, there are clear realities about making such changes. I believe that a fair takeaway from the interviews for this book is that few reform prosecutors have the funding necessary to meet the goals of their efforts. In fact, it is reasonable to conclude that the goals of many of these reform efforts are toned down by the realities of funding. Also, these efforts involve many moving parts, many other entities and individuals that need to be on board, and reallocation of resources. Moreover, regardless of how ambitious the agenda, change is incremental.

At the same time, we find ourselves in an unusual political climate—on the eve of the 2020 national election, with Trump claiming to be the law-and-order candidate and Biden the reform candidate, and the widespread protests and demands for criminal justice reform. The time may be right for moving beyond piecemeal change. Time will tell.

INDIGENT DEFENSE

The poor are punished in the criminal justice system in so many ways, including pretrial detention because bail is set too high, lack of options for diversion to treatment, and insufficient or absent representation of defense counsel. What this helps to create is the poor cycling in and out of the revolving door of American criminal justice.

There are two extraordinarily ambitious recommendations for indigent defense. One is putting the shameful underfunding of indigent defense—a profound violation of the spirit of the Sixth Amendment—in the past. The challenge is that much of that funding is another burden on local jurisdictions. It is time for states to acknowledge their responsibility in assuring that indigent defendants in their state receive more than three or four minutes of counsel.

The second recommendation goes directly to the ultimate objective of this book—effectively lowering recidivism. Reducing reoffending is not just the responsibility of judges and prosecutors. Rather, criminal defense can and should play a lead role in accomplishing the goals of criminal justice.

The wholesale embrace of holistic defense should be a primary element of the practice of criminal defense. Holistic defense is consistent with and complements the other recommendations herein, especially the focus on identifying and addressing the circumstances underlying someone's criminality, in turn reducing the likelihood of subsequent criminal justice involvement.

THE ADVERSARY APPROACH

Another consideration largely absent in discussions of reform that I believe can be essential for success is changing the context or environment in which deliberation, problem solving, and decision-making occur. I tried to make a case in chapter 6 for how the adversarial system promotes conflict, lack of collaboration, and a focus on winning. The adversarial approach, in effect, sets the stage, which in turn governs how things play out.

John Chisholm is a very dedicated reform District Attorney in Milwaukee County, Wisconsin. I believe this quote really nails the problem with the adversarial system.[10]

> I can't overstate how Milwaukee has benefitted from the culture of collaboration we have developed with our defense bar. In most other places, the system is locked in an adversarial mode and primacy is placed on the adjudication of cases. Don't get me wrong. Trade craft is important and skilled attorneys are essential to our form of justice. But the emphasis on solving problems strictly through adjudication blinds us to a wealth of information that is true evidence. We've restricted ourselves to legal evidence for too long and forced our brains to ignore other things that are powerful evidence, whether in medicine or social sciences. Prosecutors might think: "Yeah, that

makes sense, but I can't use that idea to charge someone or not. It only matters whether I can prove the case beyond a reasonable doubt." That thinking limits us.

Professor Eric Luna, another well-known expert on prosecutors, has his own concern about the adversarial system.[11]

> prosecutors are participants in America's unique form of adversarialism, where the belligerence can foster an ends-justify-the-means mentality . . . As advocates in a sometimes brutal partisan process . . . prosecutors marshal evidence and arguments in support of a conviction and sentence.

My thinking is that an adversarial setting certainly is appropriate for criminal prosecution if the questions are guilt or innocence and how much punishment, but it does not seem to be a proper environment for collaboration and problem solving.

The model I have in mind is one that is able to differentiate between those who should be criminally prosecuted (for example, violent offenders, habitual offenders, and others who simply need to be separated from society) and who is appropriate for a different approach. That different approach includes, among other things, a nonadversarial, collaborative, problem-solving setting where the goal is to utilize a broader array of information and expertise. "Winning" in this alternative setting is doing what is necessary to reduce the likelihood one reoffends by addressing key criminogenic circumstances.

It is my thinking that this nonadversarial setting is the proper venue for the expert panels to provide evidence and recommendations to prosecutors, judges, and defense counsel, who in turn collaboratively make a determination regarding the best path forward on a case-by-case basis. What is required, among many other things, is a better job of sorting who belongs in the adversarial/criminal prosecution setting and who belongs in the other collaborative diversion approach. On top of that, obviously, is the need for adequate community resources, such as treatment capacity for mental illness and substance abuse, affordable, supportive housing, and employment training, among others.

ARREST, BAIL, AND PRETRIAL DETENTION

As I mentioned earlier, one of the more consequential components of criminal justice reform is the very front of the pretrial system, especially pretrial detention and bail. Eliminating money bail, reducing pretrial detention, and increasing cite and release by the police are increasingly on the agendas of local reform advocates. It is important to note that recent research shows that the public is very strongly in support of these changes.[12]

The vast majority of Americans (83 percent) who were polled in 2018 believe that police should cite and release rather than arrest and detain individuals accused of nonviolent crimes. Two-thirds believe that individuals accused of minor crimes that are driven by mental illness and/or addiction should not be arrested, but should be referred to treatment. Eighty percent do not think people accused of minor crimes such as criminal trespass and public intoxication should be detained pretrial. Moreover, large majorities think people accused more broadly of misdemeanors and nonviolent crimes should be released from jail before trial. While most believe violent offenders should be detained, they do see exceptions for lower-level violent crimes such as a bar fight.

Nearly 60 percent of Americans surveyed do not believe that money bail keeps communities safe since being detained has more to do with how much money someone does or does not have, rather than risk to the community. Finally, two-thirds of those surveyed would like to see less money spent on jails and more money spent on mental illness and substance-abuse treatment.

It is very important that local criminal justice leaders, including law enforcement, prosecutors, judges, and defense counsel, expand the number and types of suspected offenses for which offenders can be issued a citation rather than being arrested. That initial decision to arrest or release is a pivotal point in the pretrial system, whereby suspects can avoid or incur a variety of collateral consequences that significantly increase the likelihood of recidivism.

Pre-arrest diversion is also a fundamentally important component of an effective pretrial system. How many times do experts have to keep repeating that arresting, detaining, and criminally prosecuting disordered individuals (meaning mentally ill, addicted, those with neurodevelopmental or neurocognitive impairments) is, in many circumstances, counterproductive. The criminal justice system is simply not the place for many if not most of these individuals. The Law Enforcement Assisted Diversion program, or LEAD, in Seattle is but one example of a very effective pre-arrest diversion program that other jurisdictions can modify as necessary and emulate. By the way, it was developed in collaboration with Dan Satterberg, the Seattle District Attorney.

For those who are arrested, validated risk-assessment instruments are a significant step forward for making informed decisions about detention or release. Judges and prosecutors, and for that matter defense counsel, will benefit from having a statistical tool for estimating an offender's risk. However, risk assessments alone will not provide all of the information necessary to effectively determine who should be detained, who should be diverted to services, or what conditions should be imposed for supervised release. The panel of clinical experts can provide a much broader array of evidence and recommendations that can dramatically enhance the quality of decision-making at this early point in the pretrial process. This information can help manage the risk to public safety, avoid unnecessary and detrimental detention, inform the conditions of pretrial supervision, and direct individuals to available support services such as housing and mental health treatment. Obviously, a critical piece of this is whether support services are available.

Courts have essentially four primary pretrial status options for individuals who are arrested—detention, release on bail, release on recognizance, and supervision. We need to end unnecessary detention and use of money bail. If bail is absolutely necessary, it should be set based on ability to pay, so we can end the long-term pattern of detention of the poor. In lieu of bail, something as simple as a reminder system for court appearances has been shown to be highly effective for individuals on pretrial release.

A worthwhile policy to consider is that in lieu of unnecessary detention and excessive use of bail, jurisdictions develop robust and effective pretrial supervision, diversion, and pretrial programs and services. Pretrial supervision can be used to manage the risk of reoffending, assure compliance with conditions, and reduce failure to appear, as well as serve as an intercept point to treatment and services. However, there is much to be done to effectively develop appropriate pretrial supervision systems. In many jurisdictions they are essentially nonexistent, and in others, they are underdeveloped.

There are pretrial supervision programs that can serve as models for jurisdictions to adopt. The King County (Brooklyn) New York Supervised Release program was developed[13]

> to minimize failures to appear in court, reduce reliance on pretrial detention due to an inability to afford money bail, minimize the potential collateral consequences of incarceration on defendants and their families, and enhance participant perceptions of fairness in the justice system.

The King County program targets misdemeanor defendants who cannot afford a low bail amount. In collaboration with judges, prosecutors, and defense attorneys, the program closely monitors defendants to assure they make scheduled appearances. Defendants also receive individual case management as well as referrals to community-based services. An evaluation conducted by the Center for Court Innovation found, compared to a control group, that program participants had many fewer days in detention (four days versus twenty-six days), a slightly higher failure to appear rate, a significantly lower likelihood of conviction and a significantly lower likelihood of receiving a jail sentence upon conviction, and no difference in felony rearrest. The evaluators conclude that, among other things, the program participants were able to avoid the higher conviction and incarceration effects of pretrial detention.

The King County program has key elements for managing risk, reducing failure to appear, and, importantly, improving the circumstances of individuals under supervision. It is unfortunate that in many situations contact with the pretrial system is a missed opportunity to establish a relationship with a defendant that extends beyond supervision and risk management. Pretrial can and should offer programs and services and referrals to community resources to help address the needs of individuals at the very front end of the system. Pretrial services could provide support services for issues such as housing, mental health and substance-abuse treatment, and unemployment, among others. This can be based on the information compiled by the expert panel of clinicians and other professionals discussed above.

It is also important that supervision conditions imposed by the court are as minimal as necessary to manage risk and consistent with efforts to support those under supervision. It is unfortunate that approximately 40 percent of pretrial services are housed within probation departments.[14]

Pretrial services agencies should avoid resorting to probationary tactics because they risk setting defendants up for failure. In the probation context, supervision has been shown to increase recidivism among individuals who otherwise have a low risk of reoffending. This is in large part because the sheer number of probation requirements imposes a nearly impossible burden on many offenders.

The COVID-19 pandemic has provided the opportunity to conduct a natural experiment. The National Association of Pretrial Service Agencies took this opportunity to survey nearly two hundred respondents in forty states and the District of Columbia. What was learned from the survey is that dramatic changes in pretrial practices do not compromise public safety. The primary findings are that as a result of COVID-19, jail populations were substantially reduced. This was accomplished by a 65 percent increase in cite and release by police, a 68 percent increase in release on personal recognizance for nonviolent cases, and an 81 percent increase in releases from jail for those awaiting trial. Finally, bail amounts decreased by 60 percent. In light of all of these changes, there was no evidence of a significant rise in crime.[15]

The Prison Policy Initiative has been tracking changes to jail admissions and jail populations as a result of the pandemic. They note dozens of instances, some statewide, of substantial reductions accomplished by increased cite and release, declination to prosecute certain low-level misdemeanors, judges vacating bench warrants for unpaid fees and fines, changes in detention/release decisions such as increases in release on recognizance, and the release of those at high risk for COVID-19 complications. Many of these jail reductions range from 20 percent to 45 and 50 percent and more.[16]

JUDGES

Most of the more recent discussions of criminal justice reform tend to focus on prosecutors and police. That is understandable given the elevated position prosecutors occupy in the criminal justice hierarchy, the fact that police are the most visible officials in the justice system from the perspective of the public, and the rash of officer-involved shootings, use-of-force incidents, and the massive protests that are continuing into the fall of 2020.

What seems to get somewhat lost in all of this is the role of judges in criminal justice reform. This is unfortunate since they are key decision makers in a number of essential issues such as pretrial detention, bail, and sentencing, depending on the sentencing laws in each state that dictate how much discretion judges have. Some of the most articulate advocates for justice reform are judges, for example Roger Warren (president, National Center for State Courts), Jed Rakoff (Southern District of New York), the late Michael Marcus (of Portland, Oregon), and John Gleeson (formerly Eastern District of New York), to name a few.

Many judges have been involved in local reform initiatives across the country, perhaps more quietly than some of their justice system colleagues. For example, judges in New York City have dramatically reduced bail and pretrial detention. The percentage of cases requiring bail dropped from 48 percent to 23 percent, and the percent of defendants released without having to pay any money increased from 50 percent to 76 percent. All of this was due not to changes in law or court rules, but the culture of the courthouse.[17] A recent survey of federal district judges identifies "new activist judges" who are responsible for developing diversion programs and alternatives to incarceration, often in the form of treatment and counseling.[18] While state judges have been involved in such innovations for years, these changes are relatively new in the federal system.

We are also beginning to see the election of reform-oriented judges. Harris County (Houston), Texas, in 2018 voted out of office all fifty-nine contested judicial seats, which had been occupied by Republicans, replacing them with Democrats. Top on the list of reforms for the new judges is not detaining low-level misdemeanants who cannot afford bail. There is also evidence that these new Harris County judges are making significant progress in changing the culture of the courtroom.

Reform advocates have now shifted their efforts to San Antonio and Dallas for reform judge candidates. Moreover, there has also been a notable increase in judicial candidates running as progressive judges. This is in contrast to the decades of elections where candidates ran as tough-on-crime judges.

Key to the role of judges in broader criminal justice reform is facilitating better decision-making on such matters as bail/detention, conditions of pretrial supervision, diversion, sentencing, and probation conditions and probation revocation. My coauthor and I interviewed about forty judges for the book *Confronting Underground Justice* and inquired about the idea of the advisory panels of clinicians and other experts. Essentially every judge stated that the information provided would be invaluable. Many judges feel very limited by the information they have and are not comfortable making decisions about complex situations involving mental health. They welcome the advice and recommendations the panels could provide. The collaboration of judges and advisory experts can also facilitate the development of more of a problem-solving culture in the criminal courts. However, changing the culture does not end there. I was particularly affected by two comments that several prosecutors made in the interviews I conducted—one is that decision-making is shortsighted and the other is it lacks empathy. These characteristics are not limited to prosecutors.

CHANGING CULTURE

Perhaps the greatest barrier to comprehensive criminal justice reform is our thinking about crime, criminals, and punishment. Tough on crime has been enshrined in law, procedure, decision-making, and policy at all levels of government for more than fifty years. The culture of the prosecutor's office and the courthouse go a long way in understanding resistance to change. The irony is that public opinion has changed considerably in recent years in a decidedly progressive or reform-oriented direction, but changes to law, policy, culture, and funding lag significantly behind.

A couple of years ago, a newly elected progressive District Attorney gave a speech that I attended. At the end, he took a few questions. I asked what his plans were for changing the culture of the organization, as an outsider to an office that had many old-school, tough-on-crime prosecutors. His response was that he appreciated the importance of changing the culture, and that his strategy was to lead by example. While this seems like a legitimate answer, I believe it underscores the fact that DAs are lawyers, not management experts. It's not that the lead-by-example approach is wrong; it is just a considerably incomplete strategy. The point is a simple one. District Attorneys cannot transform their offices by themselves.

In the corporate world, facilitating effective organizational change is called change management. The Society of Human Resource Management defines it as follows:[19]

> Effective change management involves leading the "people side" of major change within an organization. The primary goal of change management is to successfully implement new processes, products and business strategies while minimizing negative outcomes.

As Jack Welch, the former CEO of General Electric, put it, "The soft stuff is the hard stuff." What he was referring to is the difficulty in changing organizational culture. On the corporate side, executives nearly universally believe that culture change is the enabler of organizational change and fundamental to success. When transformation fails, it is usually a result of the failure to effectively change the organizational culture.[20]

I am not going to go into detail here regarding the various roles, responsibilities, strategies, and steps involved in managing culture change. I simply recommend that prosecutors' offices may benefit from working with experts in change management, as might other agencies involved in local criminal justice. I'm not alone in this recommendation. Stephanos Bibas, currently a US Circuit Judge for United States Court of Appeals and a former law professor at the University of Pennsylvania Law School, writes:[21]

> Another group of solutions draws on management literature to suggest ways to transform an office's structure, incentives and culture from the inside. In short, institutional design is more promising than rigid legal regulation.

There are many considerations in transforming a prosecutor's office, but one thing that came through loud and clear in the interviews sponsored by the National District Attorneys Association as well as interviews conducted by the Harvard Law School was a very strong need for new metrics for tracking and evaluating performance. Many prosecutors noted that in many jurisdictions, metrics focus on trial skills, the speed at which cases are disposed, and conviction rates. What they call for are broader measures including community involvement and recidivism. This can go a long way in helping understand where line prosecutors are in terms of their thinking, facilitating a bigger-picture understanding of the downstream consequences of their decisions. I think tracking the consequences of decisions will be a valuable tool for judges as well.

There is a lot at stake in the fundamental reform of American criminal justice—fairness, equality, legitimacy, effectiveness, public safety, victimization, recidivism, direct criminal justice costs, and the social and economic costs of crime. Changing law and policy is difficult enough, but certainly much more straightforward than changing thinking, decision-making, and culture. Chief prosecutors can and do serve as local leaders in justice reform, but they cannot do it alone. They will need help with many things, especially, I suspect, the "soft stuff." There are many barriers to successfully reinventing criminal justice, just as there are for implementing corporate change. It seems to me that one of the smartest things we can do is follow the lead of the private sector and rely on the experts.

NOTES

1. Kyckelhahn, "Justice Expenditures and Employment."

2. Sklansky, "The Nature and Function of Prosecutorial Power," 507–8.

3. Cheney v. United States District Court for the District of Columbia, 542 U.S. 367 (2004), 386.

4. Hyland, Bureau of Justice Statistics, "Expenditure and Employment Extracts."

5. Kyckelhahn, "Justice Expenditures and Employment."

6. Travis, Stewart, and Goldberg, "Prosecutors, Democracy, and Justice," 5.

7. In the interviews Judge Pitman and I conducted for our book *Confronting Underground Justice*, prosecutors were quick to say they need help in making these more clinical decisions. Common responses include "I'm not a psychiatrist" or "I'm trained in law, not medicine" or "I don't know anything about mental illness."

8. Wright, "Prosecutor Institutions ad Incentives."

9. Lowens, "How Progressive Prosecutors Came Up Short."

10. Lagratta, "To Prosecute: Interviews about Early Decision-Making," 60.

11. Luna, "Prosecutor King," 76–77.

12. Pew Charitable Trusts, "Americans Favor Expanded Pretrial Release, Limited Use of Jail."

13. Hahn, "An Experiment in Bail Reform: Examining the Impact of the Brooklyn Supervised Release Program," iii.

14. Hopkins, Bains, and Doyle, "Principles of Pretrial Release: Reforming Bail without Repeating Its Harms," 691.

15. Gelb, "'Dramatic' Reforms to Pretrial Practice Triggered by Pandemic: Survey."

16. Prison Policy Initiative, "Responses to the COVID-19 Pandemic," retrieved from https://www.prisonpolicy.org/virus/virusresponse.html.

17. Hager, "New York City's Bail Success Story."

18. Roth, "The 'New' District Court Reform Activism in Criminal Justice Reform."

19. Society for Human Resource Management, "Managing Organizational Change," 1.

20. Baker, "Chapter 11. Organizational Culture"; Aguirre, von Post, and Alpern, "Culture's Role in Enabling Organizational Change: Survey Ties Transformation Success to Deft Handling of Cultural Issues."

21. Bibas, "Prosecutorial Regulation versus Prosecutorial Accountability," 963.

References

ACLU. "Inadequately Funded Public Defender Services Threaten Criminal Justice System." March 29, 2009. Retrieved from https://www.aclu.org/press-releases/inadequately-funded-public-defender-services-threaten-criminal-justice-system-aclu.

Adcock, Clifton. "'Staggering' Caseloads for Prosecutors." *Oklahoma Watch*, September 2014.

Aguirre, DeAnne, Rutger von Post, and Micah Alpern. "Culture's Role in Enabling Organizational Change: Survey Ties Transformation Success to Deft Handling of Cultural Issues." Booz and Company, 2013. Retrieved from https://www.strategyand.pwc.com/gx/en/insights/2011-2014/cultures-role-organizational-change.html.

Alexander, Michelle. *The New Jim Crow: Mass Incarceration in the Age of Colorblindness*. New York: The New Press, 2010.

Alper, Mariel, Matthew R. Durose, and Joshua Markman. "2018 Update on Prisoner Recidivism: A 9-Year Follow-up Period (2005–2014)." Bureau of Justice Statistics, May 2018.

American Action Forum. "The Economic Costs of the U.S. Criminal Justice System." July 16, 2020. Retrieved from https://www.americanactionforum.org/research/the-economic-costs-of-the-u-s-criminal-justice-system/.

American Bar Association Commissions on Disability Rights. "Implicit Biases and People with Disabilities." American Bar Association, January 7, 2019.

American Bar Association Task Force on Preservation of the Justice System Report to the House of Delegates. Retrieved from https://static.prisonpolicy.org/scans/aba/aba_report_to_the_house_of_delegates.pdf.

American Civil Liberties Union. "Inadequately Funded Public Defender Services Threaten Criminal Justice System, ACLU Testifies." March 2006. Retrieved from https://www.aclu.org/press-releases/inadequately-funded-public-defender-services-threaten-criminal-justice-system-aclu.

American Civil Liberties Union. "Missouri Public Defenders to Shortchange Constitutional Rights." May 2018. Retrieved from https://www.aclu-mo.org/en/news/lack-adequate-funding-forces-missouri-public-defenders-shortchange-constitutional-rights.

American Public Health Association. "Health Rankings." 2019. Retrieved from https://www.americashealthrankings.org/learn/reports/2019-annual-report/executive-summary.

Anderson, James M., Maya Buenaventura, and Paul Heaton. "The Effects of Holistic Defense on Criminal Justice Outcomes." *Harvard Law Review*, January 2019.

Anderson, James M., Maya Buenaventura, and Paul Heaton. "Holistic Representation: An Innovative Approach to Defending Poor Clients Can Reduce Incarceration and Save Taxpayer Dollars—Without Harm to Public Safety." RAND Corporation, January 2019.

Anderson, Sara. "Statewide Judicial Decision-Making Study Results Announced." Illinois State Bar Association, November 7, 2017.

Anleu, Sharyn Roach, David Rottman, and Kathy Mack. "The Emotional Dimension of Judging: Issues, Evidence, and Insights." *Court Review* 52 (2016): 60–71.

APM Research Lab Staff. "The Color of Coronavirus." APM Research Lab, April 2020.

Arnold, David, Will Dobbie, and Crystal S. Yang. "Racial Bias in Bail Decisions." *Quarterly Journal of Economics* 133, no. 4 (November 2018): 1885–1932. Retrieved from https://academic.oup.com/qje/article-abstract/133/4/1885/5025665?redirectedFrom=fulltext.

Arnold Ventures. "Pretrial Research Agenda Summary." Retrieved from https://craftmediabucket.s3.amazonaws.com/uploads/Arnold-Ventures-Pretrial-Research-Agenda.pdf.

Arnold Ventures. "Public Safety Assessment FAQs." Retrieved from https://craftmediabucket.s3.amazonaws.com/uploads/Public-Safety-Assessment-101_190319_140124.pdf.

Astor, Maggie. "Left and Right Agree on Criminal Justice: They Were Both Wrong Before." *New York Times*, May 16, 2019.

Austin, James, Barry Krisberg, and Paul Litsky. "The Effectiveness of Supervised Pretrial Release." *Crime and Delinquency*, October 1985. Retrieved from https://journals.sagepub.com/doi/abs/10.1177/0011128785031004004.

Babcock, Pamela. "Tech Start-ups Look to Disrupt the Affordable Housing Industry." *Washington Post*, July 11, 2019.

Babikian, James. "Cleaving the Gordian Knot: Implicit Bias, Selective Prosecution, and Charging Guidelines." *American Journal of Criminal Justice* 42 (2015): 139–75.

Baker, Kathryn. "Chapter 11. Organizational Culture." 2002. Retrieved from https://www.semanticscholar.org/paper/Chapter-11.-Organizational-Culture-1-Baker/df0549d9dec0c29101033466f0e33c175d1441ad.

*Banks, Gabrielle. "New Harris County Bail Lawsuit Challenges Thousands Jailed on Felony Arrests." *Houston Chronicle*, January 22, 2019. Retrieved from https://www.chron.com/news/houston-texas/houston/article/New-Harris-County-bail-lawsuit-challenges-13551860.php.

*Banks, Gabrielle. "Harris County Judges Unveil Drastic New Plan for Releasing Defendants on No-Cash Bail." *Houston Chronicle*, January 18, 2019. Retrieved from. Retrieved from https://www.chron.com/news/houston-texas/houston/article/Harris-County-judges-to-unveil-drastic-new-plan-13541189.php.

Baradaran, Shima, and Frank L. McIntyre. "Predicting Violence." *Texas Law Review*, 2012. Retrieved from http://texaslawreview.org/wp-content/uploads/2015/08/Baradaran-McIntyre-90-TLR-497.pdf.

Barkow, Rachel Elise. *Prisoners of Politics: Breaking the Cycle of Mass Incarceration*. Cambridge, MA; London, England: The Belknap Press of Harvard University Press, 2019.

Barno, Matt, Deyanira Nevárez Martínez, and Kirk R. Williams. "Exploring Alternatives to Cash Bail: An Evaluation of Orange County's Pretrial Assessment and Release Supervision (PARS) Program." Southern Criminal Justice Association, July 2019. Retrieved from https://www.researchgate.net/publication/337792728_Exploring_Alternatives_to_Cash_Bail_An_Evaluation_of_Orange_County's_Pretrial_Assessment_and_Release_Supervision_PARS_Program.

Barton, Benjamin H., and Stephanos Bibas. *Rebooting Justice: More Technology, Fewer Lawyers, and the Future of Law*. New York, London: Encounter Books, 2017.

Batastini, Ashley B., Michael E. Lester, and R. Alan Thompson. "Mental Illness in the Eyes of the Law: Examining Perceptions of Stigma among Judges and Attorneys." *Psychology, Crime & Law* 24 (2018): 673–86.

Baughman, Shima. "Costs of Pretrial Detention." *Boston University Law Review* 97 (2017): 1–30.

Bayram, Seyma. "Left Behind: Public Defenders Underpaid, Have Little Oversight." *Jackson Free Press*, October 2019.

Bazelon, Emily. *Charged: The New Movement to Transform American Prosecution and End Mass Incarceration*. New York: Random House, 2019.

BBC. "How Norway Turns Criminals into Good Neighbours." July 7, 2019.

Bechtel, Kristin, Alexander M. Holsinger, Christopher T. Lowenkamp, and Madelin J. Warren. "A Meta-Analytic Review of Pretrial Research: Risk Assessment, Bond Type, and Interventions." Southern Criminal Justice Association, May 2016. Retrieved from https://slideheaven.com/a-meta-analytic-review-of-pretrial-research-risk-assessment-bond-type-and-interv.html.

Bendix, Aria. "The US was Once a Leader for Healthcare and Education—Now it Ranks 27th in the World." *Business Insider*, September 27, 2018.

Benforado, Adam. *Unfair: The New Science of Criminal Injustice*. New York: Crown Publishers, 2015.

Bennett, Mark W. "The Implicit Racial Bias in Sentencing: The Next Frontier." *Yale Law Journal Forum*, January 2017.

Bibas, Stephanos. "Prosecutorial Regulation versus Prosecutorial Accountability." *University of Pennsylvania Law Review* 157, no. 4 (2009): 959–1016.

Blakinger, Keri. "'The Place is a Jungle': Texas Youth Prisons Still Beset by Gangs, Violence, Abuse." *Houston Chronicle*, December 30, 2019.

Block, Frederic. "Let's Put an End to Prosecutorial Immunity." The Marshall Project, March 2018.

Bogira, Steve. *The Hustle of Kim Foxx*. The Marshall Project, 2018. Retrieved from https://www.themarshallproject.org/2018/10/29/the-hustle-of-kim-foxx.

Booker, Corey, Sherrod Brown, Julián Castro, Ta-Nehisi Coates, Alicia Garza, Kirsten Gillibrand, Kamala Harris et al. *Ending Mass Incarceration: Ideas from Today's Leaders*. New York: Brennan Center for Justice, 2019.

Brennan Center for Justice. "Follow the Texas Model." April 28, 2015. Retrieved from https://www.brennancenter.org/our-work/analysis-opinion/follow -texas-model.

Brennan Center for Justice. "21 Principles for the 21st Century Prosecutor." 2019. Retrieved from https://www.brennancenter.org/sites/default/files/2019-08/ Report_21st_century_prosecutor.pdf.

Brennan Center for Justice. "A Fair Fight: Achieving Indigent Defense Resource Parity." 2019. Retrieved from https://www.brennancenter.org/sites/default/ files/2019-09/Report_A%20Fair%20Fight.pdf.

Brown, Darryl K. "Criminal Law Reform and the Persistence of Strict Liability." *Duke Law Journal* 62 (2012): 285–338.

Brown, Darryl K. "The Perverse Effects of Efficiency in Criminal Process." *Virginia Law Review*, February 2014. Retrieved from https://virginialawreview.org/ sites/virginialawreview.org/files/Brown_Book.pdf.

Bureau of Justice Statistics. "Sentencing and Time Served." 1987. Retrieved from https://www.bjs.gov/index.cfm?ty=pbdetail&iid=3664.

Burke, Alafair S. "Improving Prosecutorial Decision Making: Some Lessons of Cognitive Science." *William and Mary Law Review* 47, no. 5 (2006): 1588–1631.

Burke, Alafair S. "Neutralizing Cognitive Bias: An Invitation to Prosecutors." Maurice A. Deane School of Law at Hofstra University, 2007. Retrieved from https://scholarlycommons.law.hofstra.edu/cgi/viewcontent.cgi?referer=&htt psredir=1&article=1744&context=faculty_scholarship.

Burke, Alafair. "Prosecutorial Passion, Cognitive Bias, and Plea Bargaining." Maurice A. Deane School of Law at Hofstra University, 2007. Retrieved from https://scholarlycommons.law.hofstra.edu/faculty_scholarship/672/.

Burks, Rabiah. "FAMM Applauds Introduction of 'North Carolina First Step Act.'" Families against Mandatory Minimums, March 28, 2019.

Bushway, Shawn D., and Jonah B. Gelbach. "Testing for Racial Discrimination in Bail Setting Using Nonparametric Estimation of a Parametric Model." August 20, 2011. Retrieved from https://www.law.upenn.edu/live/files/1142 -gelbachbailracialdiscriminationpdf.

Butts, Jeffrey A., and Vincent Schiraldi. "Recidivism Reconsidered: Preserving the Community Justice Mission of Community Corrections." Papers from the Executive Session on Community Corrections, Harvard Kennedy School Program of Criminal Justice Policy and Management, March 2018.

Carmichael, Dottie, George Naufal, Steve Wood, Heather Caspers, and Miner P. Marchbanks. "Liberty and Justice: Pretrial Practices in Texas." Public Policy Research Institute, March 2017. Retrieved from https://ppri.tamu.edu/pretrial -practices/.

Carpenter, Siri. "Buried Prejudice." *Scientific American*, April 2008.

Carrol, David. "Why Our Misdemeanor Courts Are Filled with Uncounselled Defendants." *Pleading the Sixth*, Sixth Amendment Center, May 12, 2015. Retrieved from https://sixthamendment.org/why-our-misdemeanor-courts-are-filled -with-uncounselled-defendants/.

Charles Koch Institute. "Survey on American Money Bail System: Americans Recognize Inequities in Pretrial Justice System and Support Reforms to Current

System." Charles Koch Institute, July 13, 2018. Retrieved from https://www
.charleskochinstitute.org/blog/pretrial-justice-bail-reform-poll/.

Clark, Dan. "How Many U.S. Adults Have a Criminal Record? Depends of How
You Define It." PolitiFact, August 18, 2017.

Cohen, Andrew. "How Americans Lost the Right to Counsel, 50 Years after
'Gideon.'" *The Atlantic*, March 13, 2013.

Coleman v. Alabama, 399 U.S. 1 (1970).

Collins, Christopher. "Potter County Criminal Defense System Is Lambasted in a
New Report." *Texas Observer*, November 2019.

Color of Change, ACLU Campaign for Smart Justice. "Selling Off Our Freedom."
Color of Change and ACLU Campaign for Smart Justice, May 2017.

Committee on Causes and Consequences of High Rate of Incarceration, Jeremy
Travis (Editor), Bruce Western (Editor), Steve Redburn (Editor), and Commit-
tee on Law and Justice. *The Growth of Incarceration in the United States: Exploring
Causes and Consequences*. Washington, DC: National Academies Press, 2014.

Constitution Project. "Justice Denied: America's Continuing Neglect of Our Constitutional Right to Counsel, Report of the National Right to Counsel Committee." Washington, DC: April 2009.

Copland, James R., and Rafael A. Mangual. "Overcriminalization America: An
Overview and Model Legislation for the States." Manhattan Institute, August
2018.

Corey, Ethan. "New Data Suggests Risk Assessment Tools Have Little Impact on
Pretrial Incarceration." *The Appeal*, February 2020.

Council on Criminal Justice. "Our Mission." No Date. Retrieved from https://
counciloncj.org/page/Mission.

Council on State Governments. Justice Center. "Confined and Costly: How Supervision Violations Are Filling Prisons and Burdening Budgets." June 2019.
Retrieved from https://csgjusticecenter.org/wp-content/uploads/2020/01/
confined-and-costly.pdf.

Crime and Justice Institute. "Pretrial Progress: A Survey of Pretrial Practices and
Services in California." August 2015. Retrieved from https://safeandjust.org/
wp-content/uploads/PretrialSurveyBrief_8.26.15v2.pdf.

Crime and Justice News. "Miami Prosecutors, Defenders Quit over Low
Pay." *The Crime Report*, March 2019. Retrieved from https://thecrimereport
.org/2019/03/27/miami-prosecutors-defenders-quit-over-low-pay/.

Crime and Justice News. "MA Official Says DA's Practices Threaten Public
Safety." *The Crime Report*, April 2019. Retrieved from https://thecrimereport
.org/2019/04/05/ma-official-says-das-practices-threaten-public-safety/.

Crime and Justice News. "MO Defender Crisis: 'You're Getting Sliver of an Attorney.'" *The Crime Report*, November 2019. Retrieved from https://thecrime
port.org/2019/11/21/mo-defender-crisis-youre-getting-sliver-of-an-attorney/.

Crombie, Noelle. "Portland Gets First Outsider District Attorney in Mike Schmidt,
Part of National Wave of Progressive Prosecutors." *The Oregonian*, May 2020.
Retrieved from https://www.oregonlive.com/politics/2020/05/portland
-gets-first-outsider-district-attorney-in-mike-schmidt-part-of-national-wave-of
-progressive-prosecutors.html.

Cueto, Emma. "Why Prosecutorial Overload Can Spark More Problems." Law360, August 2019. Retrieved from https://www.law360.com/articles/1189577/why-prosecutorial-overload-can-spark-more-problems.

Cullen, Francis T., Cheryl Lero Jonson, and Daniel S. Nagin. "Prisons Do Not Reduce Recidivism: The High Cost of Ignoring Science." *The Prison Journal* 91 (2011): 49S–65S.

Dahmi, M. "Psychological Models of Professional Decision Making." *Psychological Science* 14, no. 2 (2003):175–80.

Daniels Jr., Flozell, Benjamin D. Weber, and Jon Wool. "From Bondage to Bail Bonds: Putting a Price on Freedom in New Orleans." DataCenterResearch.org, May 2018.

Darr, Thomas. Supreme Court of Pennsylvania, Administrative Office of Pennsylvania Courts, Court Statistics, 2017.

Davidson, Janet, George King, Jens Ludwig, and Steven Raphael. "Managing Pretrial Misconduct: An Experimental Evaluation of HOPE Pretrial." Goldman School of Public Policy, January 2019. Retrieved from https://gspp.berkeley.edu/assets/uploads/research/pdf/HOPE_final_evaluation_January_2019.pdf.

Davis, Diane, Ryan Cunningham, and Jason Enox v. State of Nevada; Brian Sandoval, Governor. The First Judicial District Court of the State of Nevada in and for Carson City, Class Action Complaint for Injunctive and Declaratory Relief, 2017.

Della Cava, Marco. "New, More Progressive Prosecutors Are Angering Police, Who Warn Approach Will Lead to Chaos." *USA Today*, February 2020. Retrieved from https://www.usatoday.com/story/news/nation/2020/02/08/criminal-justice-police-progressive-prosecutors-battle-over-reform/4660796002/.

Demuth, Stephen. "Racial and Ethnic Differences in Pretrial Release Decisions and Outcomes: A Comparison of Hispanic, Black, and White Felony Arrests." *Criminology* 41 (2003): 873.

Desmarais, Sarah L., and Evan M. Lowder. "Pretrial Risk Assessment Tools: A Primer for Judges, Prosecutors, and Defense Attorneys." Safety and Justice Challenge, February 2019. Retrieved from http://www.safetyandjusticechallenge.org/wp-content/uploads/2019/02/Pretrial-Risk-Assessment-Primer-February-2019.pdf.

Digard, Léon, and Elizabeth Swavola. "Justice Denied: The Harmful and Lasting Effects of Pretrial Detention." Vera Institute of Justice, April 2019. Retrieved from https://www.vera.org/publications/for-the-record-justice-denied-pretrial-detention.

Disaster Center. "United States Crime Rates 1960–2018." 2019. Retrieved from http://www.disastercenter.com/crime/uscrime.htm.

Dobbie, Will, Jacob Goldin, and Crystal S. Yang. "The Effects of Pretrial Detention on Conviction, Future Crime, and Employment: Evidence from Randomly Assigned Judges." *American Economic Review*, February 2018. Retrieved from https://www.aeaweb.org/articles?id=10.1257/aer.20161503.

Dobbie, Will, and Crystal Yang. "Proposals for Improving the U.S. Pretrial System." The Hamilton Project, March 2019. Retrieved from https://www.hamiltonproject.org/papers/proposals_for_improving_the_u.s._pretrial_system.

Doyle, Colin, Chiraag Bains, and Brook Hopkins. "Bail Reform: A Guide for State and Local Policymakers." Criminal Justice Policy Program, February 2019. Retrieved from http://cjpp.law.harvard.edu/assets/BailReform_WEB.pdf.

Ebbesen, Ebbe B., and Vladimir J. Konechi. "Decision Making and Information Integration in the Courts: The Setting of Bail." *Journal of Personality and Social Psychology*, 1975.

Ebbesen, Ebbe B., and Vladimir J. Konechi. "An Analysis of the Sentencing System." In *The Criminal Justice System: A Social-Psychological Analysis*, edited by Ebbe B. Ebbesen and Vladimir J. Konecni, 293–332. San Francisco: W. H. Freeman, 1982.

Eisenberg, Theodore, and Sheri Lyn Johnson. "Implicit Racial Attributes of Death Penalty Lawyers." *DePaul Law Review* 53 (2004): 1539–56.

Elderbroom, Brian, Laura Bennett, Shanna Gong, Felicity Rose, and Zoë Towns. "Every Second: The Impact of the Incarceration Crisis on America's Families." FWD, December 2018. Retrieved from https://everysecond.fwd.us/downloads/everysecond.fwd.us.pdf.

Enns, Peter K., Youngmin Yi, Megan Comfort, Alyssa W. Goldman, Hedwig Lee, Christopher Muller, Sara Wakefield, Emily A. Wang, and Christopher Wildeman. "What Percentage of Americans Have Ever Had a Family Member Incarcerated? Evidence from the Family History of Incarceration Survey (FamHIS)." *Socius: Sociological Research for a Dynamic World* 5 (2019): 1–45.

Equal Justice Initiative. "America's Massive Misdemeanor System Deepens Inequality." January 9, 2019. Retrieved from https://eji.org/news/americas-massive-misdemeanor-system-deepens-inequality/.

Equal Justice Initiative. "Thousands in Florida Face Misdemeanor Charges without a Lawyer." November 2019. Retrieved from https://eji.org/news/thousands-face-misdemeanor-charges-without-counsel-in-florida.

Escobedo v. Illinois, 378 U.S. 478 (1964).

Farina, F., R. Arce, and M. Novo. "Anchoring in Judicial Decision-Making." *Psychology Spain* 7, no. 1 (2003): 56–65.

Federal Bureau of Investigation. Uniform Crime Reporting Statistics, "State Level Crime Estimates." Various years. Retrieved from https://www.fbi.gov/services/cjis/ucr/publications.

Filter Staff. "Public Defenders Are Hugely Overworked—But Also Underpaid Compared with Prosecutors." *Filter Magazine*, February 2019.

Findley, Keith A. "Tunnel Vision." University of Wisconsin Law School, May 2010. Retrieved from https://papers.ssrn.com/sol3/papers.cfm?abstract_id=1604658.

Fines and Fees Justice Center. "Paying for Jail: How County Jails Extract Wealth from New York Communities." December 2019. Retrieved from https://finesandfeesjusticecenter.org/articles/paying-for-jail-how-county-jails-extract-wealth-from-new-york-communities/.

Fish, Eric S. "Against Adversary Prosecution." *Iowa Law Review* 103 (2018): 1419–81.

Ford, Matt. "A 'Constitutional Crisis' in Missouri." *The Atlantic*, March 2017.

Frankel, Marvin. *Partisan Justice*. New York: Farrar Straus & Giroux, 1981.

Frederique, Nadine, Patricia Joseph, and R. Christopher C. Hild. "What Is the State of Empirical Research on Indigent Defense Nationwide? A Brief Overview and Suggestions for Future Research." *Albany Law Review*, 2015. Retrieved from http://www.albanylawreview.org/Articles/Vol78_3/78.3.1317%20Frederi que%20et%20al.PDF.

Freedman, Monroe H. "Our Constitutionalized Adversary System." *Chapman Law Review* 1(1998): 57–90.

Friedman, Matthew. "Just Facts: As Many Americans Have Criminal Records as College Diplomas." Brennan Center for Justice, November 17, 2015.

Furst, Bryan. "A Fair Fight." Brennan Center for Justice, September 9, 2019. Retrieved from https://www.brennancenter.org/our-work/research-reports/fair-fight.

Gabler, Neal. "The Secret Shame of Middle-Class Americans." *The Atlantic*, May 2016.

Gatowski, Sophia I., Shirley A. Dobbin, James T. Richardson, Gerald P. Ginsburg, Mara L. Merlino, and Veronica Dahir. "Asking the Gatekeepers: A National Survey of Judges on Judging Expert Evidence in a Post-*Daubert* World." *Law and Human Behavior* 25 (2001): 433–51.

Gelb, Michael. "'Dramatic' Reforms to Pretrial Practice Triggered by Pandemic: Survey." *The Crime Report*, July 2, 2020. Retrieved from https://thecrimereport .org/2020/07/02/dramatic-reforms-to-pretrial-practice-triggered-by-pandemic -survey/.

George, Justin. "What's Really in the First Step Act?" The Marshall Project, November 16, 2018.

Gershowitz, Adam M., and Laura R. Killinger. "The State (Never) Rests: How Excessive Prosecutorial Caseloads Harm Criminal Defendants." *Northwestern University Law Review* 105, no. 1 (2015).

Gifford, Elizabeth J., Lindsey Eldred Kozecke, Megan Golanka, Sherika N. Hill, Jane Costello, Lilly Shanahan, and William E. Copeland. "Association of Parental Incarceration with Psychiatric and Functional Outcomes of Young Adults." *JAMA Network Open* 2 (2019): 1–12.

Gilbert, D. "Inferential Correction." In Gilovich, Griffin, and Kahnerman (eds), *Heuristics and Biases: The Psychology of Intuitive Judgment.* New York: Cambridge University Press, 2002.

Glod, Greg. "Texas Adult Corrections: A Model for the Rest of the Nation." Texas Public Policy Foundation, October 2015. Retrieved from https://files .texaspolicy.com/uploads/2018/08/16101833/PP-Texas-Adult-Corrections-A -Model-for-the-Rest-of-the-Nation.pdf.

Godsil, Rachel D., and Hao Yang (Carl) Jiang. "Prosecuting Fairly: Addressing the Challenges of Implicit Bias, Racial Anxiety, and Stereotype Threat." *CDAA Prosecutor's Brief* 40 (2018): 142–57.

Gramlich, John. "America's Incarceration Rate Is at a Two-Decade Low." Pew Research Center, May 2, 2018.

Graves, Patrick. "Texas State Jails: Time for a Reboot?" Texas Comptroller, August 2019.

Greenwald, Anthony G., and Linda H. Krieger. "Implicit Bias: Scientific Foundations." *California Law Review* 94, no. 4 (2006): 945–78.

Gross, John P. "Gideon at 50: A Three-Part Examination of Indigent Defense in America." National Association of Criminal Defense Lawyers, October 2016.

Gross, John P. "The Right to Counsel but Not the Presence of Counsel: A Survey of State Criminal Procedures for Pre-Trial Release." *Florida Law Review*, February 2018. Retrieved from https://scholarship.law.ufl.edu/cgi/viewcontent.cgi?article=1372&context=flr.

Gross, Terry. "'Punishment without Crime' Highlights the Injustice of America's Misdemeanor System." National Public Radio, January 2, 2019.

Gupta, Arpit, Christopher Hansman, and Ethan Frenchman. "The Heavy Costs of High Bail: Evidence from Judge Randomization." Maryland Office of the Public Defender, August 2016. Retrieved from https://papers.ssrn.com/sol3/papers.cfm?abstract_id=2774453.

Guthrie, Chris, Jeffrey J. Rachlinski, and Andrew J. Wistrich. "Blinking on the Bench: How Judges Decide Cases." *Cornell Law Review*, 2007. Retrieved from https://scholarship.law.cornell.edu/clr/vol93/iss1/9.

Hager, Eli. "When There's Only One Public Defender in Town." The Marshall Project, September 2016.

Hager, Eli. "New York City's Bail Success Story." The Marshall Project, March 14, 2019.

Hager, Eli. "One Lawyer. Five Years. 3,802 Cases." The Marshall Project, August 2019.

Hager, Eli, and Nicole Lewis. "Facing Intimidation, Black Women Prosecutors Say: 'Enough.'" The Marshall Project, January 16, 2020.

Hahn, Josephine. "An Experiment in Bail Reform: Examining the Impact of the Brooklyn Supervised Release Program." The Center for Court Innovation. No date. Retrieved from https://www.courtinnovation.org/sites/default/files/documents/BK%20SRP_Research%20Report_FINAL.pdf.

Hale, Steven. "Pretrial Detainees Are Being Billed for Their Stay in Jail." Shelby County Justice Center, July 2018. Retrieved from https://theappeal.org/pretrial-detainees-are-being-billed-for-their-stay-in-jail/.

Hamilton v. Alabama, 368 U.S. 52 (1961).

Hanlon, Stephen F., Thomas B. Harvey, and Norman Lefstein. "Denial of the Right to Counsel in Misdemeanor Cases: Court Watching in Nashville, Tennessee." American Bar Association Section on Civil Rights and Social Justice, 2017.

Hanson, Mark. "Gideon's Broken Promise: America's Continuing Quest for Equal Justice." American Bar Association, 2005. Retrieved from https://www.abajournal.com/magazine/article/gideons_promise.

Harris County Public Defender's Office. "Holistic Defense." Retrieved from http://harriscountypublicdefender.org/holistic-defense-2/.

Harris, Kamala, and Rand Paul. "To Shrink Jails, Let's Reform Bail." *New York Times*, July 20, 2017.

Hastings, Deborah. "Public Defender Offices Are in Crisis." Associated Press, June 2009. Retrieved from ttps://www.sandiegouniontribune.com/sdut-us-no-defense-060309-2009jun03-story.html.

Hatton, Ross, and Jessica Smith. "Research on the Effectiveness of Pretrial Support and Supervision Services: A Guide for Pretrial Services Programs." UNC School of Government Criminal Justice Innovation Lab, May 2020. Retrieved

from https://docplayer.net/187255441-Research-on-the-effectiveness-of-pre
trial-support-and-supervision-services-a-guide-for-pretrial-services-programs
-may-2020.html.

Heaton, Paul, Sandra Mayson, and Megan Stevenson. "The Downstream Consequences of Misdemeanor Pretrial Detention." *Stanford Law Review*, March
2017. Retrieved from https://www.stanfordlawreview.org/print/article/the
-downstream-consequences-of-misdemeanor-pretrial-detention/.

Hinshaw, Stephen P., and Andrea Stier. "Stigma as Related to Mental Disorders."
Annual Review of Clinical Psychology 4 (2008): 367–93.

Hinton, Elizabeth, LeShae Henderson, and Cindy Reed. "Research Confirms that
Entrenched Racism Manifests in Disparate Treatment of Black Americans in
Criminal Justice System." Vera Institute of Justice, May 2018. Retrieved from
https://www.vera.org/publications/for-the-record-unjust-burden.

Holcombe, Madeline. "Law Students Say They Don't Get Mental Health Treatment for Fear It Will Keep Them from Becoming Lawyers. Some States Are
Trying to Change That." CNN Health, February 29, 2020.

Hood, Katherine, and Daniel Schneider. "Bail and Pretrial Detention: Contours
and Causes of Temporal and County Variation." *RSF: The Russell Sage Foundation Journal of Social Sciences* 5 (2019): 126–49.

Hopkins, Brook, Chiraag Bains, and Colin Doyle. "Principles of Pretrial Release:
Reforming Bail without Repeating Its Harms." *Journal of Criminal Law and Criminology* 108, no. 4 (2018): 679–700.

Hughes, Timothy A., Doris James Wilson, and Allen J. Beck. "Trends in State Parole, 1990–2000." Bureau of Justice Statistics, October 2001.

Hyland, Shelley S. "Justice Expenditure and Employment Extracts." Bureau of
Justice Statistics, November 2019. Retrieved from https://www.bjs.gov/index
.cfm?ty=pbdetail&iid=6727.

Iannelli, Jerry. "Despite Common Belief, Floridians Can't Always Get a Free Public Defender." *Miami New Times*, October 2019.

Illinois Circuit Court. *Illinois Circuit Court Statistics 2019*. Illinois Circuit Court,
2019. Retrieved from http://illinoiscourts.gov/CircuitCourt/CCStats.asp.

Illinois Sentencing Policy Advisory Council. "The High Cost of Recidivism." 2016.
Retrieved from https://spac.illinois.gov/publications/cost-benefit-analysis/
high-cost-of-recidivism-2018-supplemental-report.

Indiana Office of Judicial Administration. *Indiana Judicial Service Report*. Indiana
Supreme Court, 2017. Retrieved from https://www.in.gov/judiciary/iocs/
files/rpts-ijs-2017-judicial-review.pdf.

Indiana Office of Judicial Administration, Indiana Supreme Court. "The Judicial
Year in Review." 2018. Retrieved from https://www.in.gov/judiciary/iocs/
files/rpts-ijs-2018-judicial-review.pdf.

Institute for Innovation in Prosecution at John Jay College. "A Vision for
the Modern Prosecutor." July 2020. Retrieved from https://static1.square
space.com/static/5c4fbee5697a9849dae88a23/t/5f0f7ef399da432fac5a8
25f/1594851060130/Vision+Paper.pdf.

Irwin, John F., and Daniel L. Real. "Unconscious Influences on Judicial Decision-
Making: The Illusion of Objectivity." *McGeorge Law Review*, January 2010. Retrieved from https://papers.ssrn.com/sol3/papers.cfm?abstract_id=1696643.

Israel, Jerold H. "Excessive Criminal Justice Caseloads: Challenging the Conventional Wisdom." University of Michigan Law School Scholarship Repository, 1996. Retrieved from https://repository.law.umich.edu/articles/229/.

Jackson, Robert. "The Federal Prosecutor." Address by Robert Jackson, Attorney General of the United States, April 1, 1940. Retrieved from https://www.justice.gov/sites/default/files/ag/legacy/2011/09/16/04-01-1940.pdf.

Jaffe, DJ. *Insane Consequences: How the Mental Health Industry Fails the Mentally Ill.* Amherst, NY: Prometheus Books, 2017.

Jaffe, Samantha. "'It's Not You, It's Your Caseload': Using *Cronic* to Solve Indigent Defense Underfunding." *Michigan Law Review*, 2018. Retrieved from http://michiganlawreview.org/wp-content/uploads/2018/06/116MichLRev1465_Jaffe.pdf.

Jalbert, Sarah Kuck, William Rhodes, Michael Kane, Elyse Clawson, Bradford Bogue, Chris Flygare, Ryan Kling, and Meaghan Guevara. "A Multi-Site Evaluation of Reduced Probation Caseload Size in an Evidence-Based Practice Setting." US Department of Justice, June 2011. Retrieved from https://www.ncjrs.gov/App/Publications/abstract.aspx?ID=256554.

Jan, Tracy. "America's Affordable-Housing Stock Dropped by 60 Percent from 2010 to 2016." *Washington Post*, October 23, 2017.

Janosko, Jackie. "Individual Homelessness: What Are the Trends?" Alliance to End Homelessness, February 11, 2019. Retrieved from https://endhomelessness.org/individual-homelessness-what-are-the-trends/.

Jones, Alexi, and Wendy Sawyer. "Arrest, Release, Repeat: How Police and Jails Are Misused to Respond to Social Problems." Prison Policy Initiative, 2019. Retrieved from https://www.prisonpolicy.org/reports/repeatarrests.html.

Jones, Van. "Ten Reasons to Celebrate the First Step Act." Retrieved from https://www.cnn.com/2018/12/21/opinions/ten-reasons-to-celebrate-first-step-act-jones-and-jackson/index.html.

Jones, Van. "Van Jones Prison Reform Bill a Christmas Miracle." Retrieved from https://www.realclearpolitics.com/video/2018/12/19/van_jones_prison_reform_bill_a_christmas_miracle.html.

Jordan, Barbara, and Mickey Leland. "An Examination of Prosecutorial Caseloads: In Search of a Standard." Center for Justice Research, 2019. Retrieved from centerforjusticeresearch.com.

Judicial Council of California. "2018 Court Statistical Report Statewide Caseload Trends 2007–2008 through 2016–2017." Retrieved from https://www.courts.ca.gov/documents/2018-Court-Statistics-Report.pdf.

Justice Policy Institute. "The High Price of Bail." JusticePolicy.org. Retrieved from http://www.justicepolicy.org/uploads/justicepolicy/documents/high_price_of_bail_-_final.pdf.

Justice Policy Institute. "Finding Direction: Expanding Criminal Justice Options by Considering Policies of Other Nations." April 2011. Retrieved from http://www.justicepolicy.org/research/2322.

Justice Policy Institute. "Sentencing: Long Prison Terms." No date. Retrieved from http://www.justicepolicy.org/Long-Prison-Terms.html.

Justice Programs Office. "Americans' Views on Public Defenders and the Right to Counsel." 2016. Retrieved from https://static1.squarespace.com/static/

55f72cc9e4b0af7449da1543/t/5a0225139140b76ff9027de7/1510090007542/ Americans%27+Views_11-7-17.pdf.

Kahneman, Daniel. *Of 2 Minds: How Fast and Slow Thinking Shape Perception and Choice.* New York: Farrar, Straus and Giroux LLC, 2011.

Kaiser, Joshua. "Revealing the Hidden Sentence: How to Add Transparency, Legitimacy, and Purpose to 'Collateral' Punishment Policy." *Harvard Law and Policy Review* 10 (2016): 124–84.

Kang, Jerry, Judge Mark Bennett, Devon Carbado, Pam Casey, Nilanjana Dasgupta, David Faigman, Rachel Godsil, Anthony G. Greenwald, Justin Levinson, and Jennifer Mnookin. "Implicit Bias in the Courtroom." *UCLA Law Review* 59 (2012): 1124–53.

Kang-Brown, Jacob, Oliver Hinds, Jasmine Heiss, and Olive Lu. "The New Dynamics of Mass Incarceration." Vera Institute of Justice, June 2018. Retrieved from https://www.vera.org/publications/the-new-dynamics-of-mass-incarceration.

Keane, Judy. "Bishops' Conference Praises Senate for Passage of the First Step Act and Encourages Passage in the House." United States Conference of Catholic Bishops, December 20, 2018. Retrieved from https://www.usccb .org/news/2018/bishops-conference-praises-senate-passage-first-step-act -and-encourages-passage-house.

Kelly, William R. *The Future of Crime and Punishment.* Lanham, MD: Rowman & Littlefield, 2019.

Kelly, William R., and Robert Pitman. *Confronting Underground Justice: Reinventing Plea Bargaining for Effective Criminal Justice Reform.* Lanham, MD: Rowman & Littlefield, 2018.

Kelly, William R., Robert Pitman, and William Streusand. *From Retribution to Public Safety: Disruptive Innovation of American Criminal Justice.* Lanham, MD: Rowman & Littlefield, 2017.

Khazan, Olga. "What's Actually Wrong with the U.S. Health System." *The Atlantic*, July 14, 2017.

Kirk, David S., and Sara Wakefield. "Collateral Consequences of Punishment: A Critical Review and Path Forward." *Annual Review of Criminology* 1 (2018): 171–94.

Kirwan Institute for the Study of Race and Ethnicity. "Understanding Implicit Bias." 2015. Retrieved from http://kirwaninstitute.osu.edu/research/understanding-implicit-bias/.

Kleinberg, Jon, Himabindu Lakkaraju, Jire Leskovec, Jens Ludwig, and Sendhil Mullainathan. *Human Decisions and Machine Predictions.* New York: Oxford University Press, 2017.

Krugman, Paul. "Opinion: Why Does America Hate Its Children?" *Austin American Statesman*, January 21, 2020.

Kutateladze, Besiki L., Nancy R. Andiloro, Brian D. Johnson, and Cassia C. Spohn. "Cumulative Disadvantage: Examining Racial and Ethnic Disparity in Prosecution and Sentencing." *Criminology* 52 (2014): 514–51.

Kyckelhahn, Tracey. "Justice Expenditures and Employment, FY 1982–2007— Statistical Tables." Bureau of Justice Statistics, December 2011. Retrieved from https://www.bjs.gov/content/pub/pdf/jee8207st.pdf.

Lagratta, Emily. "To Prosecute: Interviews about Early Decision-Making." La-Gratta Consulting LLC, 2020. Retrieved from https://www.lagratta.com/products/to-prosecute-interviews-about-early-decision-making.

Laird, Lorelei. "Starved of Money for Too Long, Public Defenders Are Suing—And Starting to Win." *ABA Journal*, January 1, 2017.

Lam, Courtney. "Pretrial Services: An Effective Alternative to Monetary Bail." Center on Juvenile and Criminal Justice, July 2014. Retrieved from http://www.cjcj.org/news/8036.

Lam, Kristin. "Cities Are Criminalizing Homelessness by Banning People from Camping in Public. That's the Wrong Approach, Report Says." *USA Today*, December 10, 2019.

Lee, Cynthia G., Brian J. Ostrom, and Matthew Kleiman. "The Measure of Good Lawyering: Evaluating Holistic Defense in Practice." *Albany Law Review*, 2015. Retrieved from http://www.albanylawreview.org/Articles/Vol78_3/78.3.1215%20Lee%20et%20al.PDF.

Lefstein, Norman. "A Broken Indigent Defense System: Observations and Recommendations of a New National Report." National Right to Counsel Committee, American Bar Association. 2009. Retrieved from https://www.americanbar.org/groups/crsj/publications/human_rights_magazine_home/human_rights_vol36_2009/spring2009/a_broken_indigent_system_observations_and_recommendations_of_a_new_national_report/.

Leslie, Emily, and Nolan G. Pope. "The Unintended Impact of Pretrial Detention on Case Outcomes: Evidence from New York City Arraignments." *The Journal of Law and Economics*, August 2017. Retrieved from http://www.econweb.umd.edu/~pope/pretrial_paper.pdf.

Levine, Sam. "Texas Upholds Sentence for Woman Who Didn't Know She Was Ineligible to Vote." *The Guardian*, March 20, 2020.

Levinson, Justin D., Mark W. Bennett, and Koichi Hioki. "Judging Implicit Bias: A National Empirical Study of Judicial Stereotypes." *Florida Law Review*, 2017. Retrieved from http://www.floridalawreview.com/wp-content/uploads/Levinson_Bennett_Hioki.pdf.

Levinson, Justin D., and Robert J. Smith. "Forum: Systemic Implicit Bias." *The Yale Law Journal*, January 31, 2017. Retrieved from https://www.yalelawjournal.org/forum/systemic-implicit-bias.

Lin, Zhiyuan, Jongbin Jung, Sharad Goel, and Jennifer Skeem. "The Limits of Human Predictions of Recidivism." *Science Advances*, February 2020. Retrieved from https://advances.sciencemag.org/content/6/7/eaaz0652.

Liu, Patrick, Ryan Nunn, and Jay Shambaugh. "The Economics of Bail and Pretrial Detention." The Hamilton Project, December 2018. Retrieved from https://www.hamiltonproject.org/assets/files/BailFineReform_EA_121818_6PM.pdf.

Livingston, James D., Teresa Milne, Mei Lan Fang, and Erica Amari. "The Effectiveness of Interventions for Reducing Stigma Related to Substance Use Disorders: A Systematic Review." *Addiction* 107 (2011): 39–50.

Loudon Now. "Loudon Lawyers Urge Better Pay for Public Defenders." March 6, 2020. Retrieved from https://loudounnow.com/2020/03/06/public-defenders-ask-for-better-pay/.

Lowder, Evan M., Bradley R. Ray, and Jeffrey A. Gruenewald. "Criminal Justice Professionals' Attitudes toward Mental Illness and Substance Use." *Community Health Journal* 55 (2019): 428–39.

Lowenkamp, Christopher T., and Marie VanNostrand. "Exploring the Impact of Supervision on Pretrial Outcomes." Arnold Foundation, November 2013. Retrieved from http://craftmediabucket.s3.amazonaws.com/uploads/PDFs/LJAF_Report_Supervision_FNL.pdf.

Lowens, Ethan. "How Progressive Prosecutors Came Up Short (And Why They Still Deserve Appreciation)." *Harvard Civil Rights—Civil Liberties Law Review*, April 2020. Retrieved from https://harvardcrcl.org/.

Luna, Erik. "Prosecutor King." *Stanford Journal of Criminal Law and Policy* 1 (2014): 48–103.

Lynch, Gerard E. "Our Administrative System of Criminal Justice." *Fordham Law Review* 83 (2015): 2117–51.

Lyon, Andrea D. "Race Bias and the Importance of Consciousness for Criminal Defense Attorneys." *Seattle University Law Review* 35 (2012): 755–68.

McCullough, Julie. "Three Texas Inmates Have Died at the Hands of Prison Officers as Use of Force Continues to Rise." *Texas Tribune*, February 7, 2020.

Mears, Daniel, and Sarah Bacon. "Improving Criminal Justice Through Better Decision-Making: Lessons from the Medical System." *Journal of Criminal Justice* 37 (2009): 142–55.

Menefee, Michael R. "The Role of Bail and Pretrial Detention in the Reproduction of Racial Inequalities." *Sociology Compass*, February 2018. Retrieved from https://onlinelibrary.wiley.com/toc/17519020/2018/12/5.

Menendez, Matthew, Michael F. Crowley, Lauren-Brooke Eisen, and Noah Atchison. "The Steep Costs of Criminal Justice Fees and Fines." Brennan Center for Justice, November 2019. Retrieved from https://www.brennancenter.org/sites/default/files/2019-11/2019_10_Fees%26Fines_Final5.pdf.

Menkel-Meadow, Carrie. "The Trouble with the Adversary System in a Postmodern, Multicultural World." *William and Mary Law Review* 38 (1996): 5–44.

Merelli, Annalisa. "The US Has a Lot of Money, but It Does Not Look Like a Developed Country." Quartz, March 10, 2017. Retrieved from htttps://q.z.com/879092/the-us-doesnt-look-like-a-developed-country/.

Meyer, Alfred W. "To Adjudicate or Mediate: That Is the Question." *Valparaiso University Law Review* 27 (1993): 357–84.

Miller, Ted R., Mark A. Cohen, David I. Swedler, Bina Ali, and Delia Hendrie. "Incidence and Costs of Personal and Property Crimes in the United States, 2017." January 2020. Retrieved from https://papers.ssrn.com/sol3/papers.cfm?abstract_id=3514296.

Miranda v. Arizona, 384 U.S. 436 (1966).

Mirza, Mustafa Z. "In Dallas County, Bail Is Set in Secret—And Often in Seconds." *Texas Tribune*, September 5, 2018.

Missouri Circuit Court. *2018 Annual Report—Circuit Profiles*. Missouri Circuit Court, 2018. Retrieved from https://www.courts.mo.gov/page.jsp?id=137406.

Natapoff, Alexandra. *Punishment without Crime: How Our Massive Misdemeanor System Traps the Innocent and Makes America More Unequal*. New York: Basic Books, 2018.

National Association for Law Placement. "New Findings on Salaries for Public Interest Attorneys." September 2010. Retrieved from https://www.nalp.org/sept2010pubintsal?s=Public%20Sector%20and%20Public%20Interest%20Attorney%20Salary%20Report&print=Y.

National Association of Criminal Defense Lawyers. "Minor Crimes, Massive Waste: The Terrible Toll of America's Broken Misdemeanor Courts." 2009. Retrieved from https://www.nacdl.org/Document/MinorCrimesMassiveWasteTollofMisdemeanorCourts.

National Association of Criminal Defense Lawyers. "Making Sense of Pretrial Risk Assessments." June 2018. Retrieved from https://www.nacdl.org/Article/June2018-MakingSenseofPretrialRiskAsses.

National Association of State Budget Officers. "State Spending for Corrections: Long-Term Trends and Recent Criminal Justice Policy Reforms." September 2013. [Washington, DC] Retrieved from https://www.prisonpolicy.org/scans/nasbo/state_spending_for_corrections.pdf.

National Center for State Courts. "Criminal Caseload Clearance Rates in 23 States, 2016." National Center for State Courts, 2017. Retrieved from http://www.courtstatistics.org/__data/assets/pdf_file/0029/23897/sccd_2016.pdf.

National Registry of Exonerations. "Exonerations in 2018." April 2018. Retrieved from https://www.law.umich.edu/special/exoneration/Documents/Exonerations%20in%202018.pdf.

New Jersey Commission of Investigation. "Inside Out: Questionable and Abusive Practices in New Jersey's Bail Bond Industry." 2014. Retrieved from https://www.nj.gov/sci/pdf/BailReportSmall.pdf.

Nichanian, Daniel. "Rachael Rollins Announces New Prosecutorial Policies in Boston." *The Appeal*, March 28, 2019. Retrieved from https://theappeal.org/politicalreport/rachael-rollins-announces-new-prosecutorial-policies-in-boston/.

Nichanian, Daniel. "Voters Beyond Big Cities Rejected Mass Incarceration in Tuesday's Elections." *The Appeal*, November 2019. Retrieved from https://theappeal.org/politicalreport/voters-beyond-big-cities-rejected-mass-incarceration-in-tuesdays-elections/.

Nichanian, Daniel. "From Marijuana to the Death Penalty, States Led the Way in 2019." *The Appeal*, December 20, 2019. Retrieved from https://theappeal.org/politicalreport/2019-review-criminal-justice-reform-legislatures-maps/.

Nichanian, Daniel. "Progressive Winner in Portland D.A. Race Expects 'Shock Waves' in Oregon's Punitive System." *The Appeal*, May 2020. Retrieved from https://theappeal.org/politicalreport/portland-district-attorney-election/.

Nichanian, Daniel. "Eleven Prosecutors Form a Progressive Alliance in Virginia." *The Appeal*, July 2020. Retrieved from https://theappeal.org/politicalreport/virginia-prosecutors-form-progressive-alliance/.

Nichanian, Daniel. "Progressives Score New Wins in Prosecutor Elections, Adding to the Movement's Breadth." *The Appeal*, August 2020. Retrieved from https://theappeal.org/politicalreport/prosecutor-elections-pima-washtenaw-san-luis/.

Offices of the United States Attorneys. "United States Attorneys' Annual Statistical Report Fiscal Year 2017." United States Department of Justice, 2017.

OJJDP Statistical Briefing Book. "Estimated Number of Arrests by Offense and Race, 2018." October 31, 2019. Retrieved from: https://ojjdp.gov/ojstatbb/crime.

Oleson, James C., Christopher T. Lowenkamp, John Wooldredge, Marie Van-Nostrand, and Timothy P. Cadigan. "The Sentencing Consequences of Federal Pretrial Supervision." Crime and Delinquency Project, September 2014. Retrieved from https://journals.sagepub.com/doi/abs/10.1177/0011128714551406.

Oliver, Ned. "Most Public Defenders in Richmond Make Less Than a Secretary in the Prosecutor's Office. They Want a Raise." *Virginia Mercury*, September 30, 2019.

O'Neill, Ciara. "Bail Bond Businesses Buck for Bookings." FollowTheMoney.org, June 7, 2018.

Oppel Jr., Richard A., and Jugal K. Patel. "One Lawyer, One Day, 194 Felony Cases." *New York Times*, February 2019.

Oregon Judicial Branch. *Reports, Statistics, and Performance Measures*. Oregon Judicial Branch, 2018. Retrieved from https://www.courts.oregon.gov/about/Pages/reports-measures.aspx.

Ortiz, Natalie R. "County Jails at a Crossroads: An Examination of the Jail Population and Pretrial Release." National Association of Counties, July 2018. Retrieved from https://bit.ly/2Bt3mUW.

Ostrom, Brian J., and Jordan Bowman. "Examining the Effectiveness of Indigent Defense Team Services: A Multisite Evaluation of Holistic Defense in Practice, Project Summary." National Criminal Justice Reference Service, February 2020.

Ouss, Aurélie, and Megan Stevenson. "Bail, Jail, and Pretrial Misconduct: The Influence of Prosecutors." June 2020. Retrieved from https://papers.ssrn.com/sol3/papers.cfm?abstract_id=3335138.

Parcesepe, Angela M., and Leopoldo J. Cabassa. "Public Stigma of Mental Illness in United States: A Systemic Literature Review. *Administration and Policy in Mental Health* 40 (2013).

Patrick, Robert. "Judge Rules that St. Louis Jails Can't Hold Inmates Who Can't Pay." *St. Louis Post-Dispatch*, June 12, 2019. Retrieved from https://www.stltoday.com/news/local/crime-and-courts/judge-rules-that-st-louis-jails-can-t-hold-inmates-who-can-t-pay/article_f2411e60-1ba5-548a-84c6-a6ba0ff13128.html.

Peng, Tina. "I'm a Public Defender. It's Impossible for Me to Do a Good Job Representing My Clients." *Washington Post*, September 2015.

Petersen, Nick. "Do Detainees Plead Guilty Faster? A Survival Analysis of Pretrial Detention and the Timing of Guilty Pleas." Criminal Justice Policy Review, 2019. Retrieved from https://journals.sagepub.com/doi/10.1177/0887403419838020.

Petersen, Nick, Marisa Omori, Robert Cancio, Oshea Johnson, Rachel Lautenschlager, and Brandon Martinez. "Unequal Treatment: Racial and Ethnic Disparities in Miami-Dade Criminal Justice." ACLU of Florida and its Greater Miami Chapter, 2018. Retrieved from https://www.aclufl.org/en/publications/unequal-treatment-racial-and-ethnic-disparities-miami-dade-criminal-justice.

Pew Center on the States, Public Safety Performance Project. "Time Served: The High Cost, Low Return of Longer Prison Terms." 2012. Retrieved from https://www.pewtrusts.org/en/research-and-analysis/reports/2012/06/06/time-served-the-high-cost-low-return-of-longer-prison-terms.

Pew Charitable Trusts. "Americans Favor Expanded Pretrial Release, Limited Use of Jail." November 21, 2018. Retrieved from https://www.pewtrusts.org/en/research-and-analysis/issue-briefs/2018/11/americans-favor-expanded-pretrial-release-limited-use-of-jail.

Pew Charitable Trusts. "New Jersey Reform Leader Says Better Data Strengthened Bail System." May 1, 2019. Retrieved from https://www.pewtrusts.org/en/research-and-analysis/articles/2019/05/01/new-jersey-reform-leader-says-better-data-strengthened-bail-system.

Pfaff, John. "A Mockery of Justice for the Poor." *New York Times*, April 2016.

Pfaff, John. *Locked In: The True Causes of Mass Incarceration and How to Achieve Real Reform.* New York: Basic Books, 2017.

Picard, Sarah, Matt Watkins, Michael Rempel, and Ashmini Kerodal. "Beyond the Algorithm: Pretrial Reform, Risk Assessment, and Racial Fairness." Center for Court Innovation, July 2019. Retrieved from https://www.courtinnovation.org/publications/beyond-algorithm.

Porporino, Frank John. "Developments and Challenges in Probation Practice: Is There a Way Forward for Establishing Effective and Sustainable Probation Systems?" *European Journal of Probation* 10 (2018): 76–95.

Pretrial Justice Institute. "Why We Need Pretrial Reform." 2018. Retrieved from https://www.pretrial.org/get-involved/learn-more/why-we-need-pretrial-reform/.

Pretrial Justice Institute. "What's Happening in Pretrial Justice?" April 2019. Retrieved from https://university.pretrial.org/viewdocument/where-pretrial-improvements-are-hap-2.

Pretrial Justice Institute "How to Fix Pretrial Justice." Retrieved from https://www.pretrial.org/get-involved/learn-more/how-to-fix-pretrial-justice/.

Pretrial Justice Institute. "Pretrial Services and Supervision." Retrieved from https://university.pretrial.org/HigherLogic/System/DownloadDocumentFile.ashx?DocumentFileKey=24bb2bc4-84ed-7324-929c-d0637db43c9a&forceDialog=0.

Pretrial Justice Institute. "Why We Need Pretrial Reform." Retrieved from https://www.pretrial.org/get-involved/learn-more/why-we-need-pretrial-reform/.

Pretrial Justice Institute. "Why Are People in Jail Before Trial?" Retrieved from https://www.pretrial.org/get-involved/learn-more/why-we-need-pretrial-reform/.

Price, Ray, Hon. Chief Justice Supreme Court of Missouri. "State of the Judiciary." Jefferson City, February 2010. Retrieved from https://www.courts.mo.gov/page.jsp?id=36875.

Primus, Eve Brensike. "Defense Counsel and Public Defense." In *Reforming Criminal Justice: Pretrial and Trial Processes*, edited by E. Luna, 3, 121–45. Phoenix: Academy for Justice, 2017.

Prison Policy Initiative. "Detaining the Poor: How Money Bail Perpetuates an Endless Cycle of Poverty and Jail Time." 2016. Retrieved from https://www.prisonpolicy.org/reports/incomejails.html.

Prison Policy Initiative. "Responses to the COVID-19 Pandemic." Retrieved from https://www.prisonpolicy.org/virus/virusresponse.html.

Prosecutor's Office, Johnson County, Indiana. Frequently Asked Questions. Retrieved from https://www.jcpo.us/faq/.

Pyun, John. "When Neurogenetics Hurts: Examining the Use of Neuroscience and Genetic Evidence in Sentencing Decisions through Implicit Bias." *California Law Review* 103 (2015): 1019–45.

Queally, James. "San Francisco D.A. Unveils Program Aimed at Removing Implicit Bias from Prosecutions." *LA Times*, June 12, 2019.

Quiñones, Ana R., Anda Botoseneanu, Sheila Markwardt, Corey L. Nagel, Jason T. Newsom, David D. Dorr, and Heather G. Allore. "Racial/Ethnic Differences in Multimorbidity Development and Chronic Disease Accumulation for Middle-Aged Adults." *PLoS ONE*, June 2019.

Rachlinski, Jeffrey J., Sheri Johnson, Andrew J. Wistrich, and Chris Guthrie. "Does Unconscious Racial Bias Affect Trial Judges?" *Notre Dame Law Review* 84 (2009): 1196–1232.

Rachlinski, Jeffrey J., and Andrew J. Wistrich. "Judging the Judiciary by the Numbers: Empirical Research on Judges." *The Annual Review of Law and Social Science*, 2017. https://www.annualreviews.org/loi/lawsocsci.

Rachlinski, Jeffrey J., Andrew J. Wistrich, and Chris Guthrie. "Can Judges Make Reliable Numeric Judgments? Distorted Damages and Skewed Sentences." Retrieved from https://scholarship.law.cornell.edu/cgi/viewcontent.cgi?article=2552&context=facpub.

Raphael, S., and M. Stoll. "Why Are So Many Americans in Prison?" In *Do Prisons Make Us Safer? The Benefits and Costs of the Prison Boom*, edited by S. Raphael and M. Stoll. New York: Russell Sage Foundation, 2009.

Redcross, Courtney, Melanie Skemer, Dannia Guzman, Insha Rahman, and Jessi Lachance. "New York City's Pretrial Supervised Release Program: An Alternative to Bail." Vera Institute of Justice, April 2017. Retrieved from https://www.vera.org/publications/new-york-citys-pretrial-supervised-release-program.

Redding, Richard E., and Daniel C. Murrie. "Judicial Decision Making about Forensic Mental Health Evidence." *Forensic Psychology: Emerging Topics and Expanding Roles* (2010): 683–702.

Richardson, L. Song, and Phillip Atiba Goff. "Implicit Racial Bias in Public Defender Triage." *The Yale Law Journal* 122 (2013): 2626–49.

Robertson, Campbell. "Crime Is Down, Yet U.S. Incarceration Rates Are Still among the Highest in the World." *New York Times*, April 25, 2019.

Robinson, Rashad. "The People Who Undermine Progressive Prosecutors." *New York Times*, June 11, 2020.

Roth, Jessica. "The 'New' District Court Reform Activism in Criminal Justice Reform." *NYU Annual Survey of American Law* 72 (2018): 187–274.

RTI International and Zogby Analytics. "Re: Public Opinion Poll Findings on Jails and Local Justice Systems." Zogby Analytics, March 16, 2017. Retrieved from http://www.safetyandjusticechallenge.org/wp-content/uploads/2017/03/Zogby-RTI-SJC-Polling-Memo-3-16-2017.pdf.

Sanderlin, Lee O. "Prosecutors Handling More Cases Than Recommended, Data Shows." *High Point Enterprise News*, June 2020.

Satija, Neena. "How Judicial Conflicts of Interest Are Denying Poor Texans Their Right to an Effective Lawyer." *Texas Tribune*, August 19, 2019. Retrieved from https://www.texastribune.org/2019/08/19/unchecked-power-texas-judges-indigent-defense/.

Sawyer, Bradley, and Daniel McDermott. "How Does the Quality of the U.S. Healthcare System Compare to Other Countries?" Health System Tracker, March 2019. Retrieved from https://theactuarymagazine.org/the-current-state-of-u-s-health-care/.

Sawyer, Wendy, and Peter Wagner. "Mass Incarceration: The Whole Pie 2020." Prison Policy Initiative, March 24, 2020. Retrieved from: https://www.prisonpolicy.org/reports/pie2020.html.

Schauffler, Richard. "The Rise and Fall of State Court Caseloads." National Center for State Courts, April 2017.

Schauffler, Richard, and Matthew Kleiman. "State Courts and the Budget Crisis: Rethinking Court Services." The Council of State Governments, 2010.

Schlesinger, Traci. "Racial and Ethnic Disparity in Pretrial Criminal Processing." *Justice Quarterly* 22 (2005): 171–93.

Schoneman, Theodore. "Overworked and Underpaid: America's Public Defender Crisis." Fordham Political Review, September 2018.

Sentencing Project. "Fact Sheet: Trends in U.S. Corrections." June 2019. Retrieved from https://www.sentencingproject.org/wp-content/uploads/2020/08/Trends-in-US-Corrections.pdf.

Sentencing Project. "U.S. Prison Population Trends: Massive Buildup and Modest Decline." September 17, 2019. Retrieved from https://www.sentencingproject.org/publications/u-s-prison-population-trends-massive-buildup-and-modest-decline/.

Sentencing Project. "People Serving Life Exceeds Entire Prison Population of 1970." February 2020. Retrieved from https://www.sentencingproject.org/publications/people-serving-life-exceeds-entire-prison-population-1970/.

Shah, Anuj K., and Daniel M. Oppenheimer. "Heuristics Made Easy: An Effort-Reduction Framework." *Psychological Bulletin*, 2008. Retrieved from http://psy2.ucsd.edu/~mckenzie/Shah%26Oppenheimer2008PsychBull.pdf.

Shapiro, Joseph. "As Court Fees Rise, the Poor Are Paying the Price." NPR, May 19, 2014. Retrieved from https://www.npr.org/transcripts/312158516.

Shepherd, Katie. "Public Defenders Make Far Less Than Prosecutors." *Willamette Week*, October 24, 2018.

Sinayev, Aleksandr, and Ellen Peters. "Cognitive Reflection vs. Calculation in Decision Making." *Frontiers in Psychology*, 2015.

Sitter, Phillip. "Report: Prosecutors' Workloads Even Higher Than Public Defenders.'" *News Tribune*, February 2020.

Sixth Amendment Center. "Actual Denial of Counsel in Misdemeanor Courts." May 2015. Retrieved from https://sixthamendment.org/wp-content/uploads/2015/05/Actual-Denial-of-Counsel-in-Misdemeanor-Courts.pdf.

Sklansky, David Alan. "The Nature and Function of Prosecutorial Power." *Journal of Criminal Law and Criminology*, 2016. Retrieved from https://scholarlycommons.law.northwestern.edu/cgi/viewcontent.cgi?article=7590&context=jclc.

Sklansky, David Alan. "The Changing Political Landscape for Elected Prosecutors." *Ohio State Journal of Criminal Law* 14, no. 2 (2017): 647–74.

Sklansky, David Alan. "The Problems with Prosecutors." *The Annual Review of Criminology*, September 2017. Retrieved from https://papers.ssrn.com/sol3/papers.cfm?abstract_id=3044204.

Sleek, Scott. "The Bias Beneath: Two Decades of Measuring Implicit Associations." Association for Psychological Science, February 2018.

Smith, Doug. "A Failure in the Fourth Degree." Texas Criminal Justice Coalition, October 2018. Retrieved from https://www.texascjc.org/system/files/publications/A%20Failure%20in%20the%20Fourth%20Degree%20Report.pdf.

Smith, Robert J., and Justin D. Levinson. "The Impact of Implicit Racial Bias on the Exercise of Prosecutorial Discretion." *Seattle University Law Review* 35 (2012): 795–826.

Smith, Robert J., Justin D. Levinson, and Zoë Robinson. "Implicit White Favoritism in the Criminal Justice System." *Alabama Law Review* 66 (2015): 871–923.

Society for Human Resource Management. "Managing Organizational Change." Retrieved from https://www.shrm.org/resourcesandtools/tools-and-samples/toolkits/pages/managingorganizationalchange.aspx.

Steinberg, Robin G. "Beyond Lawyering: How Holistic Representation Makes for Good Policy, Better Lawyers, and More Satisfied Clients." *N.Y.U. Review of Law and Social Change*, 2006. Retrieved from https://socialchangenyu.com/wp-content/uploads/2019/09/ROBIN-STEINBERG_RLSC_30.4.pdf.pdf.

Stevenson, Megan T. "Distortion of Justice: How the Inability to Pay Bail Affects Case Outcomes." *Journal of Law, Economics, and Organization*, September 2018. Retrieved from https://academic.oup.com/jleo/article/34/4/511/5100740.

Stevenson, Megan T., and Jennifer L. Doleac. "The Roadblock to Reform." American Constitution Society, November 2018. Retrieved from https://www.acslaw.org/expertforum/roadblock-to-reform/.

Stock, Stephen, Rachel Witte, and Michael Horn. "Budget Cuts to Courts Now Affecting Criminal Cases; Creating Backlogs Similar to Civil Case Calendars." NBC Universal, February 2018.

Stuntz, William J. "The Pathological Politics of Criminal Law." *Michigan Law Review*, September 2001. Retrieved from https://repository.law.umich.edu/cgi/viewcontent.cgi?article=1908&context=mlr.

Stuntz, William. *The Collapse of American Criminal Justice*. Cambridge: Harvard University Press, 2011.

Sukhatme, Neel U., and Jay Jenkins. "Pay to Play? Campaign Finance and the Incentive Gap in the Sixth Amendment's Right to Counsel." *Duke Law Journal* 70 (2020).

Supreme Court of Ohio. "Pretrial Services Utilization Survey." 2016. Retrieved from https://www.supremecourt.ohio.gov/Boards/Sentencing/Materials/2016/September/pretrialSvcsSurveySum.pdf.

Sutton, John R. "Structural Bias in the Sentencing of Felony Defendants." *Social Science Research* 42 (2013): 1207–21.

Swanson, Ana. "The U.S Court System Is Criminally Unjust." *Washington Post*, July 20, 2015.

Taylor, Derrick B. "George Floyd Protests: A Timeline." *New York Times*, July 2020. Retrieved from https://www.nytimes.com/article/george-floyd-protests-timeline.html.

Teachman, Bethany A., Joel G. Wilson, and Irina Komarovskaya. "Implicit and Explicit Stigma of Mental Illness in Diagnosed and Healthy Samples." *Journal of Social and Clinical Psychology* 25 (2006): 75–95.

Texas Appleseed. "Bail and Pretrial Release: Summary of Recent Research on What Works." Retrieved from https://www.texasappleseed.org/sites/default/files/Bail%20Reform%20Summary.pdf.

Texas Appleseed. "An Analysis of Texas Jail Bookings: How Texas Counties Could Save Millions of Dollars by Safely Diverting People from Jail." April 2019. Retrieved from https://www.texasappleseed.org/sites/default/files/An%20Analysis%20of%20Texas%20Jail%20Bookings%20Apr%202019.pdf.

Texas Criminal Justice Coalition. "A Survey of Pretrial Service Providers in Texas: Preliminary Report Findings." March 2012. Retrieved from https://www.texascjc.org/system/files/publications/A%20Survey%20of%20Pretrial%20Service%20Providers%20in%20TX%20%28Mar%202012%29.pdf.

Texas Department of Criminal Justice. "FY 2018 Statistical Report." Executive Services, February 2019. Retrieved from https://www.tdcj.texas.gov/publications/index.html.

Texas Office of Court Administration. Statutory County Courts. "Age of Cases Disposed during September 1, 2016, to August 31, 2017." 2017. Retrieved from https://www.txcourts.gov/statistics/annual-statistical-reports/.

Texas Office of Court Administration. "District Courts: Age of Cases Disposed" 2017. Retrieved from http://www.txcourts.gov/statistics/annual-statistical-reports/2017/.

Texas Office of Court Administration. "District Court Performance Measures." November 2018. Retrieved from https://www.txcourts.gov/statistics/annual-statistical-reports/.

Texas Office of Court Administration. "Annual Statistical Report for the Texas Judiciary." State of Texas Judicial Branch, 2018. Retrieved from https://www.txcourts.gov/statistics/annual-statistical-reports/.

Texas Southern University, Barbara Jordan-Mickey Leland School of Public Affairs. "An Examination of Prosecutorial Staff, Budgets, Caseloads, and the Need for Change." 2019. Retrieved from https://phys.org/news/2019-09-prosecutorial-staff-caseloads.html.

Tonry, Michael. "Prosecutors and Politics in Comparative Perspective." In M. Tonry (ed), *Crime and Justice*, vol. 41. Chicago: University of Chicago Press, 2012.

Trautman, Lars. "The Bill of Rights 'Shouldn't Come with a Bill.'" *The Crime Report*, March 2019.

Trautman, Lars, and Jonathan Haggerty. "Statewide Policies Relating to Pre-Arrest Diversion and Crisis Response." R Street Policy Study No. 187, November 2019. Retrieved from https://www.rstreet.org/wp-content/uploads/2019/10/Final-187.pdf.

Travis County, Texas "Justice System Profile, Fiscal Years 2006–2019.

Travis County, Texas. "Justice System Profile, Fiscal Years 2010–2014." Retrieved from www.traviscountytx.gov/images/criminal_justice/Doc/justice_system_profile_fy10-14.pdf

Travis, Jeremy, Carter Stewart, and Allison Goldberg. "Prosecutors, Democracy, and Justice: Holding Prosecutors Accountable." Institute for Innovation in Prosecution at John Jay College, September 2019. Retrieved from https://static1.squarespace.com/static/5c4fbee5697a9849dae88a23/t/5d6d8d224f45fb00014076d5/1567460643414/Prosecutors%2C+Democracy%2C+Justice_FORMATTED+9.2.19.pdf.

Tsai Alexander C., Mathew V. Kiang, Michael L. Barnett, Leo Beletsky, Katherine M. Keyes, Emma E. McGinty, Laramie R. Smith, Steffanie A. Strathdee, Sarah E. Wakeman, and Atheendar S. Venkataramani. "Stigma as a Fundamental Hindrance to the United States Opioid Overdose Crisis Response." *PLoS Medicine* 16 (2019): 1–18.

Turner, Jenia Iontcheva. "Plea Bargaining." *Academy for Justice, A Report on Scholarship and Criminal Justice Reform*, March 2017. Retrieved from https://papers.ssrn.com/sol3/papers.cfm?abstract_id=2930521.

Turner, Jenia Iontcheva. "Transparency in Plea Bargaining." *Notre Dame Law Review*, June 2020. Retrieved from https://papers.ssrn.com/sol3/papers.cfm?abstract_id=3545536.

Turner, Jenia Iontcheva. *Plea Bargaining Across Borders*. New York: Aspen Publishers, 2009.

Ujiyediin, Nomin. "One in Four Kansas Public Defenders Quit Last Year, Leaving Agency 'In Crisis.'" Kansas News Service, April 2019. Retrieved from https://www.kcur.org/government/2019-04-08/one-in-four-kansas-public-defenders-quit-last-year-leaving-agency-in-crisis.

Uniform Crime Reporting Statistics. *Estimated Crime in United States—Total*. United States Department of Justice, February 2020.

United States Commission on Civil Rights. "Collateral Consequences: The Crossroads of Punishment, Redemption, and the Effects on Communities." Briefing before the United States Commission on Civil Rights Held in Washington, DC, June 2019.

United States Courts. "Criminal Cases Commences, Terminated, and Pending (including Transfers), during the 12-Month Periods Ending March 31, 2014 and 2015." United States District Courts, 2016. Retrieved from https://www.uscourts.gov/sites/default/files/data_tables/fcms_na_distprofile0930.2018.pdf.

United States Courts. "Criminal Cases Commences, Terminated, and Pending (including Transfers), during the 12-Month Periods Ending June 30, 2018 and 2019." United States District Courts, March 2020. Retrieved from https://www.uscourts.gov/sites/default/files/data_tables/fcms_na_distprofile0930.2018.pdf.

United States Courts. "National Judicial Caseload Profile." United States District Courts, 2018. Retrieved from https://www.uscourts.gov/sites/default/files/data_tables/fcms_na_distprofile0930.2018.pdf.

United States Department of Justice, Office of Public Affairs. "Department of Justice Announces New Department-Wide Implicit Bias Training for Personnel." Justice News, June 27, 2016.

United States Senate Committee on the Judiciary. "*Wall Street Journal, New York Times* Praise Trump-Backed First Step Act." November 16, 2018. Retrieved from https://

www.judiciary.senate.gov/press/rep/releases/wall-street-journal-new
-york-times-praise-trump-backed-first-step-act.

United States v. Wade, 388 U.S. 218 (1967).

Urban Institute. "A Matter of Time." Retrieved from http://apps.urban.org/
features/long-prison-terms/demographics.html.

VanNostrand, Marie, Kenneth J. Rose, and Kimberly Weibrecht. "State of the Science of Pretrial Release Recommendations and Supervision." Pretrial Justice Institute, June 2011. Retrieved from https://university.pretrial.org/Higher Logic/System/DownloadDocumentFile.ashx?DocumentFileKey=47063a15 8e11-461e-6ee5-cc109b053b08.

Vaughn, Joshua. "New Data Reveals the Racial Disparities in Pennsylvania's Money Bail Industry." TheAppeal.org, May 22, 2019.

Vera Institute of Justice. "Reform-Minded Prosecutors—Especially Black Women—Face Pushback." 2019. Retrieved from https://www.vera.org/state
-of-justice-reform/2019/prosecution.

Vergano, Dan. "The Criminal Justice System Is Bad for Your Health, Warns New York City's Health Department." Buzzfeed News, August 5, 2019.

Vogt, RJ. "In First Step's Wake, States Tinker with Mandatory Minimums." Law360, July 21, 2019. Retrieved from https://www.law360.com/articles/1180305/in
-first-step-s-wake-states-tinker-with-mandatory-minimums.

Wargo, Eric. "The Mechanics of Choice." Association for Psychological Science, January 2012. Retrieved from https://www.psychologicalscience.org/
observer/the-mechanics-of-choice.

Warren, Elizabeth. "Comprehensive Criminal Justice Reform." Medium, August 2019. Retrieved from https://elizabethwarren.com/plans/criminal-justice
-reform.

Weidner, Robert R., and Jennifer Schultz. "Examining the Relationship Between U.S. Incarceration Rates and Population Health at the County Level." *SSM Population Health* 9 (2019): 1–8.

Weiss, Douglas B., and Doris L. MacKenzie. "A Global Perspective on Incarceration: How an International Focus Can Help the United States Reconsider Its Incarceration Rates." *Victims and Offenders* 5 (2010): 268–82.

West, Emily M. "Court Findings of Ineffective Assistance of Counsel Claims in Post-Conviction Appeals among the First 255 DNA Exoneration Cases." Innocence Project, September 2010. Retrieved from https://www.innocenceproject
.org/wp-content/uploads/2016/05/Innocence_Project_IAC_Report.pdf.

White House Fact Sheet: Law and Justice. December 21, 2018. Retrieved from whitehouse.gov/briefings-statements/president-donald-j-trump-secures-land mark-legislation-to-make-our-federal-justice-system-fairer-and-our-communi ties-safer/.

White, Jeremy B. "Floyd Death Propels Police Reformers in Key Prosecutor Races." *Politico*, June 2020. Retrieved from https://www.politico.com/states/
california/story/2020/06/10/floyd-death-propels-police-reformers-in-key
-prosecutor-races-1291855.

Widgery, Amber. "Trends in Pretrial Release: State Legislation." National Conference of State Legislatures, March 2015. Retrieved from https://www.ncsl.org/

research/civil-and-criminal-justice/trends-in-pretrial-release-state-legislation
.aspx.

Widgery, Amber. "Providing Pretrial Services." National Conference of State
Legislation, June 2015. Retrieved from https://www.ncsl.org/research/civil
-and-criminal-justice/ncsl-crime-brief-providing-pretrial-services.aspx.

Wilets, Jim, and Areto A. Imoukhuede. "A Critique of the Uniquely Adversarial
Nature of the U.S. Legal, Economic and Political System and Its Implications
for Reinforcing Existing Power Hierarchies." *University of Pennsylvania Journal
of Law and Social Change* 20 (2018): 342–79.

Williams, Janice. "Serving Time: Average Prison Sentence in the U.S. Is Getting
Even Longer." *Newsweek*, July 22, 2017.

Wisconsin Court System. *Publications, Reports, and Addresses Circuit Court Statistics.* Wisconsin Court System, 2017. Retrieved from https://www.wicourts
.gov/publications/statistics/circuit/circuitstats.html.

Wistrich, Andrew J., and Jeffrey J. Rachlinski. "Implicit Bias in Judicial Decision
Making." 2017. Retrieved from https://osf.io/preprints/lawarxiv/sz5ma/.

Wistrich, Andrew J., Jeffrey J. Rachlinski, and Chris Guthrie. "Heart versus Head:
Do Judges Follow the Law or Follow Their Feelings?" *Texas Law Review* 93
(2015): 855–912.

Wodahl, Eric J., Robbin Ogle, and Cary Heck. "Revocation Trends: A Threat to
the Legitimacy of Community-Based Corrections." *The Prison Journal* 91 (2011):
207–26.

Wooldredge, John, James Frank, Natalie Goulette, and Lawrence Travis III. "Is
the Impact of Cumulative Disadvantage on Sentencing Greater for Black Defendants?" *Criminology & Public Policy* 14 (2015): 187–201.

Worden, Alissa Pollitz. "The Judge's Role in Plea Bargaining: An Analysis of
Judges' Agreement with Prosecutors' Sentencing Recommendations." *Justice
Quarterly* 12 (1995): 257–78.

Wright, Ronald F. "How Prosecutor Elections Fail Us." *Ohio State Journal of
Criminal Law*, 2009. Retrieved from https://papers.ssrn.com/sol3/papers
.cfm?abstract_id=1339939.

Wright, Ronald F. "Prosecutor Institutions and Incentives." *Criminology, Criminal
Justice, Law and Society* 18, no. 3 (2017): 85–100.

Yates, Diana. "Study: Judges as Susceptible to Gender Bias as Laypeople—And
Sometimes More So." Illinois News Bureau, April 19, 2018. Retrieved from
https://news.illinois.edu/view/6367/640610.

Yong, Ed. "A Popular Algorithm Is No Better at Predicting Crimes than Random
People." *The Atlantic*, January 2018.

Zaluska, Izabela. "Paying to Stay in Jail: Hidden Fees Turn Inmates into Debtors."
The Crime Report, September 17, 2019. Retrieved from https://thecrimereport
.org/2019/09/17/paying-to-stay-in-jail-hidden-fees-turn-inmates-into-debt
ors/.

Index

About the Author

William R. Kelly is a professor of sociology at the University of Texas at Austin. He has taught and conducted research in criminology and criminal justice for more than thirty years and has published extensively on a variety of justice matters. Kelly's consulting work spans local, state, and federal governments and has given him the opportunity to collaborate with a large number of justice agencies. He currently serves on the City of Austin Public Safety Commission and on the Magistrate Judge Merit Selection Panel for the Western District of Texas.

He has written four books on reforming the American criminal justice system. *Criminal Justice at the Crossroads: Transforming Crime and Punishment* was published by Columbia University Press in May of 2015. *The Future of Crime and Punishment: Smart Policies for Reducing Crime and Saving Money* was published by Rowman & Littlefield in July of 2016. It was revised and updated, and a new edition was published in 2019. *From Retribution to Public Safety: Disruptive Innovation of American Criminal Justice* was published by Rowman & Littlefield in June of 2017, and *Confronting Underground Justice: Reinventing Plea Negotiation for Effective Criminal Justice Reform* was also published by Rowman & Littlefield in 2018.